The Intersubjectivity of Time

The Intersubjectivity of Time
Levinas and Infinite Responsibility

Yael Lin

DUQUESNE UNIVERSITY PRESS
PITTSBURGH, PENNSYLVANIA

Published in the United States of America by
DUQUESNE UNIVERSITY PRESS
600 Forbes Avenue
Pittsburgh, Pennsylvania 15282

Library of Congress Cataloging-in-Publication Data

Lin, Yael.
The intersubjectivity of time : Levinas and infinite responsibility / Yael Lin.
     pages cm
     Includes bibliographical references and index.
     Summary: "An exhaustive look at Levinas's primary texts, both his
philosophical writings and writings on Judaism, that brings together
Levinas's various perspectives on time; concludes that we can extract a
coherent and consistent conception of time from Levinas's thought, one
that is distinctly political. Thus, this study elucidates Levinas's claim that
time is actually constituted via social relationships"—Provided by publisher.
     ISBN 978-0-8207-0463-0 (pbk. : alk. paper)
1. Lévinas, Emmanuel. 2. Time. 3. Intersubjectivity. I. Title.

B2430.L484L525 2013
115.092—dc23
                                                              2013001747

∞ Printed on acid-free paper.

CONTENTS

ACKNOWLEDGMENTS

Time for Levinas is intersubjective. It is the interruption of the other person demanding me to respond, speak, and listen. In this sense, this book is not only a material object one can pick off the shelf, hold, smell, and browse through. It is an occasion, a temporal event. It developed from listening and responding to my teachers, students, colleagues, and family who have inspired and influenced my life and philosophical thinking. These interruptions are the bedrock of this book.

This book grew out of my dissertation at the New School for Social Research, New York. I am grateful to all my teachers at the New School for the opportunity to learn from them how to approach philosophical questions and for opening before me new ways of thinking about my own field of interest. I am particularly thankful to Richard J. Bernstein, my PhD advisor, whose openness and non-dogmatic approach to philosophy as well as to students has become my model as a researcher and teacher. Agnes Heller, my MA advisor, taught me to read closely the philosophical text before turning to secondary material. Simon Critchley and James Miller, who served on my dissertation committee, offered comments and observations that enabled me to develop and enrich ideas presented in this book. I am especially obliged to Hagi Kenaan from Tel Aviv University who was the first to guide me in finding my way and voice in the wonderful world of philosophy. To paraphrase what Levinas says of Rosenzweig in the preface to *Totality and Infinity*, he is too often present in this book to be cited.

I am also indebted to the Goldstein-Goren International Center for Jewish Thought at Ben-Gurion University, Israel, for the generous postdoctoral fellowship that allowed me to write the last chapters of this book. I am grateful to the members of the department of Jewish

Thought for providing the perfect environment for researching Levinas's Jewish texts and for the advice and assistance they offered. I am particularly thankful to Haim Kreisel the head of the center for his support; to Yaakov Blidstein, who read portions of the book and offered insightful suggestions; and to Uri Erlich, with whom I had a meaningful conversation about prayer that lead to the development of chapter 5.

It has been a pleasure to work with Susan Wadsworth-Booth, the director of Duquesne University Press. I have benefited enormously from her professional guidance and the seriousness with which she approached the manuscript. I am grateful to Brock Bahler for his meticulous editorial work. His careful reading, queries, comments, and style improvement are greatly appreciated. I also thank two anonymous referees and the in-house readers of Duquesne University Press. I hope they will see the improvements their comments brought.

Portions of this book appeared in earlier and different versions. Much of chapter 3 appeared as "Finding Time for a Fecund Feminine in Levinas's Thought" in *Philosophy Today* 53, no. 2 (2009): 179–90. Part of the introduction and afterthoughts appeared in an article entitled "The Torah of Levinasian Time" in *The Heythrop Journal* 53, no. 1 (2012): 81–99. I wish to thank these publishers for permission to reprint this material.

Finally, my deepest and infinite gratitude goes to my family — my (immemorial) past, my present (instant), and my (fecund) future. I am indebted to my parents, Etty and Michael, whose infinite responsibility, love, generosity, and support are a model for my own parenting. My mother's fortitude and exceptional determination and my father's humbleness and extraordinary intelligence have tremendously influenced my life and work. Many thanks go to my brothers, sisters, and in-laws who have been a source of encouragement. While they taught my sons to appreciate cooking, music, catching waves, hiking, computer games, basketball, art, theater, and science, I was able to focus on writing. I thank Sivan Cohen, my sister-in-law, who read portions of the book and always had insightful suggestions. Finally, special thanks go to Ori and Ido, my two wonderful sons, who are always a happy interruption, and to my husband, Itai. Without his love and faith in me, I would have not been able to complete this book. I dedicate this book to them.

ABBREVIATIONS

All abbreviations are of primary works by Emmanuel Levinas unless otherwise noted. Full publication information can be found in the bibliography.

BPW   *Basic Philosophical Writings*
BV   *Beyond the Verse: Talmudic Readings and Lectures*
CPP   *Collected Philosophical Papers*
DEL   "Dialogue with Emmanuel Levinas" (with Richard Kearney)
EE   *Existence and Existents*
EI   *Ethics and Infinity: Conversations with Philippe Nemo*
GCM   *Of God Who Comes to Mind*
GDT   *God, Death, and Time*
IR   *Is It Righteous to Be?*
ITN   *In the Time of the Nations*
LR   *The Levinas Reader*
OB   *Otherwise than Being or Beyond Essence*
OS   *Outside the Subject*
PN   *Proper Names*
TI   *Totality and Infinity: An Essay on Exteriority*
TO   *Time and the Other*

OTHER ABBREVIATIONS

BT   *Being and Time* (Martin Heidegger)
CE   *Creative Evolution* (Henri Bergson)
LGC   *Logic as the Question Concerning the Essence of Language* (Martin Heidegger)
SR   *The Star of Redemption* (Franz Rosenzweig)
TFW   *Time and Free Will* (Henri Bergson)
TSM   *Two Sources of Morality and Religion* (Henri Bergson)

From My Time to the Time between Us

Time appears to be at once a constantly familiar nearness and yet a mystery. We have time, save time, spend time, and waste time, but every attempt to demystify time by grasping, thematizing, conceptualizing, and defining it seems to miss the heart of the matter. This book seeks to clarify the meaning of time in the writings of the Jewish-French philosopher, Emmanuel Levinas, with the paradoxical ambition of not entirely destroying the mystery of time. But is such an endeavor possible at all? And why should we even aspire to preserve mysteries? These concerns lie in the background of this journey into the depths of Levinas's view of time.

Throughout the history of philosophy different aspects have been taken into account when approaching the question of time. One way to think of the genealogy of the discussion of time is as an evolvement from the understanding of time as cosmological and scientific, as the time of clocks and dates, to views such as Husserl's phenomenological time, Bergson's duration, and Heidegger's temporality, which reveal a view of time as grounded upon finite, human existence. In understanding time as closely tied with the human structure of existence, but not limited to the individual's existence, the view of time offered by Levinas carries the discussion yet one step further.

Levinas is one of the most prominent and influential thinkers of the twentieth century. But in spite of the growing interest in his philosophy, his innovative view of time, although not overlooked, demands more attention.[1] A study dedicated to Levinas's interpretation of time

1

is needed. In an interview from 1988, Levinas himself stresses the importance of the issue of time for his work. To the question, "What is your major preoccupation today in your work?" Levinas answers, "The essential theme of my research is the deformalization of the notion of time." The rest of his reply can be regarded as predicting the outline of this book: he refers to philosophers Martin Heidegger and Franz Rosenzweig who, along with Henri Bergson, provide the background and the point of reference of my discussion of Levinasian time; and he concludes the answer to this question by suggesting that his own discoveries are "a preface to possible research" (*EN* 232–33).[2] Here Levinas seems to encourage further exploration that builds upon his view of time and is meant to open future conversation and reflection. In a way, this book is a response to this invitation.

Nevertheless, while time is fundamental to Levinas's thought, his view ultimately remains obscure. Time is present in the development of every key theme of Levinas's philosophy; it is revealed via themes such as the idea of the infinite, the problem of interiority against exteriority, the issue of the alterity of the other, the face of the other, the question of our ethical relations with other people, the role of fecundity, the metaphor of maternity, the ethics of language and dialogue, the constitution of the self, the notion of radical responsibility, and the concepts of proximity and substitution. Moreover, the structure of time provides the background against which these themes are understood. Therefore, a clear interpretation of Levinasian time is required for an exhaustive comprehension of principal Levinasian ideas. Although we find throughout Levinas's writings at different periods apparently inconsistent interpretations of time, a coherent and consistent structure of time can be extracted from his thought. I will try to unlock the mystery of Levinasian time by using three keys—the instant, fecundity, and diachrony. Although each key opens a different view of time, they all develop from the same objectives: going beyond the present, transcending the temporality of the individual, and describing time as constituted when the subject is interrupted by the other.[3]

Situating Levinas's views against the background of two of his most influential predecessors, Henri Bergson and Martin Heidegger, illuminates Levinas's unique views concerning the relation between time and ethics. Despite the central role of time for our social existence, Bergson and Heidegger focus on the life of the individual. Although they leave room for considering our existence with others in terms of temporality, their views of time are basically egological. Approaching the question of time from the Levinasian perspective provides a way to overcome this deficiency. For Levinas the original experience of time is neither the public dimension exterior to the subject (such as the time of clocks and calendars), nor is it tied with the individual's existence, but is intersubjective—it is constituted through the individual's relation with the other person. However Levinas is disappointingly vague as to how exactly our relations with the other person constitute time, and why such relations are required for its structure, as well as for our experience of it. I approach these crucial questions by examining concrete examples from art, literature, Judaism, Levinas's biography, and everyday life. Moreover, considering time neither from the individual's perspective, nor as a public dimension belonging to everyone, but as the difference between myself and the other person, has an ethical meaning. The ethical significance and the implications of Levinas's view of time are vital for approaching our everyday relations with the people around us. Levinasian time is not only constituted through the intersubjective relations between the subject and the other person, but it is the structure permitting the other person to show itself as an alterity absolutely independent of the subject.

SAME, OTHER, RESPONSIBILITY

Levinas examines the question of time from three different perspectives. In his early writings, *Existence and Existents* (1947) and *Time and the Other* (1948) the present instant is at the center of his discussion. In *Totality and Infinity* (1961) Levinas is concerned with the future of fecundity. In *Otherwise than Being* (1974), he is primarily interested in developing the notion of the immemorial past. Despite the apparently linear structure, we should refrain from correlating Levinas's three different views of time with the dimensions of present, future and past. Such an approach will defy Levinas's project, which presents an original interpretation that aims to go beyond the traditional view of linear, synchronic time. Furthermore, Levinas's attempt to describe a unique experience of time is linked with his endeavor to overcome the priority given traditionally to ontology and to the pursuit of knowledge.

The human venture, guided by philosophy, has been, and in some circles remains, the search of truth and knowledge, but for Levinas, ethics is not merely a branch of philosophy, but is first philosophy: it directs the process of knowing. This approach to ethics is the heart of Levinas's view that time is constituted via the ethical, intersubjective relation that shows itself in the face-to-face relationship with the other person—wherein the other calls the subject into responsibility. The other person presents the only alterity that cannot be incorporated by the subject and become the same. Levinas insists that the same and the other should not be compared or contrasted, since such an approach does not separate the two, but places them under one concept or category, and in doing so we remain within the realm of the same. He is interested in presenting a view of time, which unlike the everyday view of scientific time, does not unite the same and the other under one common framework (such as clock time). For Levinas the original experience of time is grounded in an ethical relation in which the other remains transcendent and is not assimilated by the same. Levinas creates this separation between the same and the other through the asymmetrical relation, wherein I am responsible for the other, but I cannot pass along my responsibility—no one can replace me, but I can replace every one (*OB* 59).[4] The responsible subject substitutes itself for the other, but "substitution is not an act; it is a passivity inconvertible into an act" (117). The structure of substitution involves passivity in the sense that I am chosen, and I do not choose to be responsible for the other person—my responsibility for the other is prior to my freedom. Levinas does not reject the idea that we make our own free choices, but is trying to reveal that our fundamental human condition is not grounded on free choices but upon a more original structure. From a Levinasian viewpoint, Sartre's famous statement, "We are condemned to freedom,"[5] should be replaced with the claim, "We are condemned to responsibility."

However, in forming this radical separation between the subject and the other, Levinas is faced with the question, "How can the same, produced as egoism, enter a relationship with an Other without immediately divesting it of its alterity?" (*TI* 38). From a temporal perspective, when preventing the reduction of the other to the same, we are left with two absolutely independent, separate subjects, durations, or instants, and we are confronted with a problem similar to the one emerging from Bergson's philosophy—how are we to overcome the void between the different selves, or durations? This dilemma is crucial for Levinas's interpretation of time since, as the following chapters will unfold, time is the dimension in between the subject and the other.

In Levinas's account of intersubjectivity, ethical time is closely linked with language and dialogue. The relation Levinas forms between ethics and language opens up a view of language that does not unite the same and the other, but rather provides a structure that allows the subject to appear as independent of the other and at the same time subjected to it, that is, responsible for it. Language is contact with the other, and "to be in contact is neither to invest the Other and annul its alterity, nor to suppress myself in the Other" (*OB* 86). Indeed, for dialogue to be possible some form of common ground—what Levinas will speak of as the "said"—between the subject and the other is necessary. Otherwise, we would be living like monads with no windows, similar to the biblical story of the tower of Babel. In this context it is important to clarify that Levinas's use of the terms "dialogue" or "conversation" does not entail a symmetrical or reciprocal relation as the usual sense implies (*IR* 4). Robert Gibbs, for example locates the asymmetry of conversation in the ethical difference between speaking and listening.[6] Through the structure of language the ethical relationship of responsibility for the other appears: "Language is always addressed to the other, as if one could not think without already being concerned for the other" (*IR* 235). Considering speaking as contact, tenderness, and nearness suggests that language is something more than the verbal dialogue. It is the language of the skin and the face, the nonverbal language of response to the other person, of gestures and responsible acts. In speaking, the other is not absorbed in the same, as happens in the process of knowing or recognition, but rather speech is between us. It provides the structure of an ethical relation that involves proximity in which not only the other and the same maintain their separateness, their singular individuality, but it also reveals the priority of the other over the self. In an interview, Levinas offers as an example the first word used in French when encountering the other person — *bonjour*. According to Levinas this does not mean: "What a beautiful day," but rather: "I wish you peace," much like the Hebrew greeting *shalom*, which means "peace." Greeting the other is beyond the order of simple knowledge — the other is blessed before known; it expresses one's concern for the other, and this underlies all communication and discourse (47). In allowing the proximity between the two separate, excluding, nonrelated domains of the same and other, speech and language open up a way for understanding time as the dimension, the difference, in between the same and the other.

This view of language as ethical agrees with the term Levinas introduces in his late thought, the saying (*le Dire*), which he distinguishes from the said (*le Dit*). The said is a proposition or statement, which is either true or false, whereas the saying is one's exposure to the other, an ethical act that cannot be reduced to propositions. According to another model, the said is the content, the meaning of the message, and the saying is the fact that the message is addressed to an interlocutor.[7] For Levinas the openness of communication is not the transmission of information or uncovering of truths. Rather, it involves "a proximity that is possible only as an openness of self, an imprudent exposure to the other, a passivity without reserve, to the point of substitution" (*OB* 150–51). The saying conveys the view that language "is the sound of my voice, or the figure of my gesture" (149), and like the face, every individual has its own expressions that constitute its unique signature. The dimension of the saying is a form of dialogue and communication that precedes dialogue's verbal aspect of communication, and this ethical, nonverbal, dimension is overlooked when we treat dialogue as sheer verbal communication. The saying is a wordless, contentless, exposure that is a passive responsibility for another; it is the ethical structure which grounds and allows verbal communication: "The responsibility for another is precisely saying prior to anything said" (43). Jacques Derrida summarizes this idea in an essay on Levinas: "Without that responsibility there would be no language."[8]

But between the saying and the said there is a tension that is intrinsic to the relation between the two. This tension can be described through a number of oppositions, such as the ethics of the saying versus the ontology of the said, the wordlessness of the saying versus the wordiness of the said, the passivity of the saying versus the imperialism of the said, and the singularity of the saying versus the essentialism of the said. Despite these dichotomies, the one cannot be separated from the other. "They are correlative of one another" (*OB* 6). The translation of the saying into a linguistic system and to ontology is inevitable, and although the saying has an ethical priority, it is subordinated to the said. In stating the saying, it is thematized, that is, dominated by the said. As Levinas points out, the price of manifestation is betrayal (6–7). However, at the same time, the said offers a glimpse of the saying. The saying and the said feed on one another: the former conditions the latter, whereas through the latter the former appears.

The Binding of Isaac

For Levinas time originates from the ethical relation of response and responsibility revealed in facing or speaking to the other. Levinas identifies such an ethical response in the occasion of saying, "Here I am" to the other. The phrase "Here I am," which is found numerous times throughout Levinas's writings, discloses the relation between the act of speaking and the proximity of the saying.[9] This expression appears several times in the Jewish Scripture, and the most powerful and haunting moment is in the story of the *Akedah*, the binding of Isaac (Gen. 22). Levinas identifies the expression "Here I am" (*me voici,* *hineni:* הנני), "with nothing but the very voice that states and delivers itself, the voice that signifies" (*OB* 143). A mother answers, "Here I am" to her crying baby; the baby is comforted not by the content of the sentence, which young babies are still unable to understand, but by the saying, by the mother's contact, her voice, tone, and proximity. Yet the force and ethical meaning of the phrase "Here I am" are derived not only from the voice, or expression of one person saying it to another, but from the meaning of the words, and its historical and cultural significance.

Hilary Putnam writes, "When Levinas speaks of saying *me voici* what he means is virtually unintelligible if one is not aware of the biblical resonance."[10] Here Putnam refers to the said (the question of intelligibility belongs to the realm of the said), but an element of unintelligibility of the said affects the saying. The episode of the binding of Isaac illuminates the relation between the saying and the said, as well as informs the notions of diachronic time and synchronic time to be examined in chapter 4. In this biblical story, Abraham replies with the phrase "Here I am" on three different occasions to three different callers. First, it is his answer to the call of God commanding him to sacrifice his beloved son (Gen. 22:1), who was born after years of anticipation, and only after Abraham had reached the age of a hundred. A few verses later, as Isaac follows his father to the place where he is expected to be sacrificed, Abraham again answers, "Here I am," this time to Isaac (Gen. 22:7). The third time is Abraham's reply to God's messenger, who calls him when Abraham is about to sacrifice his son and execute God's command (Gen. 22:11–12). "Here I am" means that Abraham is open, ready, and listening. It expresses Abraham's unconditional devotion to God. It is commonly interpreted that it was his responsibility for the generations to come, and his obligation to keep the covenant with God, that led Abraham to obey God's command and agree to sacrifice his beloved son. Levinas borrows the phrase to convey the subject's infinite responsibility for the other person: it indicates that I am always already accused, responsible for the other; by uttering "I," I am responsible (*GCM* 75; *OB* 114). This infinite responsibility for the other is the bedrock of Levinasian time. The repetition of the theme "Here I am" in Abraham's response to his son forms a parallel between God and the other, which suggests that the Bible is teaching us that we should be committed to the other as we are committed to God. We must approach the other with the same responsiveness, awe, respect, and openness with which we approach God. However, the use of this phrase as a reply to Isaac in these tragic circumstances seems paradoxical. How can Abraham be present for both—for God who demands the sacrifice of the son, and for the son who desires to live and continue the history of the Jewish people? Is Abraham, who is fully present to the demand made by God, equally present for his son calling out to him? One would assume that when answering, "Here I am" to a son, a father means he is there for him and will protect him. But it seems that in saying, "Here I am" to Isaac, Abraham is actually saying it to God, that he is clear in his intent to obey God's request. Apparently, Abraham considers his own interest prior to that of his son. Instead of worrying about his son's well-being, Abraham is willing to fulfill God's request and keep his commitment to the covenant that promised him he would be a father of many nations.

But Abraham is not necessarily renouncing his responsibility for his son. On the contrary, by adopting a Levinasian perspective when reading the story, we learn that Abraham is doing all he possibly can for his son: he is responsible for him, and it is this responsibility that guides him. As a father, he is obligated to lead his son and to teach him responsibility, and for Levinas this means Abraham must show the son that he is infinitely more demanding of himself than of others. As Claire Elise Katz says in a different context, we can ensure the continuation of *tikun olam*—the responsibility to make every attempt to repair the world by feeding the hungry, clothing the naked, and so forth—not only by having children, but also by raising them to be responsible.[11] In order to teach his son to act responsibly, Abraham must show Isaac that he himself is responsible, even at the risk of a dreadful and paradoxical outcome—sacrificing the son, the same person he is guiding. That is, the responsibility to the son is a trace of the responsibility to God. Or better yet, Abraham's responsibility to Isaac is the trace of God, of *illeity*. For Levinas God shows himself only by his trace. "To go toward Him is not to follow his trace, which is not a sign; it is to go toward the others who stand in the trace of *illeity*" (*BPW* 64). To respond to the other is to respond to God.

But does Abraham go toward Isaac and truly respond to him? Levinas seems to think so. Unlike most interpretations which consider most dramatic the moment in which Abraham stretches forth his hand and takes the knife to slay his son, Levinas finds the highest moment of the drama when Abraham responds to the call of God's messenger forbidding him to lay a hand on Isaac, and consequently is brought back to the ethical order (*PN* 74). For Levinas, Kierkegaard's emphasis on Abraham's commitment to God as revealing the rise of the subject to the religious level, means that God is above ethics. Unlike Kierkegaard, Levinas finds in the story the idea that ethics comes before God—loving the Torah (ethics) more than God.[12] Katz pushes Levinas's insight further and offers a perceptive reading of this event, discovering in Abraham's actions a Levinasian response to Isaac's face. The Midrash describing Abraham's tears dropping into Isaac's eyes illustrates a situation in which Abraham and Isaac are facing each other (Gen. Rabbah 56:8). According to Katz's interpretation of the event, before hearing the call of the messenger, Abraham has already shifted from God to Isaac; better yet, Abraham is attentive to the call because he has already responded to the face of Isaac, set the knife down, and returned to the ethical order.[13] This interpretation may explain Abraham's willingness to respond to God's messenger, rather than demand that God himself cancel the order that he has sent. But since Abraham has already returned to the ethical order, it was meaningless for him whether God or his messenger annul the command. Katz concludes that Abraham successfully passed a test, not in his faith in God, but in returning to the ethical order and responding to the face of Isaac. Nevertheless, these are not mutually exclusive tests since this story teaches us that faith in God is actually revealed in the ethical response to the other.

The *Akedah* is not only Abraham's tale, but it is Isaac's story as well. The numerous discussions of the event mostly overlook Isaac's perspective, but in my view, Isaac's ethical response to the other is also tested. On their journey, Isaac wonders about the whereabouts of the lamb for the offering, and Abraham replies, "God will provide himself the lamb for burnt offering my son" (Gen. 22:8).[14] According to the Midrash, here Abraham reveals to Isaac that he is the lamb for slaughter. This interpretation is probably based on reading the phrase punctuated this way: "God will provide himself the lamb—oh my son; and if not, Thou art for a burnt-offering my son" (Gen. Rabbah 56:4).[15] But even though Isaac is now aware of the situation, he stays with his father, as the sentence continues: "They went both of them together" (Gen. 22:6 KJV). Unlike Kierkegaard's emphasis on Abraham's loneliness, Rabbi Kook shows that Isaac shares the mission; however, it is not the search for the face of God that binds them together, as Kook suggests, but Abraham and Isaac are ethically bound by the response to the other person.[16] The story can be read not only as one in which Abraham is ethically bound to Isaac, but also as a story revealing Isaac as ethically bound to his father. By going with Abraham, Isaac is actually saying, "Here I am" to his father: an ethical response to the other, which reveals his faith in God. In spite of the fear and trepidation Isaac must have felt, he does not protest or escape the situation though he is old enough to do so (he is described as old enough to carry a large bundle of wood).[17] This is supported by the Midrash which describes Isaac's active participation in planning and executing his own death: "Father, I am a young man and afraid that my body may tremble through fear of the knife and I will grieve thee, whereby the slaughter may be rendered unfit, and this will not count as a real sacrifice; therefore bind me very firmly" (Gen. Rabbah 56:8). Isaac responds to the call he has never heard; he is obligated to Abraham's covenant without ever committing to it himself. Isaac passes the test. Against the natural right of *conatus essendi,* Isaac considers the other—Abraham and his contract with God—as prior to his own self-preservation.

The story ends when Abraham returns to his young men, and the Midrash wonders why Isaac is no longer mentioned in the text. One rabbi answers that Abraham has sent him to study Torah; another says that Abraham has sent him home at night, for fear of the evil eye (Gen. Rabbah 56:11). But the salient point is that Abraham and Isaac are now unbound, separated. During the entire event Abraham and Isaac are described as acting together, in unison, and this impression is strengthened by the repetition of the phrase, "They went both of them together" (Gen. 22:8 KJV). The story reveals that by accepting responsibility for the other, Abraham and Isaac are ethically bound; after the event, the two are separated and no longer exist in synchronic time. We can consider the *Akedah* as a story of individuation and separation through responsibility for the other. The ethical binding allows for the separation of Isaac and Abraham from each other: through their obligation to the other they are individuated and become independent ethical subjects. Isaac does not return home with his father because after passing the test, he is ready to embark on his independent journey as the second patriarch of the Jewish nation. This is emphasized by what follows. In the event of the death of Sarah, his mother, Isaac is not mentioned, and only Abraham buries her (Gen. 23). In the search for Isaac's future wife, Abraham is not part of the scene, as the search is conducted by his slave (but according to Abraham's instructions) (Gen. 24).

Finally, we read that Abraham has taken a new wife who gave birth to his sons (Gen. 25:1–4). The description of the new family deepens the separation between Abraham and Isaac, thus intensifying the non-synchronic temporal dimension. From this point, the Bible only says that Abraham gives all he has to Isaac, and that after his death, Isaac and Ishmael bury him (Gen. 25:5, 9). This rupture between father and son can be seen as an alienation resulting from Abraham's intention to sacrifice Isaac. But if we are to take seriously that Isaac took an active role in the event, and that he responded, "Here I am" to his father, the separation from his father can be seen as a manifestation of the *lech lecha* ("Get thee out") command to leave one's home never to return (Gen. 12:1).[18] Abraham was the first to obey this command. This is seen by Levinas as the movement toward transcendence, and the *Akedah* marks the beginning of Isaac's journey.

The trace of Abraham's and Isaac's devotion and responsibility revealed in the story of the binding of Isaac is discovered in everyday relations with other people. Even in expressions as the simple "Hello" or "After you, sir" (*OB* 117), we find the trace of the saying—response, responsibility, exposure, and welcome. Abraham's response to Isaac and Isaac's independent response to his father reveal Levinas's idea of infinite time: a time with no beginning or end. It is a time with no beginning, because responsibility is not a choice one makes but is a response to a calling that comes before every choice one makes. As the founding fathers of the Jewish nation, Abraham and Isaac are responsible for events that will occur after their death. Their responsibility does not end with their life. Abraham is responsible to raise Isaac to be the next founding father, and Isaac is responsible for his father's responsibilities. Consequently, Abraham and Isaac's responsibilities are extended by their responsibility for the other's projects, opportunities, and responsibilities to take care of others. This produces a future that extends the future of the subject.

For those unaware of the story behind Levinas's use of the phrase "Here I am," all this remains concealed. Without the narrative, without the said in the background of "Here I am," the saying is incomplete. It is through the said, through the analysis, thematization, and interpretation of this story that the saying emerges. Moreover, the saying—revealed in the faces, voices, gestures, and expressions of Abraham and Isaac—is not available to us, but only the written said, and it is only in light of the said of the story that the saying can show itself. Yet, the significance of the tale lies in the saying beyond the words and their interpretation. The ethical saying is not arrived at by reasoning, but shows itself in acts of responsibility for the other. We find in the story of the *Akedah* a gap in the narrative, which preserves the ethical moment of the saying by avoiding its translation into a thematized said. The messenger's words, "Lay not thine hand upon the lad, neither do thou any thing unto him" (Gen. 22:12 KJV) reveals a lacuna between the moment in which Abraham lifts the knife and the moment in which the knife is no longer in his hands. The Midrash fills the gap explaining that the knife is absent because the tears of the weeping angels witnessing the tragic event have fallen on it and dissolved it. But the loss of the knife does not stop Abraham, and he attempts to carry out God's command by strangling Isaac with his bare hands, leading God's messenger to command Abraham not to lay a *hand* upon Isaac (Gen. Rabbah 56:7). But once accepting Katz's interpretation that Abraham has already put down the knife from his own will, and committed himself to the ethical before hearing the messenger's call, we can consider this gap as preventing the betrayal of the saying by the said and creating the interruption required for the formation of diachronic time. The gap signifies the moment in which Abraham turns to the ethical order of the saying, and by leaving it unsaid the event is not betrayed by the said, thus going beyond the synchronic order toward diachrony.

Despite the difference between the saying and the said, one cannot be separated from the other, as the voice cannot be separated from the pronounced words. The saying, although more and other than the said, is rarely, if at all, pure. In order to be pure, the saying must be the unsaid. Perhaps in exceptional occasions the saying is revealed without the said, but for the most part it shows itself through the said.

BACK TO THE SAID

Levinas admits, "In the writing the saying does indeed become a pure said" (*OB* 170–71). Like all written texts this book is said; it aims at coherency, and strives to manifest what at times remains unsaid by Levinas. Therefore, despite the centrality of diachronic time in Levinas's thought, the synchronic structure of the book is inevitable. Its ideas are developed in a linear manner that correlates with the historical evolvement of Levinas's views of time throughout the different periods of his writings.

Chapter 1 describes the time before the time of Levinas by focusing on an important aspect of Levinas's background—the interpretations of time offered by his predecessors, Henri Bergson and Martin Heidegger. Bergson and Heidegger were among the first to overcome the cosmological view of time, and locate the locus of time in the human structure of existence. But although both Bergson and Heidegger leave room for a temporal understanding of the subject's relation with the community, they do not make the necessary move from the temporal self to an intertemporal view of time, and we are left with a relation between temporality and ethics that is basically egological and limited to the individual's perspective.

Chapter 2 is dedicated to the moment of separation—of the subject from the anonymous being of the *il y a*, and of Levinas from his predecessors. I examine Levinas's interpretation of time in relation to the views offered by Bergson and Heidegger and show the context in which Levinas's view of time begins where they left off. By focusing on the relation between time and the individual, the requirement of otherness and differences for the constitution of time, the otherness of death, and the issue of infinite time versus finite time, I show which aspects of the thoughts of Bergson and Heidegger Levinas maintains and where he parts from their interpretations.

Chapter 3 proceeds to Levinas's first mature book, *Totality and Infinity*. Here Levinas claims that the locus of time is found in the relationships formed between individuals, that time is neither interior nor exterior, but rather is the lapse in between subjects. Intersubjective time is revealed in different aspects, namely fecundity, discontinuity, and recommencement. These themes provide the framework for characterizing the ethical relations between the subject and the other, for demonstrating the ways in which such ethical encounters are the foundation of time, and for elucidating why, from Levinas's viewpoint, they are required for the constitution and the experience of time.

Chapter 4 moves on to Levinas's late view of time, and explores the themes of diachrony, the immemorial past, and the pure future. Here I examine the centrality of the ethical relation of speech and dialogue for the formation of diachronic time. Diachronic time is constituted through the intersubjective relations of responsibility, proximity, and substitution, which manifest themselves in dialogue and speech.

Chapter 5 begins with a critical assessment of Levinas's project, questioning whether Levinas is successful in presenting a view that bridges the gap inherited from Bergson and Heidegger. Then, by concentrating on Levinas's notion of *illeity*, his thought opens up a path for making the move from ethical time to a view of political time. Focusing on Jewish prayer, and borrowing from Rosenzweig the idea of linking time with cultic rites, I explore how the trace of *illeity*, of God, appears in cultural, collective experience, enabling the different individuals to form a political time through interruption. This move preserves alterity and avoids the submerging of different individuals under one totalizing order. It is a step toward a view of collective time that takes us forward in the genealogy of the discussion of time.

After examining Levinas's view of time in relation to the philosophical (i.e., Greek) tradition by situating him as continuing and going beyond the views of time presented by Bergson and Heidegger, a Jewish source of inspiration will be recognized as well. In the Afterthoughts, I form a Greek/Jew opposition, and compare the biblical stories of Abraham and Moses with Greek legends, namely the myth of Cronos devouring his children and Goya's illustration of this myth.

Despite the linearity of the book, through interruption we can go beyond the book's synchronic structure and produce diachrony. As Levinas recognizes, "A book is interrupted discourse.... They are interrupted, and call for other books and in the end are interpreted in a saying distinct from the said" (*OB* 171). Consequently, by reading this book and allowing it to interrupt the reader's synchronic temporality, hopefully a diachronic dimension between the reader and the text will open up. Levinas teaches us that without the other, without the interruption of the synchronic dimension of the same by the other, diachronic intersubjective time cannot be formed. This is the case also when it comes to books and their readers.[19]

ONE

Bergson and Heidegger
Overcoming Scientific Time

The notions of time and temporality play a prominent role in contemporary philosophical thought, and as Richard Cohen observes, these notions are as central today as eternity was in ancient and premodern philosophy.[1] In order to fully appreciate the extent to which Levinas's interpretation of time breaks new grounds, it is crucial to understand the relation between his view of time and the views provided by Bergson and Heidegger.[2] In his conversation with Philippe Nemo, Levinas mentions four philosophical texts he admires; among them are Bergson's *Time and Free Will* and Heidegger's *Being and Time* (*EI* 37–38). But despite the influence these thinkers had on Levinas, his thought goes against and beyond them. Considering the interpretations of time offered by Bergson and Heidegger, focusing primarily on these two texts Levinas esteems, will provide the background for later showing that Levinas begins his discussion of time where Bergson and Heidegger left off.

Bergson and Heidegger freed us from the cosmological, scientific notion of time after a long tradition, beginning with Aristotle, in which time had been considered in terms of an infinite succession of instants moving from the future to the past via the present, or as an infinite succession of *nows* independent of human existence. To a certain degree the liberation from scientific time continued to weaken the prominent role eternity had in contemporary philosophical thought. David Scott insightfully claims, "There remains a kind of iconicity in the scientific function of clock, whereby the clock makes time eternity, even after it is divorced from transcendence."[3] Bergson and Heidegger no longer regard time primarily as a *physis*, as a natural, even objective phenomenon, but reveal the relation between time and the human structure of existence. This innovative approach to time opened up a new vocabulary for its discussion—one that associates the primordial, real time with the finitude of human beings, entailing the emphasis of the finite aspect of time.

Consequently, both thinkers distinguish between two primary experiences of time, which in many ways exclude one another. One is the traditional, Aristotelian position, which regards time as a linear series of points that can be measured, and is seen as a modification of presence—the past is what is no longer present, and the future is what is not yet present. According to this view, time is basically infinite, public, and exterior to us. The second experience of time is the temporal perspective, which Bergson and Heidegger believe to be the more real or authentic way for understanding time. Duration, or temporality, is the understanding of time as equivalent to the individual's existence or life. However, for the most part Bergson and Heidegger focus respectively on the consciousness or existence of the individual, and this raises the problem as to whether they fail to see the possibility of an authentic communal aspect of time. Considering the relation between time and ethics in the thought of Bergson and Heidegger, and exploring the issue of political time, the question remains whether their views open the way to an original, collective time that does not unite the individuals under a totalizing structure (such as clock time), which Levinas later names synchronic time.

BERGSON: DURATION, ETHICS, SOCIETY

Bergson's innovative approach to the issue of time in general and to the question of its reality in particular bears not only metaphysical consequences but ethical implications as well. In his thought, Bergson focuses on the notion of duration (*durée*). He does so in order to show its priority over scientific clock time, or spatial time.

Duration

In contrast to symbolic, spatial time, duration is the real and concrete time: "In a word, pure duration might well be nothing but a succession of qualitative changes, which melt into and permeate one another, without precise outlines, without any tendency to externalize themselves in relation to one another, without any affiliation with number: it would be pure heterogeneity" (*TFW* 104). Spatial time, like space, is understood as made of homogeneous units (days, hours, minutes, etc.), whereas duration is heterogeneous and uncountable. This difference is derived from Bergson's distinction between two types of multiplicity: quantitative and qualitative. The first kind is the homogeneous multiplicity of material objects that are counted in space (87). This multiplicity is a numerical multiplicity, which only has a quantitative difference, a change in number. To use Bergson's example, a flock of sheep is a multiplicity that differs only in number and not in quality (76–77). Each member of the flock differs from the other in the place it occupies, in its characteristics, and so forth, but they all bear a qualitative similarity (sheep), without which they could not be counted. But duration is composed of components that differ qualitatively. This qualitative multiplicity is the internal multiplicity of states of consciousness such as memories, experiences, expectations, and so forth, which do not have a common attribute or a detected starting and ending point, as linearly ordered points in space have. Therefore, this type of multiplicity is heterogeneous; it emphasizes difference in quality, or, to use Deleuze's words—difference in kind.[4] These two types of multiplicity are the bedrock of Bergson's distinction between the spatial, everyday, physical, and conceptual public time and duration, the real and concrete time.

Duration's heterogeneity is recognized in the plurality of states of mind with their variety of rhythms, which, for example, alter from slow to rapid. However, we are incapable of noticing the continuous change characterizing duration, and we refer to our different states of mind as jumping from one situation to another. We discern the change from a feeling of warmth to a feeling of coldness, but we ignore the changes occurring during the experience of a certain state. Each experience, even a seemingly homogeneous experience, actually involves constant change—as Heraclitus's disciple puts it, we can never enter the same river even once. Each state, even one that appears to be homogeneous, like entering a river, actually includes continuous indivisible alterations. Duration is a conscious time that exists in the separate consciousness of each person and is composed of all the heterogeneous memories, experiences, and events, which the consciousness undergoes. These experiences are intertwined, and it is impossible to determine precisely when one event ends and the other begins.

The dream is a rare opportunity for experiencing duration without subordinating it to spatial concepts (*TFW* 126–27). Resembling the state of a dream, the mental events, constituting duration, are entwined, inseparable, and unrepeatable. Bergson urges us to release ourselves from the captivation of the spatial comprehension of time and reality and open ourselves to the possibility of an understanding embedded in duration and temporality. He advocates a perspective that is not confined merely to the unchanging, immobile substance, but on the contrary, it emphasizes change, mobility, difference, and evolvement. By rejecting the tendency of focusing on the immutable we dismiss the understanding that mobility is the unstable state of immobility.[5]

Ethics

Although it seems that Bergson's primary focus in his discussion of duration is metaphysical, in *Time and Free Will* he alludes to the pertinence of temporality to ethical concerns in his attempt to relate duration with the ethical problem of free will. Bergson's view of time focuses on the individual and duration, and one wonders whether the ontological structure of temporality carries ethical implications for our self-understanding. Bergson does not explicitly explore this issue, but his thought does pave the way for dealing with questions regarding the difference between a spatial and a temporal self-understanding, and we should address the question whether one perspective opens up a more real understanding of ourselves. Bergson associates with the two perceptions of time and reality two aspects of our self: "Conscious life displays two aspects according as we perceive it directly or by refraction through space."[6] The self that is perceived through space is considered as "an aggregate of conscious states: sensations, feelings, and ideas.... If he retains only their impersonal aspect, he may set them side by side for ever without getting anything but a phantom self, the shadow of the ego projecting itself into space" (*TFW* 165). Several paragraphs later he continues this line of thought and distinguishes between the spatial and temporal selves, claiming that the former conceals the latter: "We generally perceive our own self by refraction through space, that our conscious states crystallize into words, and that our living and concrete self thus gets covered with an outer crust of clean-cut psychic states, which are separated from one another and consequently fixed" (167). Bergson's distinction between two selves implies that we have two ways for understanding ourselves—spatially and temporally. The spatialized self is the shadow of the real self: it exists in spatialized time, and perceives itself as an aggregate of consecutive, fixed, refracted, clean-cut, conscious states. The temporal understanding of the self, on the other hand, is the fundamental and concrete self that exists in duration, in a sense it is duration, and it embraces its concrete, living, ever-changing aspect. But due to the fact that we commonly dwell in space and not in duration, we replace the "real," progressing, inner self with the outer, fundamentally identical to itself, ghost self.[7]

The difference between the spatial self-understanding and the temporal self-understanding is like the distinction between a conceptual understanding and an intuitive understanding. It is similar to the difference between understanding a car's motion by observing and analyzing it in comparison to experiencing the car's motion while seated in it and feeling united with its oscillations. But what do we forfeit from a captivation to a spatial self-understanding and gain from a temporal self-understanding? Bergson affiliates the spatial self-understanding with determinism and associationism, and a self-understanding initiating from any of these doctrines relies on laws and rules; it focuses on similarities and essences, and regards our choices, acts, behaviors, and so on as not uniquely ours but as belonging to a universal, repeating, public sphere.

To paraphrase Bergson's example of Peter and Paul (*TFW* 184–92), even if we assume that Peter and Paul are both present at the same events, and the circumstances and settings in which they choose, act, and live are identical (without them being one and the same person), each would still make different choices. But the spatial view that focuses on similarities leaves us confined to a self-understanding that is embedded in the unchanging and the abstract. However, instead of referring to ourselves as a thinking subject wherein our identity is preserved despite the changes we go through, we can focus on change and duration.[8] Our consciousness changes continually, and these continuous changes build up our memory, and it is memory which generates the continuity that implements our ability to understand ourselves as remaining the same person. It is not despite the continuous change that our identity is *preserved*, but rather it is due to duration, the changes and evolvements that we undergo, that our identity is *formed*. Therefore, once we divert our focus from preservation to formation we learn to see ourselves not as an entity whose identity is embedded in the preservation of an essence, but rather as a being whose individuality is a continuous creation and regeneration.

Understanding our selves as temporal beings is significant for the way we understand and live our lives. We ordinarily think of ourselves as situated in one stage of our lives, waiting to reach the next. Every time we get to a certain point (such as a new job), we are already looking forward to the next point (a better job); we tend to focus on the exterior stages and points, instead of on our temporal, internal movement and progress. We view our lives from a spatial perspective, constructed of milestones, hoping that each milestone will bring us to a better place. When adopting this approach we lose sight of life as a continuous progression and forget to experience the process. We view life as a résumé — a summary or list of goals and achievements. What may seem as the insignificant details, but which create life itself, are left out. Bergson's philosophy reveals the urgency of focusing on the whole process of our lives and our individual process of becoming. His notion of duration when applied to the way we approach our selves and our lives shows what may be gained by adopting such a perspective.

Like Zeno's paradoxes, we confuse motion with trajectory, and we see life not as a process but as a trail in which we are moving. In *Two Sources of Morality and Religion* Bergson mentions in the context of his discussion of morality that "if we think only of the interval and various points, infinite in number, which we still have to pass one by one, we shall be discouraged from starting, like Zeno's arrow" (*TSM* 36). Likewise, focusing on the exterior stages of our lives as individuals may have a discouraging effect. The difficulties of reaching point *M*, and the frustration when feeling trapped in point *O*, may seem to us that like Zeno's arrow, and similar to Sisyphus's tedious life, we are not advancing but remain at the same starting point. Such an understanding entails the view that our selves and lives are not consolidated, but are two separate things. The everyday use of metaphors such as "path," "trail," "track," and "way" when talking about our lives and our choices also shows a disassociation between our lives and our selves, as if they were not one and the same. We think of life as a route, in which we are walking, and at every intersection that we come across we choose the course and action preferable for us. We analyze life instead of experiencing it—we describe it as something exterior to us rather than living it from the inside, making this movement our own. In contrast, by embracing a temporal perspective, we concentrate on the movement rather than on the milestones, on the real rather than on the symbolic. Such a perspective imparts a more real understanding of our lives and of our selves, since it focuses on the process of becoming or learning, and avoids reducing life to a sequence of static stages.

Bergson's approach to the issues of self-understanding and the constitution of the self complies with his understanding of time as grounded in the individual's consciousness and life. But one could expect that an extensive attitude toward ethics will also include the discussion of the relations between the different individuals. Hence it is important to make the step from a self-understanding of ourselves as temporal to the view of others as equally temporal. We should consider whether Bergson's thought allows for some form of inter-temporal mode of experience to exist between different individuals, or if it requires that we remain basically independent. On the face of it there is no room in Bergson's *Time and Free Will* for intersubjective relations. Dan Zahavi severely criticizes Bergson on this point:

> Given Bergson's view on expressions — rather than revealing and artic-ulating our conscious states, they falsify and distort them — it is hard to see how he will be able to come up with a satisfying account of intersubjectivity. Not only does his position lack the resources to tackle the problem of other minds in a convincing manner, but everything he says regarding sociality suggest a rather Cartesian view on the relation between self and other. On his account, social life is a danger to the integrity of subjectivity, rather than a natural prolongation and enrich-ment of the latter.[9]

Zahavi's comment remains applicable for Bergson's *Time and Free Will*, but perhaps his later writings describe intertemporal relations. In *Creative Evolution* he makes an attempt to expand his notion of duration beyond the individual's point of view, although in the end, he is unsuccessful. His objective in this text is to determine whether the idea of duration, which is the time of the individual's conscious-ness that involves constant change, can be extended and applied to describe existence in general. He offers a way to think of duration as belonging to the universe (*CE* 8). Despite the temporal perspec-tive Bergson adopts in explaining the creation and evolution of life, this text is concerned mainly with biological evolution and not with ethics, and consequently he does not address the relation between the different individuals or the relation between the individual and the community. Moreover, Bergson's attempt to generalize duration implies that there is a duration, a time, in which everything (matter, consciousness) participates, or what Deleuze calls "a monism of time."[10] Regardless of our position toward Deleuze's conclusion that there is no contradiction between the multiplicity constituting dura-tion described in *Time and Free Will* and the coexistence in a single time in *Creative Evolution,* it is clear that *Creative Evolution* does not go beyond what Levinas calls synchronic time, which is associated with the perspective of the same. Bergson considers the universe as an organism, a unit, which like the individual involves duration. So also when discussing the universe, Bergson is adopting the viewpoint of an individual being (the universe in this case), and consequently his discussion remains confined to the perspective of totality, which from a Levinasian viewpoint, does not include real alterity.

Society

Perhaps an answer to the question of interpersonal time is found in Bergson's final book, *Two Sources of Morality and Religion. Two Sources* focuses on the question of morality and offers a political theory, so it is possible that in this text the individual's relation with the other is examined from a temporal perspective that goes beyond the spatial point of view. Referring to *Two Sources* Levinas himself says, "*Life* itself or the lived of 'profound time,' consciousness, and knowledge of *durée,* are interpreted as a relationship with the other and with God" (*EN* 224).

Bergson begins his discussion by adopting a biological perspective, claiming that the individuals of certain species in nature cannot exist on their own and require the support of a community (ants and bees, for example). But despite the biological starting point, this text is Bergson's most serious attempt to discuss ethical and particularly political issues, and he also addresses the individual's relation to society: "Each of us belongs to society as to himself. While his consciousness, delving downwards, reveals to him the deeper he goes, an ever more original personality, incommensurable with others and indeed undefinable in words, on the surface of life we are in continuous contact with other men whom we resemble, and united to them by a discipline which creates between them and us a relation of interdependence" (*TSM* 14). Bergson is suggesting here that beyond the individual's social life lies the original, deep understanding of the subject, which is grounded in one's consciousness. The distinction discussed earlier in light of *Time and Free Will* between a temporal and spatial life is now described in terms of the difference between the individual and social life.

But although the personal, internal life of duration is more real than the public life involving others encountered in spatial time, one could not cut oneself away from society even if one wished. For,

> his memory and his imagination live on what society has implanted in them, because the soul of society is inherent in the language he speaks, and because even if there is no one present, even if he is merely thinking, he is still talking to himself. Vainly do we try to imagine an individual cut off from all social life. Even materially, Robinson Crusoe on his island remains in contact with other men, for the manufactured objects he saved from the wreck, and without which he could not get along, keep him within the bounds of civilization, and consequently within those of society. (*TSM* 14–15)

Bergson seems to allude to an idea that Heidegger further develops. We live in a world that involves others, or to use Heidegger's phrasing—we are always being-with-others. Even Robinson Crusoe exists as being-with, because he thinks in the language he inherited, follows habits and traditions, obeys the rules of his community, and uses equipment he salvages from the wreckage, which has been produced by other people. And when he has the opportunity to create a cohesive community, he forces on Friday the habits, traditions, and language he inherited. But the social aspect of life covers over our real individual existence; living in a community involves obeying laws and duties, and Bergson claims, "Obedience to duty means resistance to self" (20). So although we cannot but subsist with others, with their laws, duties, and language, such an existence is in conflict with the subject's "original personality, incommensurable with others." Our existence involves the unavoidable tension between our social obligations and our self-centered desires and interests, but at the same time, the individual and society are not distinguishable (24–25, 37–38). It is when the moral obligations imposed by the society are in balance with the ego's desires and interests that the individual lives in a feeling of well-being and pleasure (58). But it would seem that only in rare occasions such a harmony is attained. Perhaps the balance is only apparently maintained because there exists "so firm a feeling of solidarity between the individual and the group that the group remains present in the isolated individual" (67). The individuals suppress and ignore their interests and embrace the community's perspective in order to live under the impression that their interests are in accord with their duties and obligations to society. This relation between the subject and society can also mean that the subject is absorbed in society, embraces the community's static viewpoint, and as a result, its singular, original existence is covered over. By ignoring one's singular existence the clash between the subject's individual existence and its existence as a social being living according to the habits and rules of other people is avoided. This view of the subject's relation with society implies that in order to disclose one's incommensurable existence, one must distance oneself from the cohesion of the community and focus on one's inner life and duration. This complies with the view alluded to in *Time and Free Will,* according to which real time, duration, involves the life of the individual person, whereas the public engagement with other people takes place in spatial time. Consequently, such an approach to the subject's relation with its community adopts the spatial perspective, and does not open up a way to consider one's relation with the other from a temporal viewpoint.

This description of the individual's relation with its society portrays what Bergson names a closed society. In closed societies, moral laws are seen as an order of nature and as the discipline that unites us as a community. Nature may be said to have equipped us with an innate disposition to obey the interests of our common and individual survival. In Bergson's words, "There is no humanity without society, and society demands of the individual an abnegation which the insect, in its automatism carries to the point of utter obliviousness of the self" (*TSM* 210). Bergson compares the human closed societies to ants in an anthill and bees in a hive: similar to the instincts of the ants and bees, for us moral laws are an order of nature. The human society, unlike the anthill or hive, consists of free individuals, and consequently the role of preserving human society is fulfilled by the system of moral laws, a role fulfilled by instincts in the case of ants and bees (55–56). From this perspective the self-preservation of humanity is achieved through a society that is characterized as a self-centered, hierarchical, disciplined, cohesive community, in which absolute authority is given to its chief (283). Like every other species, humanity has the instinct of self-preservation, but it differs from all other species by its intelligence (139). But with intelligence comes egoism, which leads to conflicts between the different individuals of a certain closed society. Such conflicts imperil the self-preservation aimed at by each closed society, so the community with its established laws and habits pressures the individuals to settle their dispute (for example, for the purpose of being united in war against the threat of a different closed community). This description of the relation between the individual and its closed society demonstrates a spatial perspective in the sense that heterogeneity and differences are ignored and even effaced, whereas homogeneity and unity are elicited. In closed societies the relation between the subject and society is grounded on doctrines, general habits, and ideas. There is no movement beyond the static conventions, and difference and singularity are disregarded, even condemned. Consequently, such a portrayal supports the claim that Bergson's view of the relation between the individual and its society does not leave room for a temporal perspective.

But although nature aims at a closed society, Bergson suggests that society can be opened by humanity:

> It is in quite another sense that man outwits nature when he extends social solidarity into brotherhood of man; but he is deceiving her nevertheless, for those societies whose design was prefigured in the original structure of the human soul, and of which we can still perceive the plan in the innate and fundamental tendencies of modern man, required that the group be closely united, but that between group and group there should be virtual hostility; we were always to be prepared for attack or defense. Not, of course, that nature designed war for war's sake. Those leaders of humanity drawing men after them, who have broken down the gates of the city, seemed indeed thereby

to have placed themselves again in the current of the vital impetus.... This being so, it was not impossible that some of them, specially gifted, should reopen that which was closed and do, at least for themselves, what nature could not possibly do for mankind. (*TSM* 57)

The open society is not the closed society of the city, but the open society of humanity; it is the society that "is deemed to embrace all humanity" (267). It is not arrived at by the force of nature, instinct, or habit, but by the force of intuition, inspiration, and creative emotion, involving a powerful insight into the unity of the human race. Bergson describes the open society as involving the love of humanity in general, the love of the other (95). This leads Nicolas de Warren to suggest understanding the opening up of society from the viewpoint of the Levinasian idea of movement toward the other.[11] But according to Bergson an open society does not yet exist, and perhaps never will (95). It has the temporal dimension of the future, perhaps even that of a pure messianic future—a future that will never become present. The two modes of society are connected with the distinction between closed and open morality, which like the case of the society, do not exist in their pure state but are intermingled. The closed morality is limited in its scope, since it is a group loyalty, and the open morality on the other hand is universal.

A closed society, which aims at self-preservation, involves the pressure of the society on the individual to obey its duties, whereas the open society involves attraction and aspiration rather than pressure, and implicitly contains the feeling of progress (*TSM* 49, 51). But even though the open society does not exist, closed societies can be opened by the genius of humanity, by the specially gifted individuals who "have broken down the gates of the city" (57) and leap beyond the limits of the closed society. As an example, we can think of the American society after the Civil War. During the Civil War two closed societies were in battle for the sake of the self-preservation and expansion of their conventions and rules. But after the war, through specially gifted people such as Abraham Lincoln, slavery was revoked, and the North and South communities began the process of unification.

As a result closed societies became more open. Bergson understands this moral progress as evolutionary and irreversible (like duration), because the opening of a society involves "a new social atmosphere, an environment in which life would be more worth living, I mean a society such that, if men once tried it, they would refuse to go back to the old state of things" (80). Although interesting, it is beyond the scope of this book to discuss how Bergson would have reacted to the recent closing up of societies in Europe, including his homeland France, marked by the spreading of a xenophobic attitude toward the foreigners residing there.

But the question remains: does Bergson's view of the open society expose a relation between the subject and its community that can be described as temporal? Another way to put it, does the open society allow the individual to be in a relation with its community in a way that reveals rather than conceals its individual existence? It seems that Bergson's preference of the open society over closed societies, and his description of the open society in terms of movement and change that remind us of his view of duration, alludes to the possibility of describing one's relation with its society as temporal. As noticed by A. R. Lacey, Bergson returns to ideas that have appeared in his earlier works.[12] Similar to his previous distinction between real time (duration) and spatial time, in *Two Sources* Bergson suggests two types that differ in essence (in kind) and not only in degree (in number)—open and closed morality and society. The closed morality focuses on brotherhood, that is, on similarities between individuals, and on static and general conventions. It unites members with some common background, trait, nationality, religion, and so forth, which differentiate them from all others that are not part of the group. The open morality, on the other hand, acknowledges diversity, and requires movement, mobility, and change (*TSM* 58). Analogous to Bergson's discussion of spatial time and duration, in which he regards the heterogeneous perspective as superior to the homogeneous perspective, the open and mobile society is considered superior to the closed and immutable society. From this analogy we might deduce that in a closed society the individual is in a spatial relation with its community, whereas in the open society the relation between the individual and the community is temporal. However, every society according to Bergson, involves both modes—open and closed (84). That is, one's relation with society is never completely temporal, and always includes also the spatial facet of common rules, obligations, and traditions. More importantly, Bergson's distinction between open and closed morality, although grounded on his distinction between space and duration, homogeneity and heterogeneity, does not address the question of one's relationship with the other. So even if to some extent the open morality reveals a possibility of a temporal understanding of one's relation with society, at stake is the evolution of a society and its morality, and thus the society is analogous to the individual.

As in *Creative Evolution,* in which Bergson considers the universe as a unit that is similar to the individual and involves duration, in *Two Sources* he describes "human society with its members as linked together like the cells of an organism" (*TSM* 82, 94), and as a unit that can develop and open itself. So also when discussing society, Bergson adopts the viewpoint of an individual being, and preserves the limited perspective of the same. Consequently, Bergson makes no real attempt to reveal the way in which different people characterized by their individual durations form intertemporal relations. Although *Two Sources* concentrates on ethical and moral issues, for the most part it does not use the temporal perspective and vocabulary in order to explain the relation between one individual and another, or even between the individual and its community; nor does it provide a profound discussion of ethical concerns regarding the individual's possibility to form a temporal relationship with the other or with its community. The only concrete temporal relationship between the individual and its society is between the community and the specially gifted person—such as an Abraham Lincoln, Martin Luther King Jr., or Jesus—who for Bergson is the image of an individual who loves all humanity. These relationships are temporal because through them the society becomes closer to what Bergson characterizes as duration: by opening the society, the morality is opened as well, and with it the once rigid and static doctrines go through change. But more importantly, in a temporal relation heterogeneity and singularity are promoted. Unlike the spatalized relationship between the subject and its society, in which the individual is absorbed in the obligations and static habits enforced by the community, in this type of relation with society the subject's singularity is not covered up. For example, Martin Luther King Jr. does not accept the limits of the group, the common conventions and norms, but acts to go beyond the solidarity laid down by nature and leaps beyond the limits of the closed community in a way that complies with his views. So instead of succumbing to the public's rigid traditions, he creates new habits that convey his ideology, his true beliefs. But he does not do so through compulsion, but by attraction—"They [great moral leaders] communicate to us something of their fervor, and draw us in their wake" (96). Yet most of us are not specially gifted leaders but ordinary people, and Bergson's thought does not seem to open up the way to a temporal relation between one ordinary person and another or even between one ordinary person and its community. No matter how open the society is, it always has a closed aspect, and for most of us our public existence involves covering up our singularity, merging in the collectivity, and accepting the common habits and traditions as our own. Bergson does not seem to offer us a way to form an intertemporal relation with another individual or society in which one's temporal and singular existence is not compromised through the existence with others.

Even if to some degree his thought opens up a way to view temporality as not only a crucial aspect of the individual, but also as essential to one's relation with a community or society of individuals, the point of view belongs to the individual. Bergson does not provide the foundation or vocabulary for understanding the relation between the individual and another as forming an intertemporal experience, and thus, his thought is insufficient for addressing the issue of intertemporality.

HEIDEGGER: TEMPORALITY, ETHICS, POLITICS

Similar to Bergson's distinction between duration and spatial time, Heidegger distinguishes between temporality (primordial time) and natural time (ordinary time) as belonging to nature and in which events take place. Unlike Bergson, Heidegger adds an additional mode of time—world time—that is the understanding of time as belonging to the structure of the world and involving events relevant to the way human beings lead their lives. William Blattner suggests understanding natural time, world time, and temporality in terms of an ascending relation of degeneration.[13] Heidegger determines natural time as the leveling down of world time. Unlike natural time, which is the cosmological time independent of human beings, world time is defined in terms of our human interests—lunchtime, teatime, happy hour, wartime, between the World Wars, the Middle Ages, the Golden Era, and so forth. Although world time reveals the relevance of time to human existence, it is temporality, the time grounded on the individual's existence, which is the primordial understanding of time and the basis of the other two experiences of time. Thus, even though Heidegger's analysis of time is different from Bergson's, both thinkers are motivated by their dissatisfaction with the traditional, Aristotelian interpretation of time; they refrain from considering time as an entity, but rather consider time as a lived process.[14] Both thinkers attempt to present what they believe to be a more real or authentic approach to time—one that is pertinent to our existence as individual human beings.

David Scott offers a different perspective for arguing the similarity between Bergson and Heidegger's motivation. He claims that Heidegger's analysis of clock time in Division Two of *Being and Time* shares a certain affinity with the Bergsonian position, because of their shared refusing of the neo-Kantian perspective assumed for interpreting the theory of relativity, and its resulting characterization of the being of time. In the context of these similarities, it is surprising that Heidegger does not acknowledge Bergson's contribution to his own philosophical project, and insists that Bergson's view of time is grounded in the traditional, Aristotelian perspective (*BT* 16, 23, 44). Similarly, Jean-Louis Vieillard-Baron claims that without Bergson there is no Heidegger as presented in *Being and Time*.[15]

Temporality

Heidegger's distinction between primordial temporality on the one hand and the leveling down of world time, vulgar time, on the other hand, reveals his agenda in *Being and Time* regarding the ethical issues relevant to Dasein's existence as an individual surrounded by others. For the most part Heidegger provides a negative picture of the other.[16] Heidegger stipulates that others and Dasein are on the same ontological level, and that being-with (*Mitsein*) is essential for the constitution of Dasein as an entity existing in the world.[17] But even though Dasein is not alone in the world, Heidegger focuses on Dasein as lost in the other, and he argues that Dasein must purify itself from *the they* (*das Man*) to become an authentic individual. Tina Chanter notices that unlike the traditional problem of attempting to connect an isolated I to others, Heidegger sees the opposite problem—the difficulty of freeing the absorbed I from the they, from the public in general. Chanter's observation of the primacy that Heidegger renders to the individual and his overall negative attitude to the other is furthered by Heidegger's analysis of time and temporality. According to Heidegger, the public, everyday time belongs to the they—to everyone and to no one—whereas primordial time is interpreted through the existence of the individual Dasein. Similar to Heidegger's reasoning that authentic Dasein should free itself from the public and overcome the leveled down way of being, primordial time is revealed when Dasein frees itself from the traditional perspective of the vulgar approach to time. It is via an authentic approach to time and death that the possibility of living the life of an authentic individual released from the they is revealed to Dasein. So although temporality is grounded in care (*Sorge*), and therefore is embedded in the existence of every Dasein, it is when Dasein discovers itself as temporal and understands temporality to be the origin of time that

Dasein can break away from the traditions and opinions of the they and lead an authentic life.

Heidegger's engagement with the question of time is not from the scientific or cosmological perspective, but from the existential onto-logical point of view. He insists that in the philosophical tradition the meaning of time is concealed because it neglects to consider the notion of temporality, and it focuses only on the public aspect of time. Heidegger shifts his inquiry from the traditional question, "What *is* time?" to the question, "What does it mean *to be in* time?"—or more accurately, "What does it mean *to be as* time?" For Heidegger, primor-dial time should not be interpreted in terms of motion and change, but should be understood from the perspective of Dasein's existential structure of care. He characterizes care by existentiality (having to be ahead of itself), facticity (already being in the world), and falling prey (being engaged with other things in the world) (*BT* 178–83). Each element of this definition of care constitutes an aspect of Dasein's temporality (*Zeitlichkeit*)—future, having-been (past), and present.

Temporality is neither the chronological order of now points, and nor does it arise from joining together the present, past, and future; rather, it is derived from Dasein's structure of existence. Dasein is the very locus of temporality, and it is from Dasein's modes of existence that an understanding of time comes forth. In being-ahead-of-oneself Dasein is futural in the original sense. The ahead-of is not a *before* in the sense of a not-yet-now; it is future not in the traditional sense of an *out there*, but it is Dasein's projection toward its future pos-sibilities, which reveal its concern about its potentiality of being. The ahead-of indicates the future as the realm of possibilities open before Dasein and Dasein's awareness of advancing toward the end, death. But Dasein also comports toward what already has been. Having-been is not merely the past left behind, but it is a characteristic of Dasein's temporality and factical existence as thrown into a world already existing. Having-been is everything Dasein has been that determines its existence.

Additionally, Dasein always acts and creates situations in a world that involves other entities with which Dasein is entangled. As engaged with entities in the world, Dasein makes things present and produces circumstances and conditions in which Dasein encounters other entities inhabiting the world. The present in the primordial sense requires focusing on our actual actions rather than regarding the present as the point in time in which events occur. As temporal beings we are the unity of the three phases, or ecstasies, of future, having-been, and present. Heidegger claims, "Temporality temporalizes itself in the ever current unity of future, past [having-been-ness] and present."[18] Contrary to the average understanding of future, present, and past as consecutive parts of linear time, these three ecstasies of temporality are equiprimordial. From the perspective of care, Dasein does not merely exist as a thing that comes into being, endures, and perishes; rather, as a temporal being, Dasein is at every moment the unity of a future, which makes present in the process of having been (*BT* 299–301, 321).

According to the Aristotelian interpretation, time is constructed as future, present, and past, in which the present moment is its point of reference. Only this present now actually exists, whereas the future and the past are either present in potential (not-yet-*present*) or an exhausted present (no-longer-*present*). Or to use Heidegger's words, the "past is irretrievable, future indeterminate."[19] However, for Heidegger the present is the least significant of the three ecstasies, and it is rather the future that bears the locus of existence. The future is the ground of the three-fold structure of care: "The future has priority in the ecstatic unity of primordial and authentic temporality, although temporality does not first originate through a cumulative sequence of the ecstasies, but always temporalizes itself in their equiprimordiality.... Primordial and authentic temporality temporalizes itself out of the authentic future, and indeed in such a way that, futurally having been, it first arouses the present. The primary phenomenon of primordial and authentic temporality is the future" (*BT* 302–03). The having-been and the present arise basically from the future. Existing as futural is the ultimate presupposition of authentic existence, since the future is Dasein's projection ahead-of-itself toward fulfilling Dasein's possibilities. The future is open in the sense that numerous possibilities are available to us, and from them we have to choose and become who we are. But this understanding of the future is frequently concealed. We tend to accept the everyday understanding, according to which the future is indeed open, but in the sense that unknown and indeterminate possibilities are awaiting us, as if events wait for us to encounter while we proceed along our path of life (this approach to the future is found in everyday idioms such as when we speak of "what the future holds"). Our past, according to Heidegger, emanates from our futural mode of existence—"in a way, having been arises from the future" (299). As long as we are futural we have possibilities, and the horizon of choices and possibilities available to us as futural includes also the possibility to return to our past and reinterpret the choices we have made. However, we can come back to what we have been, reinterpret our past, only as long as we are futural, that is as long as we have possibilities, since once our possibilities end, we actually no longer exist.

The momentousness of the future lies also in Dasein's being-toward-death. Being-toward-death is not the unavoidable termination of Dasein's life, but is the anticipatory appropriation of death to its own existence that makes Dasein finite. As historical, the possibilities that are open before Dasein are clearly bound by its birth and death; however, it is through being-toward-death and by anticipating death, that Dasein fully understands its being-ahead-of-itself. The future is the realm of possibilities, but, unlike all of Dasein's other possibilities, "as possibility, death gives Dasein nothing to 'be actualized' and nothing which it itself could be as something real" (*BT* 242). It is only through anticipating death that Dasein is able to understand itself as a possibility rather than as an actualized, fallen, ontical being. If Dasein turns its attention to its death, it does not understand time as a public sequence of nows, but rather as its own. And since Dasein is finite so is its time. Through the acknowledgment of the mineness (*Jemeinigkeit*) of my death the corresponding thought is revealed to me: only I can live my life, and only I can be responsible for the meaning that my life has for me.

But although temporality is primordial time, we generally avoid referring to time as belonging to the individual Dasein, and consider it to be a public entity that belongs to our everyday world. For Heidegger, Dasein is always preoccupied with and concerned about the world and the inner-worldly beings it encounters. One of the manifestations of this mode of existence is Dasein's being-in-time. Factical Dasein always reckons with time, is absorbed in the average interpretation of time, and since it adopts the view that time belongs to the world, it regards time as common to everyone. This world time belongs essentially to Dasein.[20] As the time taken care of, world time has the features of datability, spandness, significance, and publicness. Datability is the relational structure, which regards the *now* as constituting the *then* and *on that former occasion*. Datability is not understood according to terms such as objectivity and nature, but is experienced according to events: now I am working, on the former occasion I drove my son to kindergarten, and then I will pick him up. As William D. Blattner clarifies, we do not experience time as the seconds continuously ticking away, but as the now:[21] the now of reading, then the now of writing my thoughts, then the now of answering the phone, and so on. But every now, then, and on that former occasion lasts for a period of time—they are spanned and stretched—they have duration. The now that I am writing my thoughts spans from the former occasion of reading until the next now of answering the phone. This reveals the now as the point of reference of world time, separating the earlier from the later. Every now is understood as *time for*. We say, "It is time for this or that," "It is the appropriate time for this," or "It is the inappropriate time for that." These relations of significance, which are grounded in temporality, determine the structure of the world. For example, if it is bedtime then it is not the appropriate time for play. The morning is not the time for drinking alcohol, but happy hour is.

The time that is expressed through now, then, and on that former occasion has the feature of publicness, since it is derived from conventional occurrences that are grounded in being-with-one-another-in-the-world and that determine when lunchtime, dinnertime, happy hour, or bedtime are. Also the statement, "Now," is a public claim that expresses an understanding of time in terms of the world taken care of—in terms of the time that the they reckon with. Each one of us can be occupied with different tasks, but when I say, "Now," the other person understands what I am referring to.

Nevertheless, Heidegger recognizes that our common understanding of time, manifested explicitly in the use of the clock and in the measurement of time, does not comply with his description of world time. On account of the publicness of time, we assign to it objectivity—calendars, dates, and clocks are measurements of this time that belongs to nature and is independent of human existence. This average way of comprehending time is the leveling down (*Einebnung*) of world time, which is carried out by the covering over of the structure of temporality in which datability and significance are embedded (*BT* 387). Instead of admitting that our understanding of time is made of the datability of our actions, we ordinarily understand time as made of independent, objectively present moments. Similarly, we generally ignore the structure of significance, and instead add significance to an event we refer to as occurring in time. This vulgar, conventional interpretation of time does not only lack datability and significance, but also regards time as made of a series of objectively present nows that move in time. Consequently, Heidegger names this way of understanding time "now-time" (*Jetzt-Zeit*) (386). The most distinct outcome of the vulgar interpretation of time is that by the covering over of world time, temporality too is covered, thus, entailing a comprehension of time as an infinite succession of nows. In this context it should be mentioned that although Heidegger regards temporality as the primordial time, he acknowledges the legitimacy of the ordinary understanding of time, which is derived from temporality. The common understanding of time is not "wrong," and "the vulgar representation of time has its natural justification" (390). However, when this interpretation of time claims to provide the only "true" framework for understanding time, it loses its "exclusive and distinctive justification" (390).

For Heidegger, temporality is embedded in Dasein's existential structure of care, which generally describes the mode of existence of every Dasein. However, Heidegger's analysis of temporality is not limited to a general characterization. Rather, the general features of care that ground temporality—existentiality (having to be ahead of itself), facticity (already being in the world) and falling prey (being engaged with other things in the world)—are given a different sense and significance through the different lives of each individual Dasein. Moreover, when focusing on the temporal aspect of the individual, Dasein's authentic existence as separated from the they is revealed. As being-with other entities, Dasein is lost in the they but by awareness of its temporality, mainly of its being-toward-death, the individual authentic Dasein is extracted from the anonymous crowd. This leads Joseph J. Kockelmans to conclude that "time is the genuine principle of individuation."[22] According to Heidegger, the authentic self is constituted through its separation and differentiation from the they. In *Being and Time* he claims, "Understanding can turn primarily to the disclosedness of the world, that is, Dasein can understand itself initially and for the most part in terms of the world. Or else understanding throws itself primarily into for-the-sake-of-which, which means Dasein can exist as itself. Understanding is either authentic, originating from its own self as such, or else inauthentic" (*BT* 137). Dasein has the possibility of understanding itself in an authentic way, as an individual that forms the unique meaning of its existence despite the factical situations into which it has been thrown. Or it can understand itself inauthentically, as an individual absorbed in the world, living according to the beliefs and opinions of the they. These two opposing modes of self-understanding are closely tied with the two different approaches to time. This can be seen in Heidegger's discussion revolving around the issue of Dasein's "connection of life" between birth and death. This notion reveals a view that is not the ordinary historical self-understanding.

Heidegger's discussion of the temporality grounded in care focuses on Dasein's basic way of being-toward-death. But Dasein's existence also has a beginning—birth. To correct this, Heidegger examines the issue of Dasein's "connection of life" between birth and death. Dasein stretches out between its beginning in birth and ending in death, and it is this span of life that constitutes the whole history/

story (*Geschichte*)²³ of Dasein (*BT* 342). Heidegger refrains from understanding the idea of the "connectedness of life" as issuing from the Aristotelian interpretation of time. For Heidegger, "Dasein does not exist as the sum of momentary realities of experiences that succeed each other and disappear" (343). Moreover, unlike the Aristotelian view that considers only the present now (or actual experience) as real, the Heideggerian perspective emphasizes that as long as Dasein exists, both its "ends" (birth and death), as well as its "between," *are*. Similar to Heidegger's view that death is not a nonexisting event awaiting us in the future, birth is not a nonexisting event lying in the past. Dasein does not move, progress, or evolve *in* time the way a flower grows or an iceberg melts in time. Rather, "factical Dasein exists as born, and born it is already dying in the sense of being-toward-death" (343). Birth and death are aspects of Dasein that are always relevant to its existence. As Miguel de Beistegui illuminates, Dasein is born again and again, since it never ceases to be thrown into the world and into a life, which it has to live as being-toward-death.²⁴ Dasein continuously interprets and reinterprets itself.

Ethics

The primary objective of *Being and Time* is to examine the sociality of the life of an individual Dasein. At a basic level Dasein is individualized, detached, and to some extent is required to attain its authentic existence by releasing itself from all bonds to traditions, social principles, and moral values. But does Heidegger leave room for understanding the relation between Dasein and the other in terms of temporality, or does the authentic Dasein remain basically independent? Does Heidegger consider any form of intertemporal realm or mode of experience in which the different individuals exist or interact? Or does he, like Bergson, refrain from making the move from the temporal individual to the view of a temporal interpersonal community? Similarly, de Beistegui asks, how can we move from the encounter with one's self to a shared temporality, a cohistory? Does resoluteness open onto a more authentic way of being with others?²⁵

Jean-Luc Nancy defines this problem as the question concerning the way in which many Daseins can be *there* (*da*) together. He describes three possible ways of the "common": (1) a being-with in which each Dasein opens its own *there* (what Heidegger would consider as democracy); (2) a *there* in which the different openings intersect each other without merging into a unique Dasein; (3) and a common relation to a *there* that is beyond the singulars (what may lead to some form of totalitarianism).[26] What Nancy refers to as "the intermediary regime" correlates with the idea of an intertemporal dimension that I wish to explore.

The notion of historicity in section 74 of *Being and Time* is particularly relevant for examining the possibility of an intertemporal dimension between different Daseins. This section received much attention among scholars discussing the relation between Heidegger's attraction to Nazism and his philosophical views in *Being and Time*.[27] However, in reading this section my purpose is to examine whether the notion of temporality is reserved for the individual, and it is only within the bounds of the public time that Dasein interacts with the other, or, if Heidegger's discussion of historicity and its related ideas of fate, heritage, and destiny reveal a positive interpretation of Dasein's relationship with the community, which can lead the way to an intertemporal dimension.

As an historical being, Dasein inherits a heritage (*Erbe*). Dasein exists in a world with traditions to which Dasein "comes back" resolutely in its thrownness. Dasein inherits possibilities and opportunities, but by retrieving them Dasein does not merely repeat the inherited customs, but also chooses them, interprets them, appropriates them, and becomes committed to their significance. In taking over what has been handed down by tradition, Dasein forms its fate (*Schicksal*) and future-directed possibilities. Fate for Heidegger is not the Greek description of an inevitable future that is forced upon Dasein by chance, causality, or divinity, but is associated with Dasein's awareness of its finitude, that is, its anticipation of its death. Heidegger writes, "The interpretation of the historicity of Dasein turns out to be basically just a more concrete development of temporality"

(*BT* 350). Dasein is historical only because in a deeper sense Dasein exists as a temporal individual, and fate and heritage disclose the relation between historicity and temporality: "Only a being that is essentially futural in its being so that it can let itself be thrown back upon its factical There, free for its death and shattering itself on it, that is, only a being that, as futural, is equiprimordially having been, can hand down to itself its inherited possibility, take over its own thrownness and be in the moment for 'its time.' Only authentic temporality that is at the same time finite makes something like fate, that is authentic historicity, possible" (352). Heidegger's analysis of historicity opens up a way for Dasein to be authentic and resolute and at the same time rooted in its legacy, in its inherited past. In Heidegger's view, history is the context out of which Dasein's inherited possibilities emerge. But unlike the thrownness of Dasein, which reveals the tendency of Dasein to understand itself in terms of the public's language, customs, and practices, historicizing reveals Dasein's own particular fate. Through the reinterpretation and reappropriation of its heritage, Dasein determines its own fate and becomes authentic.

However, since Dasein exists as being-with, its own history or fate occurs with others, with the community of the people.[28] Hence, Dasein's individual historicizing is in fact historical in the sense that it exists as part of the shared history of a community of people, and this Heidegger names destiny (*Geschick*):

> But if fateful Dasein essentially exists as being-in-the-world in being with others, its occurrence is an occurrence-with and is determined as destiny. With this term we designate the occurrence of the community of people. Destiny is not composed of individual fates, nor can being-with-one-another be conceived as a mutual occurrence of several subjects. These fates are already guided beforehand in being-with-one-another in the same world and resoluteness for definite possibilities. In communication and in battle the power of destiny first becomes free. The fateful destiny of Dasein in and with its "generation" constitutes the complete, authentic occurrence of Dasein. (*BT* 352)

In order to better understand what the term "destiny" conveys, it may be helpful to distinguish it from the two other terms that accompany it in section 74—fate and heritage. Like fate, destiny is futural, and is made of authentic choices, but Heidegger explicitly says that destiny is not made of individual fates. The choices that constitute destiny do not belong to the individual Dasein (as in the case of fate), but destiny involves the choices made authentically by the community of Daseins. Hence, unlike heritage, which involves the past, and is described as including all the possibilities out of which the individual Dasein chooses, destiny is futural and involves the authentic possibilities that promote the mission of a certain community of Daseins. According to the interpretation suggested by Charles Guignon, the authentic Dasein understands its life as bound up with the life of the community of people and sees its own future-directed existence as interlaced into the wider undertaking of the mission or destiny, of an historical people.[29]

In the analysis of Johannes Fritsche, who for the most part disagrees with Guignon's interpretation, destiny rather precedes the Daseins and determines their fates. For Fritsche, destiny involves the authentic possibilities of the community of Daseins from which the individual Dasein cannot distance itself. The authentic Dasein who recognizes its fate understands that the past is the grounds of its ethos and identity, which allows for positive relations with the other.[30] This view is shared by Lawrence Vogel, who claims that "the fate of the individual is conditioned by the destiny in which he stands."[31] Whereas Mark Blitz, siding with Guignon, argues that destiny is subordinate to fate "because the popular destiny within which fate is possible is first freed by the anticipatory resoluteness that uncovers individual fate."[32] Despite the essential difference between the two positions, it seems that both Guignon and Fritsche agree that destiny offers a way in which Dasein can be in an authentic relation with other Daseins. Hence, the possibility of forming an authentic relation with one's community opens up a way for understanding Dasein's relation with the other as temporal rather than limited to and affiliated with vulgar time.

Consequently, some sorts of social relationships, although unspecified at Heidegger's ontological level of inquiry, can help Dasein move from an inauthentic to an authentic mode of existence. Moreover, after emphasizing aspects such as mineness and death that individualize and set apart authentic Dasein from the social world, Heidegger says earlier in *Being and Time*, "As *authentic being as self*, resoluteness does not detach Dasein from its world, nor does it isolate it as a free floating ego" (*BT* 274). Heidegger appears to be insinuating that an authentic existence as being-with is possible, and continues by saying, "The resoluteness towards itself first brings Dasein to the possibility of letting the others who are with it 'be' in their ownmost potentiality-of-being, and also discloses that potentiality in concern which leaps ahead and frees. Resolute Dasein can become the 'conscience' of others. It is from the authentic being of a self of resoluteness that authentic being-with-one-another first arises, not from ambiguous and jealous stipulations and talkative fraternizing in the they and in what they wants to undertake" (274). So even though the authentic Dasein must distance itself from the inauthentic modes of being-with-others, here Heidegger appears to allude to an authentic relation with the other.[33] The possibility of an authentic mode of existence as being-with-one-another opens up a way for describing Dasein's existence with other Daseins as not affiliated with public time, but as revealing a temporal authentic political existence.

However, even if we acknowledge that Heidegger's thought opens up the possibility of an authentic temporal community, he leaves this idea unexplored. Heidegger does not discuss the elements and actions that might join authentic individuals into a community, nor does he make an explicit move from the temporal individual to a communal temporal existence by showing how such a community can be related with his notion of temporality. Furthermore, it seems that such a temporal community would include only authentic Daseins. Therefore, even if such a temporal communal existence can be extracted from Heidegger's thought, it is offered to a limited number of individuals, and most aspects of social existence involve vulgar, public time. More importantly, even though we find in Heidegger a favorable description of one's relation with the other and allows for a temporal relation with other Daseins, he is explicit about the priority given to the authentic individual. For the other Dasein to be awakened and lead an authentic life, first the individual Dasein must be resolute and authentic, which involves a certain distancing from its lostness in the they. Richard Wolin makes a similar point from a different perspective, suggesting that "the historicity of Dasein, prompted by the 'anticipation of death' and grounded in categories such as 'heritage' and 'fate,' both frees Dasein for authentic self-individuation and forms the basis for an authentic Being-with-others."[34] Consequently, even if Heidegger does leave room for an intertemporal existence between one Dasein and another, it is grounded on the individual's authentic and temporal egological perspective.

Ed Wingenbach suggests that destiny as the cohistorizing of being-with, is the medium through which the being-with of each Dasein liberates one another and opens each to its own fateful situation.[35] This would open up the path to an authentic temporal existence of being-with. Yet, the community of cohistorical Daseins that Heidegger is describing is a homogeneous unit or organism (such as the German people) that has a shared destiny and thus actually leaves no room for the other. As Heidegger clearly states, the community and its destiny are not made of the plurality of fates of individual Daseins, and therefore the community can be seen as a subject analogous to Dasein. Just as the life of the individual is determined primarily by its being toward its future, the community is defined by its movement toward the realization of its destiny. So it appears that Heidegger does not offer an intertemporal existence involving the various fates and temporalities of different Daseins, and he is confined to the point of view of the same—whether it is an individual Dasein or a community of people.

More importantly, in his discussion of community and destiny Heidegger adopts the viewpoint of the individual Dasein. This corresponds both to Guignon's view and to the opposing view offered by Fritsche. According to Guignon's interpretation, the tripartite temporal structure, which springs from a projection onto future possibilities, draws on the past, and acts in the present can be described also from the viewpoint of history and historicity. The authentic mode of the individual's temporal existence involves its encounter with the future as destiny, the past as heritage, and the present as a world-historical situation.[36] So according to this interpretation, the discussion of history is presented from the individual's viewpoint. For Guignon, the authentic Dasein acts toward the community's shared mission and destiny, while in Fritsche's analysis, it is the other way around where the choices and the fate of the authentic Dasein are determined by the destiny of its community. Yet both consider the relation of the individual Dasein with its community as pertinent to Dasein's authenticity. This idea is found also in Wolin's interpretation of the relation between fate and destiny. According to Wolin, as an individuated subject, Dasein has a fate, but it is incomplete and unfulfilled. Only when Dasein's fate is inserted within a collective historical destiny is its authentic existence with others attained, and the true realization of Dasein's selfhood emerges.[37] In all three interpretations the focus is on Dasein's authenticity, and consequently on Dasein's temporality. Therefore, *Being and Time* does not truly open up the possibility of an intertemporal existence of Daseins, but merely reveals a way in which Dasein can become authentic through its relation with its community. As Dana Villa writes, although a role for politics can be detected in *Being and Time,* "Heidegger's supposed entrapment in the philosophy of the subject does not really answer the question of what a politics extrapolated from *Being and Time* would look like."[38] The relation with the community is just one more aspect involving the formation of Dasein's authentically temporal existence, and this view of temporality is confined to the perspective of the individual, and therefore does not go beyond egological time.

Politics

It is possible that a view of political, collective time can be extracted from Heidegger's later thought. After *Being and Time* the notions of time and temporality seem to lose their centrality in Heidegger's thought, but the question of the political becomes particularly salient.[39] It is a well-known fact that during the 1930s Heidegger was enthusiastic for the National Socialist party and he expressed an interest in the relation between philosophy and the *Volk*—a potentially authentic (German) community.[40] In Heidegger's later works where he reformulates the question of the meaning of Being, we notice many statements that have either direct or indirect political bearing.[41] The locus of the event of Being is no longer understood from the individuated perspective of Dasein, but, as Wolin suggests, in these later writings Heidegger is preoccupied with the truth of Being itself and with the "historical life of the *Volk*."[42] Heidegger's notorious rectoral address, "The Self-Assertion of the German University," for example, is dominated by the pronoun *we,* which is in contrast with the emphasis given in *Being and Time* to the individuality and mineness of Dasein. And in Heidegger's 1934 lecture course on logic, he asks, "Who (and not 'what') are we ourselves?" Heidegger replies, "We are the *Volk*" (*LGC* 52, 93).

The emphasis on the we leads Miguel de Beistegui to ask if politics begins when the I says, "We."[43] We may conclude that the priority given in Heidegger's later thought to Being and *we* over the point of view of the individual Dasein reveals the precedence of the collective, political perspective of the *Volk*, the people. A different view is provided by W. J. Korab-Karpowicz who argues, "Heidegger rejects any forms of collectivism, in which, by forsaking reflection on their existence, human beings surrender themselves to something 'greater' than themselves. Therefore, if there is any political theory implied in his writings, it is certainly not one that can be associated with fascism or Nazism."[44] Nevertheless, even if we reject this view and accept that in Heidegger's later writings the focus is on the collectivism of the we, a coherent intertemporal political dimension cannot be extracted from these writings. Heidegger does not go beyond the egological perspective but replaces one subject (the individual Dasein) with another (the *Volk*). For example, in claiming, "As long as we say 'we,' we are" (*LGC* 94), Heidegger rephrases Descartes's account of the indubitability of the *cogito* by replacing the I with we. Wolin argues that just as Heidegger's *Being and Time* seeks to justify the individuality of each Dasein, the later thought supports the view that the existential particularity of Germany's Dasein is as *Volk*.[45] Gregory Fried notices that in Heidegger's discussion of a community of the *Volk*, he employs the term "fate"—a term that in *Being and Time* is reserved for the individual.[46] There is also a correlation between *Being and Time*'s emphasis on the *who* of Dasein and the focus in the later writings on the who of the we rather than on the *what*. Moreover, despite Heidegger's shift of focus from the individual Dasein to the we, he stresses that "the concept 'We' is not to be conceived as plural" (48). Consequently, Heidegger is still confined to the perspective of the subject (the same), whether it is the individual Dasein or the *Volk*, and he ultimately leaves no room for plurality or alterity. As Villa concludes regarding the texts of the 1930s, namely "The Origin of the Work of Art," Heidegger perpetuates an organic notion of community that is devoid of genuine plurality.[47]

Such a lack of plurality is demonstrated also in Heidegger's remarks on conversation. In his 1936 essay, "Hölderlin and the Essence of Poetry," the poet's words "since we have been a conversation" provide Heidegger the background for discussing how the event of language occurs. Conversation (or dialogue) obviously implies a relation with an other, as the poem continues: "And able to hear from one another." Heidegger explains that "language is essential only as conversation" and "speaking mediates our coming to one another."[48] Heidegger's view that the essentiality of language is conversation as well as his claim that being able to hear is the presupposition of language, appear to anticipate Levinas's view of language and dialogue. But unlike Levinas for whom language via responsibility preserves the alterity of the other, Heidegger follows Friedrich Hölderlin's words "we have been *a* conversation" (my italics), and claims that we are *one* single conversation. From a Levinasian perspective this means that the same and the other are united through dialogue, and the result is the effacement of the other's alterity. This idea is emphasized by the link Heidegger forms between conversation and history, claiming that both "belong together, and they are the same."[49] Given that for Heidegger history is central for collective commitment, conversation assumes the role of uniting the individuals of the community in their commitment for the collective mission or destiny of the

Volk. Consequently, Heidegger's views on conversation do not open up a way for describing an intertemporal relation with the other. Heidegger does not focus on the relation between the individuals, nor does he reveal dialogue as a dimension in between the interlocutors, but rather considers dialogue as a structure that unites the individuals within one totalizing order. Such a view of dialogue complies with the synchronic structure of time (such as scientific time) that Levinas strives to overcome.

One of the important changes that occur in Heidegger's philosophy during the 1930s includes a move from concern with Dasein's temporality (*Zeitlichkeit*) to a concern with Temporality (*Temporalität*). As William McNeill notices, this signifies a philosophical shift in Heidegger's thinking from the historicity of Dasein and the temporal enactment of Dasein's individuated ownmost potential-for-Being, to the concern with the historical destining of the world.[50] This indicates a move beyond the perspective of the individual Dasein toward the point of view of the *Volk*. But despite the fact that the viewpoint of the individual is replaced with that of the *Volk*, the homogeneous notion of community in Heidegger's later writings does not open up a way to an intertemporal political conception of time. This can be especially observed in two of his texts from 1934, *Logic as the Question Concerning the Essence of Language* and *Hölderlin's Hymns: Germania and the Rhine.*

In the first part of *Logic,* Heidegger's overall concern is with a two-part question: "In which realm does language belong, and what is language?" In the attempt to address this question, Heidegger claims that language lies in the realm of human beings. Continuing, he asks further, "Who is the human being," and replies that the human being is historical, leading Heidegger to the question, "What is history?" (see *LGC* 1–100). In the second part, Heidegger moves from the question of history to the question of time. Similar to his view expressed in *Being and Time,* he claims, "The question concerning the human being is from the start the question concerning temporality" (115). Yet he rephrases the relation between temporality and history discussed in *Being and Time,* claiming that the original experience of temporality is necessary for becoming an historical *Volk* "in the distinctive sense," and concludes that "time is the fountain of the historical *Volk* and of the individuals in the *Volk*" (110).

Although Heidegger mentions the notions of care and being-toward-death to which temporality is tied in *Being and Time,* here the emphasis is on labor. As Wolin notices, labor is treated by Heidegger as "an essential modality whereby humanity realizes itself histori-cally."[51] Unlike care and being-toward-death in which the focus is on the existence of the individual Dasein detached from the they, he continues, "Labor as fundamental comportment of the human being is the ground for the possibility of being-with-one-another. Labor as such, even if it is done by one individual, transports the human being into the being-with-and-for-another" (*LGC* 133). Hence, it may seem that labor is a collective, political action that opens up a way for developing an original intertemporal experience of time. But in the following section Heidegger states, "This kind of being-human lets us first of all comprehend *how* and *who* the being [*das Seiende*] must be to satisfy alone such being [*Sein*]. This being [*Seiende*] is never subject, nor an assembly of several subjects, who by virtue of agreements first ground a community, but the originally united being [*Seiende*] bearing exposedness, transportedness, tradition, and mandate can only be what we call 'a *Volk*'" (133–34). This implies that Heidegger actually is not concerned with the relation between one Dasein and another, or even between Dasein and the commu-nity. Rather, he keeps moving from the perspective of the individual Dasein to the homogeneous perspective of the *Volk,* the we, that is not the sum total of individual yous, but is the "We who stand under a certain mandate, who find ourselves in a special situation" (37).

Heidegger also expresses his political thinking and his concern for the destiny of the German people in his discussions of Hölderlin's poetry.[52] His later works on art and poetry are closely linked with the question of Dasein's authentic historical existence as a communal being. Also in the context of these discussions the issue of time is reexamined. For example, in section 6 of *Hölderlin's Hymns,* while thinking of the original time of the peoples (*Völker*), Heidegger asserts, "'We' must be determined from the horizon of the question of time."[53] The focus on the relation between we and time, and particularly the opposition between the original time of the *Volk* and the measurable time of the individual suggest that Heidegger is presenting here an interpretation of time that differs from the one presented in *Being and Time*. He no longer associates original time with the temporality of the individual, he avoids examining time from the perspective of Dasein's individuated existence as care and as being-toward-death, and describes the time of the individual as the computable number of years between the date of birth and death.[54] Here Heidegger uses the verb *berechnen* (calculate, reckon) to describe the time of the individual, whereas in *Being and Time* he uses this verb, usually in the active form *rechnen* (reckon), to describe the leveled down world time. For the later Heidegger the time of the we is considered as original, whereas the time of the individual is characterized as calculable and measurable—aspects that in *Being and Time* portray the leveled down world time and cosmological time. Heidegger describes the historical, original time of the peoples as the time of poets, thinkers, and state founders, meaning, those who found and justify the historical existence of a people.[55] This suggests that the people have one common historical, original time that unites them (through poetry, for example). Such a view of time implies a totalizing, homogeneous (synchronic) structure that is not a dimension between individuals, but rather encompasses them.

Heidegger, like Bergson, provides a view of time that is egological, restricted to the perspective of the subject—whether the subject is the individual or the homogeneous society of people. Even though we detect in Heidegger's writings a concern for the political, his thought lacks the plurality, difference, multiplicity, and alterity necessary for going beyond the homogeneous perspective of the same. Nancy arrives at a similar conclusion claiming that what he calls "the intermediary regime" remains underdeveloped both in *Being and Time* and in Heidegger's later works.[56] We are now faced with a number of questions: Is it at all possible to go beyond views of time dominated by the same? Is there a way for understanding time as intertemporal, as a dimension, which does not belong to the public and at the same time is independent of the perspective of the subject (such as the individual person or the community of people)?[57] With these problems in mind, and against the background of the thoughts presented by Bergson and Heidegger, Levinas's view of time continues the move initiated by Bergson and Heidegger in tying time with the human mode of existence, but at the same time it leaves room for considering time as constituted by our existence among other people. The question to consider, however, is whether Levinas's view merely combines the demand for an understanding of time embedded in the human structure of existence with the traditional view of time as public, or rather, provides a view that reveals an independent perspective for considering the question of time.

Two

On the Way to Intersubjective Time

Levinas presents an understanding of time that in many significant ways preserves the model of time provided by Bergson and Heidegger, who find the locus of time in the human structure of existence. As discussed in the previous chapter, Bergson and Heidegger were among the first to break away from the traditional interpretation of time, to overcome the cosmological, scientific view, and to tie the constitution of time with the human structure of existence. Since Levinas's interpretation of time begins where Bergson and Heidegger left off, it is important to note how his approach to time corresponds with the views offered by Bergson and Heidegger but also goes against and beyond them.

Many discussions of Levinas's philosophy in general, and of his interpretation of time in particular, are formed in comparison with the thought of Heidegger. Robert Manning, for example, claims, "Levinas's philosophy is a constant arguing against and interpreting otherwise than Heidegger's phenomenological ontology, but always within the context of and after the manner of Heidegger's phenomenological project in *Being and Time*."[1] And Tina Chanter suggests, "Levinas's thoughts on time will remain inaccessible unless they are understood as having emerged out of what was, at least initially, his wholesale immersion in Heidegger's critique of the traditional metaphysical view of time in *Being and Time*."[2] These attempts are certainly right to situate Levinas's thought in relation to Heidegger's philosophy; however, even though Levinas explicitly acknowledges Bergson's significance,[3] the relevance of Bergson's thought to the philosophy of Levinas and to his understanding of time has not received sufficient attention.[4] Bergson's philosophy is no less important and pertinent for understanding Levinas's originality. In an essay examining the relation between Levinas's early view of time and Bergson's views in his late writings, Robin Durie concludes, "Levinas's thought emerges from a profound engagement with the philosophy of Bergson, an engagement whose complexity challenges us to think anew about the most fundamental problems of the philosophy of time."[5] Durie suggests that Bergson has anticipated the distinctive ways of conceptualizing the movement of time that are advanced by Levinas in his early essays. Durie seems surprised that although Levinas recognizes Bergson's influence on his thought, he does not acknowledge a "Bergsonian anticipation of his theory of time." But when examining Levinas's view of time in the context of his philosophical project in general, it becomes clear why he is critical of Bergson (and Heidegger). From a Levinasian perspective, the views of Bergson and Heidegger are confined to the perspective of the individual, whereas at the heart of Levinas's view of time lies an attempt to go beyond the ontology of the same.

Despite the similarities between the views of Bergson and Heidegger, we notice an essential difference between their approaches to the question of subjectivity, which reflects upon their views of time. Simon Critchley summarizes Heidegger's relation with the Cartesian tradition stating that in defining Dasein as being-with, Heidegger displaces Descartes's starting point of the thinking subject. The individual Dasein is not closed up in itself and is not separated from being, but rather is expanded to the world.[6] Bergson, on the other hand, can be seen as belonging to the tradition that privileges the Cartesian thinking subject, since for him the subject is formed from an amalgamation of inner experiences, which constitute its duration. Although both Bergson and Heidegger require a mode of change for the creation of time, this difference determines where each thinker locates the locus of change. Bergson, who focuses on the individual's consciousness in understanding duration, locates the necessary change in the subject's heterogeneous experiences and thoughts. Whereas Heidegger, who reveals the tension between Dasein's existence as being-with and its authentic existence as detached from the crowd, concentrates on Dasein's relation to its own death as the aspect of change that enables it to individuate itself from the they, and which is required for the constitution of its temporality. Levinas follows Bergson and Heidegger in requiring a mode of difference or otherness for the constitution of time, but from his viewpoint, what they determine as otherness is an insufficient alterity, and he locates elsewhere the difference necessary for the creation of time.

THE INSTANT AND THE SUBJECT

The most prominent connection between the interpretation of time offered by Levinas and those suggested by Bergson and Heidegger is the role the human structure of existence plays in the interpretations of all three thinkers. Similar to Bergson and Heidegger, Levinas insists on the temporal structure of the existent, but also acknowledges the traditional understanding of time. The aspect of everyday, public time, which Bergson names "spatial time" and for Heidegger is "vulgar time," Levinas calls in his early writings "the time of economic life." Like Bergson and Heidegger, Levinas distinguishes this everyday time from a more deeply lived time: "There then is no question of denying the time of our concrete existence, constituted by a series of instants to which the 'I' remains exterior. For such is the time of economic life, where the instants are equivalent and the 'I' circulates across them to link them up....We ask then whether the event of time cannot be lived more deeply as the resurrection of the irreplaceable instant. In place of the 'I' that circulates in time, we posit the 'I' as the very ferment of time in the present, the dynamism of time" (*EE* 95). Levinas's distinction between the time of economic life and the deeply lived time is analogous to the contrast Heidegger establishes between cosmological time and temporality, and particularly to the opposition Bergson forms between spatial time and duration. Before developing his own unique view of time, it seems that in his early thought Levinas is relying on Bergson's perspective and vocabulary.

Like Bergson's spatial time, Levinas's time of economic life is characterized as a series of equivalent (homogeneous) instants, which are exterior to the subject. This resemblance suggests an approach, which similar to Bergson's spatial time, considers time to be experienced as an entity exterior to the subject. The view of time as external is opposed to Bergson's duration, which is an understanding of time as a heterogeneous inner time made of the experiences of each individual. Therefore, for Bergson, duration is tied with the individual's history and becoming, with the processes and evolvements that it undergoes.

Bergson has influenced Levinas to distinguish the time of economic life from what he calls a more deeply *lived* time. In lived time the subject does not experience time from the outside, as exterior to it, does not live (circulate) *in* time, as if time were an objective, public, or — to use Bergson's perspective — spatial entity. Rather the subject is "the ferment of time," that which is responsible for the dynamism, the movement of time, and its constitution. Thus, for Levinas the deeply lived time is first and foremost a time that is grounded on the individual's life.

But even in his early writings, before presenting his original view of time, Levinas goes beyond the interpretations of his predecessors. Contrary to Bergson and Heidegger, who consider all dimensions, aspects, or ecstasies of time as grounded on the individual's existence, for Levinas the dimension that is embedded in the subject and related with its unique existence is limited to the present. The present is the aspect in which the individual is bound to itself and keeps returning to itself. As long as the individual is isolated without a world or others it is restricted to the present. Moreover, even when we concentrate on the individual's temporality, as Bergson and Heidegger do, we are confined to the present — the time of the subject is what Levinas calls the present.[7] In his late thought he continues to develop this idea, and refers to such a view of time as synchronic. But in his earlier work, *Existence and Existents* (and to some extent also in his following work, *Time and the Other*), Levinas examines the notion of the present and its relation with the individual subject by focusing on the emergence of the human being from the anonymous, impersonal existence, the *il y a*.

Edith Wyschogrod makes an illuminating suggestion in comparing the *il y a* to the Judeo-Christian description of chaos. Unlike the apocalypse that follows the final collapse of the world, from which existents cannot materialize since it is so radical that it cannot be overcome, the chaos, *tohu va-vohu* (without form and void), portrayed in Genesis provides a picture resembling Levinas's description of the impersonal *il y a* from which existents emerge.[8] Shmuel Wygoda seems to make the opposite move: he reads the first verses opening the Bible by adopting a Levinasian perspective and focuses on the moment of separation as a description of being without time.[9] Similar to the biblical description of the creation of the world, from the *il y a*, the impersonal and timeless being, the subject arises. Levinas names this moment of separation when being becomes the existent's attribute *hypostasis* (*TO* 51–54). Once the existent is separated from the anonymous existence, "there is not only, anonymously, being in general, but there are beings capable of bearing names" (*EE* 103). Hence, through its separation from the impersonal existence, the existent acquires its identity. This separation and formation of identity involves solitude. "Solitude is the very unity of the existent.... The subject is alone because it is one." And further, "A solitude is necessary in order for there to be a freedom of beginning, the existent's mastery over existing—that is in brief, in order for there to be an existent" (*TO* 54–55). For the existent to be separated from the impersonal existence and acquire its own unity and identity, it must become a solitary instant.

This requirement of separation and solitude for the constitution of the present might seem similar to Bergson and Heidegger's interpretation of time as embedded in the individual's existence. But contrary to Heidegger and Bergson, who focus on the individual as the origin of the constitution of real or authentic time, for Levinas the instant in which the individual existent (being) arises as a separate entity from existence (Being) in general is defined as the present, and therefore "the present is the beginning of a being" (*EE* 102). The subject has a present once its self is separated from the anonymous being and acquires its identity, but for Levinas this phase does not yet involve time. Consequently, the notion of the present occurs before and outside the structure of time (*TO* 52). The view of the present as outside time is found also in Aristotle's interpretation of the now in book 4 of the *Physics* when he says, "The now is not a part of time. . . . Time, however, does not seem to consist of nows."[10] Nevertheless, Levinas obviously offers a different understanding of the present, and considers it exterior to time for a different reason.[11] As Levinas himself states, throughout the history of philosophy the present instant "gets its significance from the dialectic of time; it does not have a dialectic of its own" (*EE* 72). So although the now is not part of time, it "determines time,"[12] to use Aristotle's words. But for Levinas the instant, the present, has its own function. It is in this instant that the subject is extracted from the chaotic, anonymous *il y a*.

But at this instant of separation the solitary subject is still trapped and entangled within itself: "A being capable of beginning in the present is alone encumbered with itself" (*EE* 79), and "The present refers only to itself, but this reference that should have dazzled it with freedom, imprisons it in identification" (78). Thus, the individual, solitary subject is bonded and confined to its identity, and in its inability to escape itself it is also unable to escape its presence. It is caught up in the present "as in a winter landscape where frozen beings are captives of themselves" (78). Therefore, the only movement that is available to it is "its inevitable return to itself" and to its present (78). We can understand this idea of the present in light of the correlation we find between Levinas's effort to provide a view of time that is not restricted to the perspective of the individual and his objection to the understanding of time as dominated by the present.

Heidegger already noted that time is traditionally conceived in terms of the present—the past and the future are merely modifications of the present. For example, Aristotle defines the future as the not-yet-present and the past as no-longer-present.[13] But in Levinas's view, Heidegger is unsuccessful in going beyond the present, and "he never escaped from the Greek language of intelligibility and presence," for "while Heidegger heralds the end of the metaphysics of presence, he continues to think of being as a coming-into-presence; he seems unable to break away from the hegemony of presence that he denounces" (DEL 20). According to Levinas, being is a temporal modality that is thought by reference to the present, and consequently, Heidegger's philosophy is still a philosophy of the present. Moreover, for Heidegger, as well as for Bergson, in recollection and anticipation the past and the future are brought into the present. That is, the subject tries to make all of time its own time by gathering the past and the future into the duration of the *cogito* or as constituting the temporality and history of Dasein. This too results in a philosophy that is dominated by the temporal mode of the present and in the subject's inevitable return to itself. Fabio Ciaramelli suggests that Dasein is trapped in the present, since its apparent movement is actually a return to the same through the self-reference of care.[14] Consequently, from Levinas's perspective, the views of duration and temporality offered respectively by Bergson and Heidegger manifest a restriction to the present. If we are unable to go beyond the individual's perspective then we are confined to egological time, meaning that we are doomed to keep returning to the present. However, Levinas's criticism does not imply a rejection of such views of time. If we adopt the individual's viewpoint, as Bergson and Heidegger do, then there is room for an egological understanding of time such as duration or temporality. But if we follow Levinas, who urges us to overcome the subject's limited perspective, then the real meaning of time will reveal itself.

The disparity between the approach of Levinas to the issue of time, particularly his concept of the present, and the views presented by Heidegger and Bergson may be discussed by focusing on the subject's relation with the other. Heidegger considers Dasein as already existing in a world with others and he finds alterity in the world, yet his focus is on detachment from the they as a condition of Dasein's authentic existence: "Dasein is authentically itself only if it projects itself, as being-together with things taken care of and concernful being-with…, primarily upon its ownmost potentiality-of-being, rather than upon the possibility of the they-self" (*BT* 243). Heidegger, as well as Bergson, believes that the authentic, or real, time is grounded on the individual's existence. In respect to the conception of time offered by these thinkers Levinas claims, "The subject in question was always a solitary subject. The ego all alone, the monad, already had time" (*EE* 96). However, for Levinas, "positing hypostasis as a present is still not to introduce time into being" (*TO* 52). Although the emergent of the existent out of the *il y a* provides the present, hypostasis is the event of the individual instant or monad, and as such it does not give us the movement or lapse required for there to be time. Hypostasis starts from itself and therefore does not receive anything from the past. It also does not involve a new moment, and therefore, it does not give a future. Levinas insists that the solitary subject is confined to the present and to itself, and as a result "the alterity of another instant cannot be found in the subject, who is definitively himself. This alterity comes to me only from the other" (*EE* 93). The subject does not include change or alterity, which is required for the formation of time, and without encountering the other, time is not produced.

Levinas's insistence that the alterity required for the constitution of time is found only in the subject's relationship with the other goes beyond Bergson's and Heidegger's focus on the constitution of time by adopting the point of view of the individual subject. It should be emphasized that Heidegger does consider the other and the world in his analysis of time and temporality; we even find moments in which the relation with the other is not characterized as inauthentic. Yet Heidegger's view of time is limited to the perspective of the individual. Bergson refrains from explicitly acknowledging the other in his discussion of duration, although to some degree his thought opens up a way to view temporality as essential to one's relation with a community or society of individuals. Nevertheless, the point of view is restricted to the individual. For Bergson duration is an inner time, so even if the subject would be totally isolated without any apparent external change—for example if it existed alone in a windowless, symmetrical white-walled room—there would still be duration. Even in this secluded state the individual will endure incessant internal changes, and experience the entire range of duration consisting of past, present, and future. But for Levinas such an event can be viewed as one that is limited to the present. The situation describing a solitary subject, a monad imprisoned in a windowless, symmetrical white-walled room can be seen as an illustration of the individual being against the anonymous impersonal being. In such conditions no world or others exist, and as a result there is no possibility of movement toward others. The subject is confined to itself and to its present, and thus, its movement is always a return to itself. Consequently, according to Levinas, without the other there is nothing but the present: "The I is not independent of its present, cannot traverse time alone" (*EE* 96). Hence, as noted by Aristotle, time requires a movement from the present to an entirely new moment, and therefore, "the definitiveness which comes to pass in the present is not initially connected with time" (79). As long as there are no new moments there is no time, but only a single now, and the subject is trapped in the present. In Levinas's view it is only through a relationship with the other that we go beyond the present and time is constituted.[15]

Similarity and Difference

Levinas criticizes the views of egological time offered by Bergson and Heidegger. To understand his critique, it may be helpful to clarify where each thinker locates the origin of change, or alterity, which all three agree is necessary for the constitution of time. Bergson, Heidegger, and Levinas all accept the Aristotelian condition for the creation of time—time requires change or alterity[16]—but each thinker finds the locus of this change elsewhere.[17]

In book 4 of the *Physics* Aristotle defines time as "a number of change with respect to before and after... number in the sense of that which is numbered, not in the sense of that by which we number."[18]

Hence, in order for time to elapse, a distinction between a before and an after state of motion (change) must be noticeable. Therefore, time is not change, but it depends on change. Time is that in movement which is counted—it is counted in relation with "any and every change,"[19] and is experienced through the before and after. In his commentary on Aristotle's *Physics,* W. D. Ross clarifies that when claiming that time is that in movement which is counted, Aristotle does not imply that by noticing the difference between nows change is recognized. It is the other way around. By noticing change we detect different nows and the lapse of time between them. Through transition, such as a body's transition from one point to another, we observe the different nows and consequently—the elapse of time between them.[20] According to Aristotle, it is only through change that we can distinguish between two nows, and it is only by distinguishing between two nows that we experience a passage of time.

Although Bergson accepts the requirement of change for the formation of time, he offers a unique approach when describing time in terms of *qualitative* change and not only as quantitative change that can be divided into homogeneous, countable, parts (*TFW* 75–85). Bergson challenges the traditional Aristotelian claim that time is the countable different nows that are founded on change. For Bergson such an interpretation reveals the captivation to the spatial perspective. In his view, countable things are different in degree not in kind, and since countable things must exist together simultaneously, they must exist in space (and if—like colors—they are abstract, we must substitute them for things that exist in space). Contrary to spatial time, duration does not consist of things that are qualitatively the same, and he was among the first to focus on heterogeneity, on qualitative differences when discussing time.

Levinas follows the tradition of understanding time as closely connected with change, or to use his term, alterity, but he provides a different interpretation of change and finds its origin elsewhere. He neither accepts the Aristotelian tradition that focuses on time as tied with quantitative change that is found in the physical world surrounding us, nor does he embrace the Bergsonian perspective that

grounds time on the qualitative change occurring in the inner consciousness of every individual. Jean-Louis Vieillard-Baron suggests
that Levinas's withdrawal from the tradition dominated by ontology
can be traced to Bergson's criticism of spatial time and his attempt to
release us from the dominance of science and knowledge.[21] Indeed,
like Bergson, Levinas wants to break away from the tradition that overlooks differences, strives to understand the many through the One,
disregards alterity, and transmutes otherness into the same. However,
from Levinas's perspective, Bergson is still confined to the perspective
of ontology. In Levinas's thought the *same* and *other* receive a much
more extreme interpretation than has been offered before. The same
includes not only the subject and its thoughts, but also the objects of
consciousness, the representation of objects, "because in representation the I precisely loses its opposition to its objects; the opposition
fades, bringing out the identity of the I despite the multiplicity of its
objects.... To remain the same is to represent to oneself" (*TI* 126).
Through representation and comprehension the object is no longer
exterior and opposed to the subject but is integrated into the ego and
contained in it, and as a result, the object's otherness is reduced to the
same. At the same time, despite the multiplicity of the represented/
comprehended objects, "the unalterable character of the I" (126),
that is, the identity of the same, remains unchanged and "is not alien-
ated by the other" (42). Consequently, if we accept Levinas's interpretation of the same, then we must agree that the changes occurring
within the individual's consciousness are an insufficient alterity.[22]

Similar observations are presented by Elena Bovo and Robert
Legros regarding Husserl's phenomenology of internal time-
consciousness. Legros claims that Husserl's temporality is restricted
to the perspective of the same, and Bovo suggests that the individual's future and past experiences create alterity, but this alterity
does not transcend consciousness.[23] Thus, for Levinas even Bergson's
notion of duration and Husserl's phenomenology of internal time-
consciousness are based on inadequate account of alterity. According
to Levinas the same is tied with the identity of the individual, which

"consists in being the *same*—in being oneself, in identifying oneself from within" (*TI* 289). So although Bergson's duration is heterogeneous in the sense that it is constructed of different, changing, and uncountable experiences, and even though, as Bovo suggests, Husserl's phenomenology of temporality is linked with an absence created by alterity,[24] these views of time are formed by the subject's consciousness, and therefore, from Levinas's perspective, they remain within the realm of the same. Leonard Lawlor presents this idea from a slightly different perspective. He claims that in a sense the present repeats the past through the addition of memory images, and as a result the singularity of the future does not give newness but only difference.[25] Consequently, for Levinas, newness and alterity are not contained in the individual, but must remain exterior.

Refusing the tradition that assimilates the other to the same is pertinent to Levinas's approach to time. In *God, Death, and Time* Levinas asks: "How to lend a meaning to time, when for philosophy identity is the identity of the Same, when intelligibility thrives in the Same, when it thrives on being in its stability as the Same, when it thrives on assimilating the Other into the Same—when every alteration is senseless, when understanding assimilates the Other into the Same?" (*GDT* 107). In order for time to be constituted, an alterity that is absolutely other that goes beyond the same, is required. Hence, the change required for the creation of time is not found within the individual subject. For Levinas the solitary ego is mired in itself and in the present, and without a new moment it remains at the state of an unchanging eternal present. The constitution of time demands the relationship between the present and a new moment. "The absolute alterity of another instant cannot be found in the subject, who is definitely himself. This alterity comes to me only from the other" (*EE* 96). Therefore, it is only the other person that provides the new moment, the future, which is necessary for the creation of time. Hence, "the condition of time lies in the relationship between humans" (*TO* 79), and time is constituted through the face-to-face encounter with the other.

THE OTHERNESS OF DEATH

Levinas inherits from Heidegger the importance of death, but he revises the meaning attached to it.[26] Heidegger focuses on the death of the individual, whereas Levinas ties his discussion of death with his discussion of the other's absolute otherness. He refers both to our relationship with death and to our relationship with the other as a relationship with a mystery (*TO* 70, 75). Richard Cohen explains that social life and death have in common the experience of an encounter with radical alterity (75n52). Adriaan Peperzak also remarks on the similarity between death and the other and claims that both shock me in their absolute otherness, since neither can take place within the unfolding of my possibilities.[27] And Paul Olivier states that in face of the other, as in face of death, "I cannot anymore."[28] Death can be considered as a model for one's relationship with other people. The relationship with death, similar to the relationship with the other, is a relationship with something that is absolutely unknowable, ungraspable, and incomprehensible—it is one's relationship with what does not come from within oneself but is absolutely exterior. In this context Cohen makes a helpful observation, claiming that characterizations such as *ungraspable* and *unknowable,* although not incorrect, concentrate excessively on grasping and knowledge, which are bound to the philosophical tradition of ontology and epistemology. Death is not known, but it is not simply unknown, since it exceeds the realm of knowledge, and for this reason death is described as a mystery.[29] The relation with the death of the other provides an ethical relation with an alterity that is beyond the same.

Levinas's approach is opposed to Heidegger's focus on the aspect of the mineness (*Jemeinigkeit*) of death. For Heidegger an authentic approach regards death as "always essentially my own" (*BT* 223). Heidegger insists that death is one's ownmost possibility since it is the only experience that is inescapably one's own, and in standing before itself in its ownmost potentiality-of-being "all relations to other Dasein are dissolved" (232). Moreover, for Heidegger death is the essence of the future, and by accepting death as its own,

Dasein's temporal existence is revealed to it, as well as its ecstatic projection toward the future. Consequently, in Heidegger's thought the certitude of death does not come from the experience of the death of others, but only through my relation with the possibility of my own death. As Levinas observes, the death of the other is for Heidegger merely an event coming to pass within the world (*GDT* 48, 51).

Heidegger considers death as nothingness, and claims that Dasein's "death is the possibility of no-longer being-able-to-be-there.... Death is the possibility of absolute impossibility of Dasein" (*BT* 232). This suggests an understanding of death as the annulment of one's existence, which is contrasted with Dasein's being or with temporality, and thus can lead to interpreting death as an alterity, as an otherness that is opposed to Dasein's existence. Hence, for Heidegger the alterity required for the constitution of time is found in death—it is the relation with the otherness of the nothingness of my death that constitutes temporality. The understanding of death as our ultimate end inflicts upon our experiences, providing them their temporal and finite structure. Without the threat of death our basic state would not be the temporal structure that is grounded in care. Hence, our sense of mortality and finitude are the grounds for our temporal existence, and consequently, they are the basis for our understanding of time, including scientific and astronomical time. Therefore, if Dasein were not characterized by a structure of existence that involves the alterity of death, it would have been indifferent even to cosmic processes which we generally call time. It would have been oblivious to events and processes that occur within time regardless of its existence. Events such as the origination of life on earth four billion years ago, or the creation of the universe as the result of the Big Bang ten billion years ago, are meaningful for us solely by virtue of our temporal mode of existence. For if we were not mortal, these events would have remained unnoticed and meaningless. Levinas admits that Heidegger "introduced an element of alterity into his own phenomenological description of time in *Being and Time,* when he analyzed time in terms of our anguish before death," but still he thinks that although

Heidegger allows a degree of alterity, his ecstatic temporality remains basically totalizing (DEL 26).

Robert Manning suggests the difference between Levinas's understanding of death as otherness and Heidegger's approach to death as mineness reveals that for Levinas it is through death one becomes aware that even its own existence includes a foreign aspect.[30] There are two problems with this interpretation. First, as seen above, the aspect of the otherness of death as located in my own existence can be found in Heidegger's thought as well. Although Heidegger understands death as mineness, this does not contradict his view of death as including an aspect of one's annihilation, of its nonbeing. Even though Heidegger focuses on death as mine, his notion of being-toward-death brings into the subject an alterity, an element of otherness, which is necessary for the constitution of Dasein's temporality as well as for its understanding of cosmological time. Second, Manning's interpretation focuses on death as an otherness that is included in one's own being, and consequently Manning interprets Levinas's notion of death as an element, which even if it is a foreign one, is still integrated into the subject's own existence. According to his interpretation of Levinas, although death is an otherness, it is still within the boundaries of the subject, and consequently it remains restricted to the same. From Levinas's perspective one's relation with its own death is not an adequate description of a relation with otherness. He is advocating a more extreme notion of otherness, which must remain beyond the subject's existence.

Although Heidegger's analysis of death does introduce alterity, which is the basis for the constitution of temporality, for Levinas this is an insufficient otherness. Cohen explains the insufficient alterity of death by concentrating on the fact that for Heidegger death does not shatter Dasein, but shatters only its inauthentic possibilities, its escape to the anonymous they, and as a result, death does not break Dasein but individualizes it.[31] Moreover, from Levinas's viewpoint, the alterity required for the constitution of Heideggerian temporality is insufficient for the same reason that the alterity Bergson demands for the constitution of duration is unsatisfactory. The otherness in

Heidegger's philosophy, as in Bergson's thought, does not exceed the limits of the same. Indeed the Heideggerian notion of death can be considered as otherness, because it instills into the individual's being its nothingness, its possibility of not being-in-the-world. But since such an alterity is contained in the subject, it is still confined to the realm of the same. Consequently the Heideggerian understanding of death as nonbeing or nothingness is not sufficiently other to account for Levinasian time.

Furthermore, although Levinas maintains that death "indicates that we are in relation with something that is absolutely other, something bearing alterity not as provisional determination we can assimilate through enjoyment, but as something whose very existence is made of alterity," still "the future that death gives, the future of the event, is not yet time" (*TO* 74, 79). For Levinas, time is the connection between the present and the new moment, the future, and even though death presents a future, it is a future that I cannot connect to my present. "There is an abyss between my present and death, between the ego and the alterity of mystery," and for time to be created, some form of relationship between the same and the other, between the present and the future, is necessary (*GDT* 81).

In Heidegger's thought nothingness is experienced in time, and therefore death is not absolutely separate from time. According to Levinas, Heidegger interrogates everything under the question, "What is being?" and "shows that dying is not what marks some final instant of Dasein but what characterizes the very way in which man is his being" (*GDT* 51). Hence, in Heidegger's thought, not only time but also death is a mode of being—to have to be is to have to die (41, 43). Another way to put it, in approaching death from the perspective of mineness, Heidegger opens a way for viewing death as that which reveals the issues of being and existence. This suggests an understanding of death that is not exterior to being but remains under the totalizing category of being. Since for Levinas such an approach to death is still connected with the realm of the same, the otherness of death in Heidegger's thought is inadequate. According to Levinas the alterity required for the constitution of time must be an absolute other, that is, an other which is exterior to the same, and cannot be interiorized or integrated into it.

The difficulty Levinas is facing is precisely to find such a relationship that enables the subject to both be in a relationship with alterity and to maintain the separateness between the same and the other. One's relationship with its own death does not provide such a relationship. But perhaps such a relationship could be found in the subject's relationship with the death of the other, and Levinas characterizes such a relationship as such: "In the being for death of fear I am not faced with nothingness, but faced with what is against me, as though murder, rather than being one of the occasions of dying, were inseparable from the essence of death, as though the approach of death remained one of the modalities of the relation with the other. The violence of death threatens as a tyranny, as though proceeding from a foreign will" (*TI* 234). Levinas rejects the understanding of the relation with death as "an experience of nothingness in time" (*GDT* 13). He seems to agree with Bergson, who criticizes the concept of nothingness, claiming that since death is the degradation of energy it cannot be thought of as nothingness (*CE* 255–59, 299). Levinas suggests that we refuse the traditional understanding of death through the alternative of being and nothingness, since death is neither being nor nothingness: "It is neither to see being as in Plato, nor to aim at nothingness, as in Heidegger" (*GDT* 16). Rather, we experience death as a menace, similar to murder that comes from an exterior otherness, in the face of which we are powerless. In other words, death is out of our reach, it is other, and not because it is nothingness, but because we cannot grasp it and cannot evade it (*TI* 232–33).

Tina Chanter summarizes three connections between death and otherness that can be found in Levinas's thought. First, death presents itself as murder. Like murder, death includes the possibility of evading being—it approaches as other, not as nothingness but as a fear of being. Second, death is unknowable. These two features of fear and unknowablity exhibit the aspects of death that are precisely inauthentic according to Heidegger—to fear death is an inauthentic relation to death, whereas an authentic relation is the understanding of one's finitude and accepting death as one's own. Third, alterity is inseparable from death because the subject is implicated by the death of the other.[32] But this third aspect requires clarification and development in order to determine the sense in which the alterity of death comes from one's relationship with the other and its implications on the constitution of time.

In *God, Death, and Time* Levinas asks, "Is death separable from the relation with the other [*autrui*]?" (*GDT* 8). Heidegger's response to such a question would be positive: "Dying, which is essentially and irreplaceably mine, is distorted into a publicly occurring event which the they encounters" (*BT* 234). Levinas raises a question that goes deeper than the question of whether or not the knowledge of death comes to us only secondhand. The relationship with the other's death is not designated to offer *knowledge* about the death of the other, nor to enable us to acquire knowledge about our own death (*GDT* 16). The issue at stake is not doubt in our ability to fully comprehend and accept death without experiencing the death of other people in our lives, but rather, a suspicion that the death of the other offers me something that my own death cannot offer. Therefore death must not be separated from the relationship with the other, a view that is opposed to the Heideggerian approach to death. Levinas is arguing against Heidegger's idea that death individualizes the subject, when insisting, "My solitude is thus not confirmed by death but broken by it" (*TO* 74). In the subject's relation to death, an ethical approach toward the other emerges: it does not dissolve the relationship with the other, but quite the opposite—it reveals a genuine concern for the other: "It is not my nonbeing that causes anxiety, but that of the loved one or of the other, more beloved than my being. What we call, by a somewhat corrupted term, love, is par excellence the fact that the death of the other affects me more than my own....We encounter death in the face of the other" (*GDT* 105). Here Levinas is reinterpreting Heidegger's observation that death involves anxiety, and asserts that our anxiety emerges not from the possibility of our nonbeing, but from the possibility of the annihilation of the other, the loved one. My relation to my own death provides a false alterity, and it is the death of the other and our ethical response to it that introduces an otherness that in Levinas's view is adequate for the constitution of time: "Time will have to be presented on the basis of this relationship, from this deference to the death of the other" (43).

From Levinas's perspective both Bergson and Heidegger situate in the realm of the same the otherness necessary for the constitution of time. For Bergson and Heidegger time can be defined as an other-*in*-the-same, whether this otherness is the heterogeneity of the different states of the consciousness or the nothingness induced in the subject by its acceptance of its death as its own. Levinas demands that we think of *in* otherwise than presence, and rethink the relation of other-*in*-the-same. Levinas insists that "the *in* does not signify an assimilation. It is rather a situation where the Other disturbs the Same and where the Same desires the Other and awaits it" (*GDT* 116). Therefore, the alterity required for the formation of Levinasian time is not found *in* the same, but is found in the interruption of the same by the other. Consequently, time cannot be formed within the solitary individual, but rather is constituted by the ethical relationship of the same with the other, and through its relationship with the death of the other.

INFINITE TIME VERSUS FINITE TIME

In the *Physics* Aristotle asks whether time will ever fail, that is, if time is finite, and immediately replies, "Presumably not, since change is everlasting.... Time will not fail, because it is always at a beginning."[33] Heidegger challenges the claim that time is infinite. For him, the traditional, Aristotelian understanding that time is constituted of an infinite succession of nows only provides a picture of the public, everyday, leveled down time, whereas primordial time, the time embedded in the human structure of existence, is finite. In associating duration with the subject's life, Bergson, although not explicitly discussing the question of the finitude of time, would agree with Heidegger's assertion that real time is finite.

In this context, Levinas's claim that time is infinite is surprising. In *Totality and Infinity* Levinas makes a curious move when stating that it is infinity rather than finitude that constitutes the essence of time (*TI* 284). This statement is made deliberately against Heidegger; the emphasis on infinity that we find in Levinas's thought is contrasted with its lack of significance in the thought of Bergson and Heidegger. After the groundbreaking interpretations of time presented by Bergson and Heidegger, the claim that time is infinite may seem at first as rehabilitating and reinstating the traditional, Aristotelian picture of time. However, we must avoid comprehending Levinas's view of time as a return to the conventional view. In a certain sense, Levinas would agree that the time associated with the human structure of existence is finite, but for him it is the infinite dimension of time that is the primordial and more original experience. It is critical, then, to illuminate the meaning of the idea of the infinite against the Heideggerian notion of temporality and its focus on Dasein's finitude.

We can distinguish between two modes of understanding infinity. One way is to consider the infinite as the negation of the finite, as simply more and more of finitude. According to this understanding, the infinite, unlike the finite, is that which can always extend itself further into space, time, and so forth. The second way is an intrinsic understanding of infinity, as being infinite in itself. Here the idea of the infinite, despite the misleading term "in-finite,"[34] is not the negation of the idea of the finite, but rather is a wholly positive infinite that is understood independently of the finitude. In his proof of the existence of God, Descartes adopts the second interpretation of the infinite, and for him the idea of the infinite is prior to the idea of finitude (cf. *TI* 49–50, 197; *TO* 117). The Cartesian *thinking subject* knows that it is finite only because it has in it the idea of the infinite; by first encountering the innate idea of perfection the human being is confronted with its limited, finite existence. Levinas, like Descartes, believes that the infinite is prior to the finite, but for him the relation between the finite and the infinite concretely appears not in the subject's relation with God. (Even though for Levinas God is an absolute uncontainable otherness, God is not an *Autrui*—an other person.) Rather, the infinite is revealed in the face-to-face encounter with another person, in which the other's face cannot be integrated into the same.

From the perspective of the question of time, the Cartesian model of an infinite unbridgeable exteriority is central to Levinas's later thought, yet already in *Totality and Infinity* infinite time is found. The infinity of time is revealed in terms of the negation of the finite, whereas in Levinas's late thought, time is an intrinsic, wholly positive infinite. We notice this type of infinity in Levinas's ideas of the pure future, the future that cannot be anticipated, as well as the absolute, immemorial past, the past that is not susceptible to the work of recollection. In "Diachrony and Representation" Levinas discusses the immemorial past, "which had neither been present nor represented by anyone," and the future "which no one anticipates" (*TO* 102). Concerning the future, Levinas writes, "The futuration of the future does not reach me as a to-come [*à-venir*], as the horizon of my anticipations or pro-tentions" (115). As for the past, it is an "immemorial past, signified without ever having been present" (113). And in a different text Levinas says, "no memory could follow traces of this past. It is an immemorial past—and this also is perhaps eternity."[35]

Like the other that remains beyond the same, like the metaphysical desire that is never satiated, Levinas's notion of the pure future is a positive, intrinsic infinite. Fabio Ciaramelli notices a parallelism between desire and time in the sense that neither involves a return, and both involve the inaccessibility of the other.[36] The pure future entails a dimension of an absolute future that remains open, is always a not-yet, and can be contrasted with the Heideggerian closure of death. In "Meaning and Sense," Levinas says, "to be for a time that would be without me, for a time after my time, over and beyond the celebrated 'being for death,' is not an ordinary thought which is extrapolating from my own duration; it is the passage to the time of the Other" (*BPW* 50). Levinas's unique views of death and dying are relevant for understanding the idea of the pure future. As Simon Critchley comments, in Levinas's thought dying reveals the possibility of a future without me, that is—dying discloses a future that is not my future.[37] In this sense dying opens up an understanding of a future that I will never realize, that will never become (my) present, but a future that belongs to the other. The pure future is the future that always remains futural and is beyond one's projections and possibilities and therefore is never realized. Similarly, the absolute past, is a past that was never realized. The immemorial past is not an "effect of weakness of memory" (*OB* 38), but is an absolute past that is beyond one's recollection, and therefore it was never present.

The past and the future maintain their exteriority by not being reduced to the present—they are not "presentified" (*présentifié*) or "*re*-presented" (*TO* 100, 102–03). The pure future and the immemorial past are never gathered into the present or contained in the presence of the *I think*. The irreducibility of the future and past to the present can be tied with Levinas's correlation between the solitary individual and the present. In Levinas's thought the individual is confined to the present, and it is through the relationship with the other, who is absolutely exterior to the subject and does not share its present, that time is constituted. So, the pure, ungraspable future and the absolute, immemorial past are never present, never gathered by the same, and remain exterior to it as does the other. Consequently, since the pure future and immemorial past cannot be contained in the present, they belong to the other and not to the subject. Therefore, the relation between the same and the other is analogous to the present's relation with past and future, and time is constituted through these parallel relations: same-other and present/future, past.

These ideas of a future horizon and an immemorial past that are never present are an original contribution of Levinas. We cannot find a similar idea in the traditional understanding of time, which tends to consider the future and the past in terms of the present. Neither are such ideas available in the thoughts of Bergson and Heidegger. According to Levinas, they too offer a philosophy of being, that is a philosophy of the present. Although for Bergson and Heidegger the future and the past are not regarded as events that are awaiting us or that have passed us like milestones on a road, still our future possibilities can be anticipated and achieved, and in this sense the future becomes present, and the past is retrievable since it exists in one's memory or is one's history. Legros's observation that in Husserl's account of temporality past and future are always experienced from the present is also relevant to Bergson's and Heidegger's views.[38] Protention and retention bring the future and the past into the present. That is to say, expecting the future and retrieving memories involve re-presenting, since they entail an understanding of the future and the past as secondary forms of the present, and consequently express an assimilation of the future and the past to the present.

The ideas of pure future and immemorial past seem to be connected with Levinas's claim that time is infinite. These notions can be seen as enhancing the idea of infinite Levinasian time, since they open up an understanding of infinite time as involving a future that cannot be fulfilled and a past that was never present. Moreover, the irreducibility of the past and the future to the present is closely tied with the irreducibility of the (infinite) other to same. The subject is infinitely responsible for the other. As Alphonso Lingis rightly claims, in responsibility infinity is revealed. The Levinasian subject is responsible for processes that go beyond the limits of its foresight and intention, beyond what it willed or can steer, beyond its death (*OB* xx). Hence, the same is responsible for all the others, for processes and events that are beyond the limits of its time. Therefore, infinite time can be understood not only as tied with the other's exteriority, the absolute otherness of which is required for the constitution of time, but also as a responsibility for the other that introduces a view of the future and past that cannot be encompassed, that are unreachable, that is, are never present.

Another perspective for considering the idea of infinite time is in relation to Levinas's notion of messianic time. In "Revelation in the Jewish Tradition" Levinas says, "Waiting for the Messiah is the actual duration of time," and should not be equated with waiting for Godot who will never come, but testifies "to the relation with something that cannot enter into the present, because the present is too small for the Infinite" (*BV* 143). In this context we can understand messianic time, which Levinas mentions at the end of *Totality and Infinity* but leaves unexplained. The other is the infinite that always remains beyond the same, and in this sense the other is the future that can never be contained in the present—that is, a future that is never realized, that will always remain future. Graham Ward comments, "Each person is the messiah for every other. Each one bears the messianic task and its responsibility."[39] Pascal Delhom considers messianic time as the time of patience that includes aspects such as responsibility for the other and working for others.[40] Since, the responsible relation with the other constitutes infinite time, the ideas of the other, the Messiah, the infinite, and time are closely related.[41] In contrast, Fabio Ciaramelli offers a different view. His analysis focuses on Levinas's assertion, "Truth requires both an infinite time and a time it will be able to seal, a completed time. The completion of time is not death, but messianic time, where the perpetual is converted into the eternal" (*TI* 284–85). Ciaramelli argues that messianic time is a "completed time" in the sense that desire reaches its fulfillment. However, this way of understanding messianic time is contrary to Levinas's entire phenomenological project that ties the insatiable desire with infinite time.[42]

In claiming that the essence of time is infinity, clearly Levinas is offering a new and unique understanding of infinite time, and is not returning to the Aristotelian, traditional approach. The infinity that Levinas is referring to is not an infinite succession of nows, but rather is an intrinsic, wholly positive infinite; it is the absolute otherness found in the other person, which is required for the constitution of time. Levinas is continuing the tradition of Bergson and Heidegger in understanding time as closely associated with the human structure of existence; however, at the same time he is also going beyond their interpretations. For Bergson and Heidegger real or authentic time is associated with the individual, and as a result it is related with mortality, finitude, and death (particularly in Heidegger's case). For Levinas infinity is the essence of time, but it should be emphasized that he insists that time is infinite even though it is embedded in the relation between finite individuals. Approaching time only from the perspective of the individual subject ignores a fundamental condition of human beings—our temporal existence is intertwined with the temporal existence of other individuals. Even though our social existence with others is acknowledged by Bergson and Heidegger, duration and temporality remain egological. For Levinas it is through one's relationship with the alterity of the other that infinite time is formed. Locating alterity beyond the subject can be seen as the bedrock of the difference between the Bergsonian-Heideggerian focus on the finite aspect of time and Levinas's claim that the principle of time is infinity. For the purpose of clarifying Levinas's view of time, the following chapters reveal the function and meaning of absolute alterity within the structure of time and examine how the subject's relation with the other person releases it from its confinement to the present, thus creating intersubjective time.

THREE

Intersubjective Time
Fecundity

Levinas presents an interpretation of time that is not merely a different way for considering the topic but an entirely new approach. For Levinas time is neither egological nor cosmological, neither interior nor exterior (see *TI* 290), neither Heideggerian-Bergsonian nor Aristotelian. His criticism of both the Aristotelian, traditional analysis of time and the Heideggerian-Bergsonian reading is tied to his attempt to show that "man's ethical relation to the other is ultimately prior to his ontological relation to himself (egology) or to the totality of things that we call the world (cosmology)" (DEL 21). Levinas's understanding of time reexamines egological and cosmological views of time, and it may overcome the gap that Bergson and Heidegger formed by leaving the discussion of temporality in the realm of the individual, and for the most part, reduced the time relevant to our existence with other human beings to the spatial, the inauthentic, clock time. On the one hand Levinasian time does not ignore the relevance of time to the human structure of existence, and on the other hand it reinterprets the everyday view of public time and locates the significance of time in our ethical existence among other people. Thus, although Levinas does not reject the egological or cosmological views of time, he insists that the original, primordial way for experiencing time is constituted by one's ethical relationship with the other person. As he details, "Is not sociality something more than the source of our representation of time: is it not time itself? If time is constituted by my relationship with the other, it is exterior to my instant, but it is also something else than an object given to contemplation. The dialectic of time is the very dialectic of the relationship with the other, that is a dialogue which in turn has to be studied in terms other than those of the dialectic of the solitary subject" (*EE* 96).

In presenting a view that regards time as rooted in our relations[1] with the other person, Levinas is considering time as intersubjective. The term "intersubjective" does not refer to the view of time as a public, common dimension, but rather it is the literal sense of the time existing *in between* the subjects constituted through their interaction. Consequently veritable time, although embedded in the human structure of existence, is not an inner time that is limited to the perspective of the individual, but rather, is revealed precisely in our ethical face-to-face encounter with the other person. While one must not overlook the significance of the interpretations offered by Bergson and Heidegger, in limiting their views of temporality to the perspective of the individual, they do not present an intertemporal understanding of time and seem to neglect a crucial aspect of human life, namely, that time is meaningful for our ethical existence among other individuals. Therefore, it appears that Levinas is correct in his effort to understand time from the ethical perspective and in his endeavor to provide a view that not merely acknowledges the social aspect of time, but rather, considers it to be the primordial approach.

By focusing on fecund time, I begin examining Levinas's claim that the locus of time is found in the relationships formed *between* individuals, that time is neither interior nor exterior. The three themes of fecund, intersubjective time—fecundity, discontinuity, and recommencement—provide the framework for characterizing the ethical relations between the subject and the other, for demonstrating the ways in which such ethical encounters are the foundation of time, and for elucidating why, from Levinas's viewpoint, they are required for the constitution of time.

FECUNDITY

Since fecundity provides for Levinas a concrete illustration of inter-human relations, an elucidation of the role he assigns to fecundity and its outcomes (such as discontinuity and recommencement) in the formation of time reveals a way of thinking of time as grounded in our ethical relations with other people. But Levinas was not the first to connect fecundity and time, and such a link can be found already in Plato's *Symposium*.[2] In the first part of Diotima's discussion of love she claims, "Pregnancy and procreation instill immortality in a living, mortal being."[3] Diotima explains this procreative activity, which may be regarded as an aspect or outcome of fecundity,[4] as the mortal creature's pursuit of immortality.[5] By creating and leaving behind something new, the mortal being can overcome the finite aspect of his or her temporality and take part in immortality. In other words, we transcend our mortality, finitude, and limited existence and go beyond it through our legacy, such as offspring, works of art, or poems, which we create and remain after we die.[6] In this sense, Diotima is presenting a view that regards procreation, or fecundity, as enabling us to extend our existence toward immortality, that is, overcome temporality.

Plato's dialogues are considerably relevant to Levinas's philosophy. For example, Levinas mentions the *Phaedrus* as one of the top five philosophical texts that have impressed him (*EI* 37–38). Throughout Levinas's texts we can find influences of Plato's thought and references to his dialogues. Some of the most significant terms in Levinas's thought, such as the pivotal opposition between same and other, are borrowed from Plato or are a response to Plato's thought. For example, in *Totality and Infinity* his idea of unsatisfied metaphysical desire is a criticism of the understanding of desire (*eros*) as a lack, presented by Plato in the *Symposium* (*TI* 33–35, 254). Even though Levinas does not explicitly refer to Plato in his discussion of fecundity, I find it interesting to begin by considering the Levinasian fecundity and its relevance to time in comparison to Plato's thought.[7]

For both Plato and Levinas the starting point of fecundity is *eros*. Diotima interprets *eros* not as a desire to possess beautiful things, but as a desire to procreate and give birth in beauty.[8] That is, *eros* is a desire for fecundity. These notions of *eros* and fecundity are found also in Levinas's thought. In *Time and the Other* the erotic relationship is presented as a model, which detaches the analysis of the subject's relation with the other from the approach that understands it in terms of knowledge (*EI* 65–66). *Eros* provides the model of the subject's encounter with the other's radical alterity. As Diane Perpich clearly puts it, in the erotic situation the desire is a desire to keep on desiring, and thus it requires as a condition that the object of desire remains unattained.[9] This aspect is crucial, since for Levinas the erotic situation provides a model in which the subject is affected by the existence of the other person, and yet the other is not subjugated or dominated by the same (*TO* 84–90). But then Levinas asks, "How in the alterity of a you, can I remain I, without being absorbed or losing myself in that you? . . . How can the ego become other to itself? This can happen only in one way: through paternity" (91). And later in *Totality and Infinity* he claims that the relationship established between lovers is the very contrary of the social relation, since voluptuousness isolates the lovers, as if they were alone in the world (*TI* 264–65; cf. *CPP* 33). He continues, "The encounter with the Other as feminine is required in order that the future of the child comes to pass from beyond the possible, beyond projects" (*TI* 267).

Tina Chanter views the erotic relation with the feminine as proclaiming the time of fecundity, which Levinas describes from the father-son perspective, and thus, "Paternity is needed to complete the movement toward alterity that the feminine had begun."[10] And Richard Cohen explicates this shift in the location of absolute alterity from the feminine to fecundity as tied to Levinas's growing interest in ethics in *Totality and Infinity*.[11] So, as Hugh Miller correctly claims, the erotic relation is not the final model for describing the relation between the subject and genuine exteriority, and as Perpich explicates, "The erotic is not sufficient as prototype of transcendence because the ego does not *become other* in erotic love, but only aims at alterity."[12]

Hence, Levinas proposes a new relation that will provide the model for the relation between the subject and the other: "My child is a stranger, but a stranger who is not only mine, for he is me. He is me a stranger to myself" (267). Fecundity, the product of *eros*, becomes the prototype for the relation with the other, the model for all social and ethical relationships between subjects, through which intersubjective and ethical time is formed.

Similar to Plato's Diotima, Levinas begins his discussion of fecundity from the biological aspect and refers to the fecund relation between father and son. The biological aspect of fecundity demonstrates that as a result of the erotic relationship between the same and the other—in this case the female and male—something new is produced: "The same and the other are not united but precisely—beyond every possible project, beyond every meaningful and intelligent power—engender a child" (*TI* 266). Hence, Levinas, like Diotima, associates the notion of fecundity with the creation of something new, a child for example. Also similar to Diotima, he refrains from limiting fecundity to a biological relation and affirms that fecundity "delineates a structure that goes beyond the biologically empirical" (277; cf. 247). However, if in Diotima's speech fecundity opens up the possibility of immortality, it seems that Levinas's focus is on infinity rather than on immortality. In his thought, the newness created by fecundity engenders infinity, an infinite future, rather than immortality. Infinity and immortality may seem to be synonymous expressions when discussing human related issues—immortality can be defined as an infinite existence, as an existence without limits, and Levinas himself says that "to be infinitely—infinition—means to exist without limits" (281). However, the different choice of terms implies that for each thinker a different issue is at stake.

Diotima's discussion of immortality resonates Plato's examination of the immortality of the soul in dialogues such as the *Republic* and the *Phaedo*. The question whether Diotima's views on immortality are compatible with the views Plato is promoting in those other dialogues is beside the point.[13] The relevant issue is that all these texts, including Diotima's speech in the *Symposium*, refer to the individual.

These dialogues concentrate on the life the individual should pursue in order to assure, or at least approach, his or her own immortality. Even when immortality is discussed as the outcome of procreation, we still remain in the domain of the individual—the focus is not on the relation between the parent and the offspring, but rather on the individual's pursuit of immortality via the offspring. This is true also in respect to those who are not "pregnant in body" but are "pregnant in soul," and that give birth to their "offspring" through conversation with another soul.[14] However, for Levinas, fecundity is not a means for an individual to attain immortality, but rather it opens up a time that is beyond the subject's own time: "the relation with the child—that is the relation with the other that is not a power, but fecundity—establishes relationship with the absolute future or infinite time" (*TI* 268). Here Levinas defines fecundity as the relationship with the child, who is the other, through which a relationship with the future is established and constitutes time. I understand this relation differently than Irigaray, who seems to consider Levinas's interpretation of fecundity to be similar to Plato's view. Criticizing Levinas, she writes, "The child should be for himself, not for the parent.... The son should not be the place where the father confers being or existence on himself."[15] I do not think that it is Levinas's intention to discuss fecundity from the viewpoint of the father. Levinas's perspective is different than the one conveyed by Diotima—his aim is precisely to go beyond the subject, and focus on the *relationship* with the other; he thinks of time as constituted by the difference *between* individuals rather than within the independent individual. The difference in between the same and the other opens up another way for understanding Levinas's claim that time is infinite.

Another theme found in Socrates' recapitulation of his conversation with Diotima worth mentioning—the idea of the "in between"[16]—is also present in Levinas's understanding of time as intersubjective. Diotima develops the idea that *eros* is a being which is "in between" by providing two myths. One is the myth that determines *eros* as the offspring of *Poros* (Resource) and *Penia* (Poverty) and characterizes it accordingly. As the son of Poverty, *eros* is tough, wrinkled, barefoot, and homeless, but as the son of Resource, it desires beauty and wisdom. Consequently, as a seeker of wisdom, *eros* does not possess wisdom but rather "is in between being wise and being ignorant."[17] However, the second myth is more relevant. Here, Diotima describes *eros* as a kind of being (a *daimōn*) that is in between human beings and gods, in between mortality and immortality. In other words, the separation between the two distinct realms of gods and human beings is bridged through *eros*, which also enables communication between human beings and gods, since one of its functions is interpretation.[18] According to one myth, *eros* is neither wise nor ignorant, and according to another myth it is neither god nor human, but *eros* is an "in between" that enables a connection between the two absolutely separate realms. Similarly, Levinas claims that time exists between us (*entre nous*). And since for Levinas "the relation between the same and the other is primordially enacted as conversation" (*TI* 39), time may be regarded as the dimension that enables communication between the two separate, excluding domains of same and other.

This view of an "in between" may reveal that Levinas does not attempt to convey an understanding of time that serves as the *common* ground between the traditional and the Bergsonian-Heideggerian interpretations, but rather as the *intermediate* ground between these two views. Similar to Diotima's interpretation of *eros,* which is neither god nor human and consequently cannot belong to the world of gods nor to the world of humans, Levinasian time should be understood as independent of both the Aristotelian understanding of time as exterior and the Bergsonian-Heideggerian interpretations of time as linked with the subject. Levinas claims that time is embedded in our existence as human beings, but as social beings and not as independent individuals. Although this interpretation gives room to the understanding of time as both grounded in our human existence and as involving relationships with other people, it cannot be described by applying the Bergsonian or Heideggerian vocabulary nor by using the Aristotelian terminology.

The relation between time and fecundity in Levinas's thought can further explain his view of time as intersubjective, as in between the understanding of time as public and the understanding of time as intrinsic to the individual. As already discussed above, Levinas begins describing fecundity from the biological perspective and characterizes the relationship with the son as a relationship with the other. This relationship is a relationship with the future: "the other is the future. The very relationship with the other is the relationship with the future" (*TO* 77). One way to understand this claim is by emphasizing the resemblance between the future and the other and by focusing on Levinas's view that both are ungraspable, both are a mystery. Another way is to concentrate on the significance and relevance of our relationship with the other to the formation of the future. The relationship with the other—the son in this case—provides the subject (the father) with a future that is beyond his own present. Hence, according to Levinas, my future is "both my own and non-mine, a possibility of myself but also a possibility of the other" (*TI* 267). But this raises the question—in what sense does the relation with another person provide me a future, and in what sense is this future both mine and not mine, both my possibility and the other's possibility?

Levinas claims that time is constituted according to the category of the father (*TO* 91), and paternity is "the way of being other while being oneself" (*TI* 282). The ego becomes other to himself, since it involves a relationship with a son who is both other and the same—the father both is and is not his son. Perpich clarifies this relation claiming that in being one's child alterity is not reduced, but increased. In paternity the father possesses the child but without losing himself and without negating the child's otherness.[19] This familial context of paternity incorporates fecundity. Due to this relation of fecundity, the other (the son) provides his father with a new beginning, a future that goes beyond the father's anticipated present—what is impossible for the father becomes possible through his son. This can be found in everyday relationships between parents and their offspring. But according to Levinas, this relation should not be described merely in terms of "sympathy and compassion," but rather it is an existence the self shares with the other: "The I springs forth without returning, finds itself the self of an other: its pleasure, its pain is pleasure over the pleasure of the other or over his pain—though not through sympathy or compassion" (271). Through the son's life and the possibilities open before him, the father's life or future is extended.

Although Levinas focuses on father-son relations, I would like to offer an example describing a mother-daughter relation. My mother's wish for my siblings and myself was that we have options that were not available to her as an immigrant child growing up in Israel during the first years of its independence. Parents usually have in mind concrete prospects, which they desire their children to fulfill—perhaps a star athlete, a doctor, or a lawyer. For my mother it was ballet. She insisted that I take ballet lessons, because as a child she herself was eager to dance ballet but did not have the opportunity to fulfill this wish. Thus when ballet lessons became possible for me, they became possible for my mother as well.[20] My mother was presented with a new possibility, and in this sense, through my possibilities, my mother's future was extended. In other words, I gave my mother a new future that connects to her present. This future beyond the subject's own future, which is a crucial dimension of time, becomes concrete through such parental relationships.

But the interesting aspect about fecundity and its relevance to the constitution of time is that Levinas does not limit it to familial relations, but rather considers it as a model, a prototype, for the relationships between individuals. In *Ethics and Infinity* Levinas explicitly affirms that the biological filiality[21] is only the first form of filiality, and different forms of fecundity that do not involve biological relations exist as well. A person can have a paternal attitude toward an other, even if they are not related. When seeing the other as a son or daughter, we consider the other's possibilities as our own, and that enables us to go beyond our identity toward something that was not given to us and yet is ours (*EI* 69–72). And in *Totality and Infinity* he states, "Biological fecundity is but one of the forms of paternity. Paternity, as a primordial effectuation of time, can, among men, be borne by the biological life, but be lived beyond that life" (*TI* 247). Although Levinas does not provide an analysis of nonbiological occasions in which we may find fecund relations that constitute time, in his dialogue with Philippe Nemo, he agrees that such relations can be found, for example, between a teacher and a student, but are not limited to them (*EI* 71). Similar to the relation between father and son, through their students, teachers may be presented with new possibilities that before were not available to them. Through the paternal act of preparing a promising student to accomplish achievements that the teacher was never capable of achieving, the student's possibilities become the teacher's possibilities as well.

In another interview Levinas says, "The father-son relationship can exist between beings who, biologically, are not father and son. Paternity and filiality, the feeling that the other is not simply someone I've met, but that he is, in a certain sense, my prolongation, my ego, that his possibilities are mine—the idea of responsibility for the other can go that far."[22] It may be suggested that fecundity goes beyond the production of possibilities available to the subject: it is the generating of responsibilities beyond my agency. The subject's responsibilities are also extended by his or her responsibility for the other's projects, opportunities, and responsibilities to take care of others. This produces a future that extends the future of the subject. This idea is developed by Levinas in his later writings, such as when he argues that substitution means that one must bear responsibility for the way the other is dealing with his or her responsibilities. So a fecund relationship that constitutes time is one that involves responsibility in which the other is the prolongation of the subject, and his or her possibilities (responsibilities) become the subject's possibilities (responsibilities). Adriaan Peperzak, for example, suggests that activities such as fighting for human rights or writing are also forms of paternity relevant to fecundity.[23] Although Levinas does not explicitly state that fecundity goes beyond the biological structure until his later interviews, Stella Sandford is too conclusive in her assertion that in *Totality and Infinity* each time Levinas claims fecundity overflows its purely biological signification, the biological origin of the concept is affirmed.[24] *Totality and Infinity* not only allows an understanding of fecundity that exceeds the biological model, but even an understanding that exceeds the paternal structure.

Some scholars such as Luce Irigaray and Tina Chanter have criticized Levinas for his account where only the father, through his relation with his son, is fecund, and as a result the feminine is merely the means for fecundity and in itself is not fecund. This way of understanding fecundity raises problems regarding the role of the feminine in Levinas's thought. Irigaray claims that in Levinas's thought the female is deprived of subjectivity, of a face, and only supports the temporal becoming of the male in producing a son who, in being both same and other, allows the male subject to become other to himself.[25] But this is not the only difficulty.[26] The view of fecundity as embedded in paternity also generates a difficulty regarding Levinas's interpretation of time. It appears that for Levinas time is meaningful to and relevant only for the male. The understanding of fecund time as formed only through paternal relationships engenders a narrow structure of time, which is constituted through limited forms of relationships. Consequently, from this perspective Levinas's view of time as intersubjective seems less forceful. It is important, then, to understand if the father-son model can be cleansed of its patriarchal assumptions, or whether we must understand fecundity as embedded only in the asymmetrical paternal structure of relationships. Is there room for a fecund feminine in Levinas's thought? And does his thought open up the possibility of constituting time also via relationships such as those between siblings, friends, and even colleagues?

Collegial and friendly relationships may seem to be founded on a more symmetrical, synchronic structure than that of paternal relationships—but does Levinas consider these relationships to be in fact symmetrical and synchronic? Are not all relationships—even those between friends and colleagues—asymmetrical in one way or another? And if so, does not this imply that fecund time can be produced not only via paternal relationships but also through a variety of modes of relationships without violating Levinas's requirement that time maintains an asymmetrical, nonsynchronic structure? If Levinas's philosophy is rejecting the possibility that time is created also through nonpaternal modes of interrelations, we must ponder if it is not leaving out of its discussion of time a significant part of relationships that encompass our intermingling and ethical relations with other people. Moreover, if this is the case, then either it is inconsistent with Levinas's assertion that time is formed via our relationships with the other, or the other he has in mind in this context of his discussion of time is limited to the son, to the male. But before going beyond specific examples, with the prospect of revealing the structure that underlies the interpretation of time as fecundity, another concrete example might shed more light on Levinas's interpretation of time as fecund—that of the relationship between Levinas and his colleague and friend, the novelist and critic, Maurice Blanchot.

Blanchot and Levinas met in 1926 while both were studying at the University of Strasbourg. During World War II Blanchot provided Levinas's wife and daughter a refuge from persecution. This action exhibits a responsibility for the other both in the sense that Blanchot saw himself responsible for Levinas's family as well as for the conduct of his fellow European Christians. Blanchot's act reveals that the other concerns him. He takes responsibility for Levinas, who at the time was held captive, and in correcting the wrong done to Levinas's family he takes responsibility for the behavior of their persecutors. Although the relationship should not be described in terms of the narrow sense of paternity and filiality, according to which one sees the other as a son, their relationship could be seen as an example of fecundity in the capability of going beyond one's identity and future.

One way to think of the relationship between Blanchot and Levinas in terms of fecundity is by focusing on the influence their relationship had on each other and their respective careers.[27] For example, after the early 1960s Blanchot embarked on an intense engagement with questions of a certain sort of ethics, sometimes explicitly in debate with the thinking of Levinas; and Levinas, for his part, discussed Blanchot's writings and considered his poetics as "an invitation to leave the Heideggerian world" (*PN* 135). This fecund interrelation between Levinas and Blanchot opened up for them a new horizon of thought relevant to their future and fate. The influence their thoughts had on one another may be seen as pertinent to the constitution of time, since it reveals a type of relationship that engenders newness through conversation and openness.

But the personal friendship between these two thinkers opens up a far more interesting way to think of Levinas's understanding of fecundity. In his act of providing Raïssa and Simone Levinas a refuge from persecution, Blanchot, who was born to a rural Catholic family, exceeded his own identity, possibilities, and responsibilities. As a Christian living in France during the war, Blanchot's future was bound to be different from the future of Levinas, the Jew, and his family—he was not persecuted nor imprisoned, and if it were not for his act of helping Levinas, his life would not have been in real danger. From Levinas's perspective, Blanchot gives Levinas a future that is beyond his future, beyond his own possibilities and responsibilities. While Levinas, as well as his possibilities, were literally confined, his future and fate changed via his relationship with Blanchot. By helping the family of his friend, Blanchot exposed himself to *their* fate of being persecuted, and by accepting his aid, Levinas's family and through them Levinas himself as well, were given *Blanchot's* future and possibilities including safety and a limited form of freedom.

Blanchot and Levinas's friendship is a concrete illustration of Levinas's understanding of time as intersubjective and involving ethical relationships. It expresses how through ethical relationships the other provides the subject a new moment, and as a result, time flows from the other to the subject, releasing the subject from his or her own present. Yet, it should be stressed that it is not the case that through, or in, time, the same and the other are fused into one. The duality of Levinas and Blanchot is not transformed into a unity, and their futures are not united into one. The multiplicity of their temporalities and lives is maintained. What we have here is an intersection between the same and the other, between two different temporalities or durations.

However, one may argue that since the structure of such a relationship is not paternal but rather describes a collegial relation between friends, it represents a more reciprocal relationship, and consequently the time revealed is more symmetrical than one would expect from a paternal, fecund relationship (both biological and nonbiological). This objection may originate from Levinas's criticism of the Buberian I-Thou symmetrical relation, in which "the I is related to the Thou as to someone who in turn relates itself to the I" (*LR* 68; cf. *TI* 68–69, 137). Levinas's response to Buber's reciprocal I-Thou relation is the asymmetrical relation between the self and the other: "In the case of ethical relations, where the Other is at the same time higher than I and poorer than I, the I is distinguished from Thou not by the presence of specific attributes, but by the dimension of height, thus implying a break with Buber's formalism. The primacy of the other, like his nakedness, does not qualify what is a purely formal relation to the other, posterior to the act of relating, but directly qualifies otherness itself. Otherness is thus qualified, but not by any attribute" (*LR* 72).

Consequently, we should bear in mind that for Levinas every ethical relation with the other is asymmetrical. Therefore, asymmetrical relationships are not limited to paternal relations, but every relationship between the ego and the other is basically asymmetrical—"Multiplicity in being, which refuses totalization but takes form as fraternity and discourse, is situated in a 'space' essentially asymmetrical" (*TI* 216). So even fraternal relations that may seem founded on reciprocity are in fact asymmetrical. Blanchot's actions exemplify the philosophy of Levinas according to which the subject has a responsibility to respond to the other person, to the alterity of the other. The persecution of Levinas and his family was on the grounds of their otherness—their Jewish origin. Thus, in choosing to help them, Blanchot was also taking responsibility for their alterity.[28] In responding to the call of the other, Blanchot sacrifices his own freedom, and consequently he is exercising Levinas's belief, "In ethics, the other's right to exist has primacy over my own, a primacy epitomized in the ethical edict: you shall not kill, you shall not jeopardize the life of the other. The ethical rapport with the face is asymmetrical in that it subordinates my existence to the other" (DEL 24). Blanchot is implementing the primacy of the other's right to exist by risking his own life in order to prevent the jeopardizing of the life of the other. Therefore, the example of the relationship between Levinas and Blanchot, although it may be described as fraternal or collegial, can still depict an asymmetrical ethical relation, in which the other's relation to the ego is not equivalent to the ego's relation to the other, in which the other takes priority over the self, and in which the self is responsible for the other.

Blanchot's response to Levinas should be seen not only as an ethical demeanor, but also as an act that is relevant to Levinas's interpretation of time. The purpose of examining the relationship between Blanchot and Levinas is an attempt to think of fecundity, and particularly fecund time, as not limited to father-son or teacher-student relations, but as also including relationships that at first may appear to be symmetrical. It should also be emphasized that the example of this relationship is not intended to evince that such relations are rare or exceptional. On the contrary, this and similar relationships are at the basis of our human existence as people living among other people, and it is through these relations that time is constituted. Moreover, if by exploring these relations I have congealed them in some way, it should be clear that for Levinas the relations between people are not permanent states of affairs, but rather are continuous and perpetual, and consequently are pertinent to his analysis of time. Now, in order to clarify the sense in which such relationships are not merely unique and singular events, but rather belong and even constitute the structure of time, it is necessary to reveal the place of fecundity in the structure of Levinasian time.

In *Totality and Infinity* Levinas writes, "A being capable of another fate than its own is a fecund being" (*TI* 282). Although in the following sentence Levinas mentions paternity again, if we focus on the idea of fecundity as a dimension through which the subject is given a different future and fate than his or her own, then such an interpretation opens up the possibility of thinking of fecundity as not limited only to relationships that involve paternity and filiality but as also including other forms of intersubjective relationships. This was demonstrated in Levinas and Blanchot's relationship, but many encounters we experience with other people reveal this Levinasian idea. Consequently, fecundity and its relevance to time can be viewed as a model of the subject's relationships with other people, in which a future that is beyond the subject's own future, is discovered.

Considering the future as linked with the opening up of possibilities is relevant to Heidegger's thought as well. For him the future indicates the realm of possibilities open before Dasein and reveals Dasein's concern about its own potentiality of being. In other words, the future is Dasein's awareness of anticipating its own possibilities and projecting itself toward its own future; Dasein projects itself into the future, while in its engagement with the present it carries its past. Dasein exists with other people, and its possibilities cannot be isolated from the world in which it exists, but Heidegger's focus is on the unique life of the individual. Contrary to Heidegger, for Levinas the self's possibilities demand engaging in relationships with other people. The subject's possibilities do not emerge from its individual existence as temporality, but rather are grounded in one's relation with the other. The Levinasian subject does not aspire to liberate him or herself from the other, and it is through the links between one's life with the other's that new moments, new possibilities become available, and as a result, a different future or destiny is possible.

For Levinas without the other the self is confined to his or her present, and only through encountering other people, new moments and possibilities are available to it. This is the meaning of fecundity. Levinas himself, in the last page of *Totality and Infinity* suggests, "The biological structure of fecundity is not limited to the biological fact. In the biological fact of fecundity are outlined the lineaments of fecundity in general as a relation between man and man" (*TI* 306). Therefore, even though Levinas's discussion of fecundity focuses on paternity and filiality, it does not exclude a broader approach that considers fecundity in terms of a variety of intersubjective relations that enable the subject to go beyond his or her present and acquire a future, as well as to surpass his or her own limited possibilities and become capable of other fates.

Such an understanding of fecundity is not only broad enough to include relationships that at first might seem symmetrical in comparison to the paternal structure, but also allows a fecund feminine. Perhaps Levinas should be criticized for using a sexualized vocabulary when discussing fecundity. But using the paternal metaphor does not necessarily mean that Levinas is reiterating the supremacy of the patriarchal power in which the feminine is not part of the time of sociality. When approaching the notion of fecundity, we should attempt to go beyond the said, that is, beyond propositions, beyond the thematized content, beyond—to use Chanter's words—"the paternal logic of Levinas's texts,"[29] and consider it from his perspective of the saying. Fecundity is grounded on Levinas's ethical views of the subject's infinite responsibility for the other, and the saying is precisely an ethical nonthematizable interruption that escapes comprehension, and is the manifestation of the movement from the same to the other. The saying conveys the view that language is not merely a common content but a form of expression, and like the face, every individual has his or her own expressions that constitute a unique signature. But the saying, which communicates more than can be presented by the said, must be thematized, that is, translated to the uttered and written language—into the language of the said. So when considering fecundity, the said speaks of father-son relations, but the impression of the said, the saying, exceeds the paternal structure. What precedes the thematized notion of fecundity that we find in the said of Levinas's text is the ethical and temporal movement from the same to the other.

Fecundity opens the subject to other fates, destinies, and responsibilities through which it exceeds his or her otherwise limited possibilities. Such an approach reveals another way for considering Levinas's claim that time is infinite. In fecundity the formation of new possibilities reveals the infinity of time in terms of the negation of the finite—more and more fates and options become available to the subject. This opening up of new horizons of possibilities and responsibilities means that time always begins anew, is always reborn, and consequently is infinite.

Levinas's example of the possibility of pardon provides yet another way to think of the infinity of time. Through the work of pardon the infinity of time is revealed in terms of the past. In forgiveness the past receives a new meaning, since "pardon acts upon the past, somehow repeats the event, purifying it" (*TI* 283). Furthermore, forgiveness is a manifestation of the Levinasian relation with the other. In offending or hurting me the other's alterity appears in its ultimate manifestation, the otherness of the other affects me.[30] But pardon means accepting the other's alterity; by forgiving a bad event the subject returns to the past and changes its meaning. Consequently, forgiving the other reveals time as an interruption of the subject's temporality, as a movement or flow from the other to me, rather than an infinite succession of instants linked to one another indifferently. It reveals time as beyond the subject's present since, as Rudolf Bernet explains, pardon (and hope) transforms the past (and future) into a past (and future) that were never the subject's present.[31] The ability of revising the past through forgiving the other, constitutes the infinity of time, and in this sense for Levinas "pardon is the work of time" (282).

Discontinuity and Recommencement

Time as fecundity also means that time is discontinuous. In the course of his discussion of fecundity, Levinas writes, "Time is discontinuous; one instant does not come out of another without interruption" (*TI* 284). On the face of it we may find the statement that time is discontinuous puzzling. This view may place Levinas in disagreement with approaches such as Bergson's notion of duration, Heidegger's temporality, and in a way even with traditional approaches, such as Aristotle's. In Aristotle's treatise of time, one of the models for understanding his view of time is the continuous model.[32] According to this model, time is not an instant but rather a period of time, a continuous duration like an interval on a line, whereas the now—like a point with no length—is an instant with no duration. For Bergson the continuous aspect of duration is significant. When challenging the traditional interpretations of time, Bergson rejects the discrete model for understanding time, and suggests that real time is a continuous time composed of indivisible, heterogeneous changes that occur in one's consciousness. Heidegger's approach to time also supports the view that time is continuous. For him temporality involves Dasein's continuous life span or "connection of life"—Dasein stretches itself out between its beginning in birth and ending in death. But birth and death are not regarded as merely the limits of one's life, and since Dasein is a temporal unity, birth, death, and their between lie continuously in the being of Dasein. In this context, Levinas's claim that "this discontinuity [of time] must be emphasized" is surprising, since at first it may seem to advocate a discrete model for understanding time (282). According to the discrete model, time is measured by using homogeneous units (such as seconds, minutes, or hours), and consequently the length of a finite segment of time is the number of units that constitute it. If Levinas is indeed supporting this model, it may seem that he is embracing a traditional view of time as rationalized and conceptual, as made of a series of homogeneous instants.

However, Levinas may consider time as discontinuous without supporting the view that time is discrete,[33] and the question to be answered concerns the meaning of discontinuous time in his thought. Returning to the two examples I discussed earlier—my relationship with my mother in light of my childhood ballet lessons and the relationship between Levinas and Blanchot—may clarify the matter. In these two events the time of the ego is interrupted by the time of the other—my mother's time is interrupted by my time, while in the second event, the time of Levinas is interrupted by the time of Blanchot and Blanchot's time is interrupted by Levinas's time. When I participated in ballet lessons, an interval was formed in my mother's present life, since her present was interrupted by my present, liberating her from her limited fate and providing her with a new destiny and future. In this case, my mother's fate of never attending a ballet class had been altered through the interruption of her time, her possibilities, by my time, my possibilities. Similarly, Blanchot's possibilities (his freedom from being persecuted) became Levinas's possibilities, and Levinas's possibilities (being persecuted and imprisoned) became possible for Blanchot as well. By being given the other's possibilities, that is, a new fate and future, the subject is changed and transcends his or her own life. A rupture in the continuity of the subject's present is produced, revealing time as discontinuous. Fecundity reveals that through the subject's relation with the other, a horizon of new possibilities is opened up, and this presents the subject with a new future and destiny. When the subject is given these new possibilities, there is a rupture in the continuity of its present life, as well as its liberation from its limited destiny.

Levinas's interpretation of time as discontinuous results in the understanding of time as recommencement and rebirth: "The discontinuous time of fecundity makes possible an absolute youth and recommencement" (*TI* 282). Again, such a view of time is contrary to Heidegger's approach, and to some extent it is even opposed to Aristotle's conception of time. Heidegger relates time with the movement toward corruption and death, and even Aristotle makes a similar connection. Traditionally, time is considered to involve aging; it is a movement from the unripe to the ripe, which ends with decomposition. Or to use Levinas's description, "The new sinks into the older and older" (*TO* 123). This idea appears in the *Physics* when Aristotle claims that "time is in its own right responsible more for ceasing to be than for coming to be."[34] Here Aristotle is focusing on time as responsible for destruction and ceasing to be, that is—death.[35] For Levinas, however, time is not associated with death. It is not a movement toward death or annihilation, but "is essentially a new birth" (81)—it is a dimension that brings newness. Therefore, Levinas neither gives corruption and death a primordial significance over generation, nor does he render generation and corruption an equiprimordial value. Against the Heideggerian being-toward-death, Levinas emphasizes generation and recommencement, rather than corruption and death, and stresses, "Resurrection constitutes the principal event of time" (*TI* 284). Hence, as Robert Manning puts it, "Time itself is fecund"—it always recommences, and should be understood in terms of continual rebirth.[36] This difference between Heidegger and Levinas is grounded in their different starting points and their different assumptions regarding time. It is Heidegger's consideration of time and temporality from the individual's perspective that leads him to the association of time with a movement toward death and finitude. Shifting the focus from the individual's perspective to the understanding of time as constituted through the subject's encounters with the other person enables Levinas to offer an understanding of time as recommencement and resurrection. The possibilities that before were unavailable to the subject become accessible through its relationship with the other. This reveals not only the characteristic of time as discontinuous but also as recommencing. Hence, for Levinas fecund time is associated with youth rather than ageing, with new birth rather than death.

Nevertheless, Levinas's concentration on recommencement in his discussion of time requires clarification, particularly the ways in which newness and recommencement, which for him are pertinent to the constitution of time, are attained through the subject's encounters with the other. Again, the two examples I have been discussing throughout this chapter—my relationship with my mother and Levinas's relationship with Blanchot—illustrate Levinas's claim that fecund time entails that time always recommences. In the case of biological fecundity, such as my relationship with my mother, this appears more clearly. Through their children, parents are presented with options that before were not open to them, and thus undergo what Levinas calls "trans-substantiation" (*TI* 267, 269). The term originally means the transfusion of one substance into another, and in the Christian tradition it is used to describe the change of the substance of bread and wine into that of the body and blood of Christ. Levinas borrows this term to portray the relation between the son and the father—that is, the other and the subject—in which a transition from the other's time to the time of the subject occurs. Similar to the Christian tradition, this movement involves resurrection. This transition is grounded on the new possibilities that the other offers the subject, which then renew the subject's future. Being offered a fate different from his or her own that renews his or her future, the subject "prolongs itself in the other, time triumphs over old age and fate by its discontinuity" (282). This approach reveals that time is not tied with finitude and death, but rather "time adds something new to being, something absolutely new" (283).

However, not only biological relations, but also relationships such as the one between Levinas and Blanchot, are relevant to the assertion that fecund time always recommences. Levinas and Blanchot present each other new opportunities and occasions that were not part of their individual, future possibilities. The opening up of new options that are beyond the subject's original fate ties time to the birth of new moments. In other words, these new possibilities that the other offers the subject provide the subject with a new future that is continually reborn. Through the relationship with the other, there is a transition from the subject's time to the time of the other, and as a result time is renewed—it recommences and is resurrected. So according to Levinas, the future involves newness not in the traditional sense of a new moment or occasion awaiting us, or even in the Heideggerian sense of the horizon of unrealized possibilities available to the individual, but rather in the sense that a new chance, a new beginning, is always available to the accomplished individual. Even though the subject's possibilities are limited, through its relation with the other person, new beginnings are opened up; what seems realized can still change, and in this sense time is infinite. As Alphonso Lingis summarizes, "This is the sense of time not as a determinate infinity of instants, but rather of the infinition, the ever recommencing of the definitive" (*EE* xxvi). Time is infinite not because with the recurrence of the now it extends itself further into the future. But, as the examples I have discussed reveal, through the relation with the other, the finite person has another chance and can always begin anew.

The association of time with the themes of rebirth and recommencement opens up another perspective for showing that Levinas's view of time does not exclude the feminine. Understanding time as involving recommencement and resurrection can be considered as incompatible with what Julia Kristeva describes as masculine time. In her essay "Women's Time," Kristeva characterizes masculine time as linear time—the time of history and becoming. According to her, this time rests on its own stumbling block—death. Women's time is linked both to cyclical time (repetition) and monumental time (eternity), which according to Kristeva are conceptualized from the perspective of maternity and reproduction. The cyclical time is an infinite, circular, repetitive structure of time that follows the patterns of nature's cycles—the cycles of seasons, of sunrise and sunset, of biological rhythms of life and death.[37]

It is not Levinas's attempt to overcome the cosmological, linear time that situates his view in opposition to masculine time. The attempt to overcome cosmological time has also been undertaken by thinkers such as Bergson and Heidegger who are still thinking within the framework of masculine time. Bergson considers real time from the perspective of the cogito. For him duration is the time of consciousness, and as Alice Jardin writes in her introduction to Kristeva's essay, "History is linked to the cogito...to the paternal function."[38] So even though Bergson's notion of duration overcomes the cosmological view of time, it is still linear in the sense that it is grounded on the subject's history and memory. Even Heidegger's notion of temporality, which also goes beyond the traditional view of linear time as made of a series of infinite moments and avoids tying time with the consciousness of the thinking subject, in a way, does not succeed in overcoming the linear structure (or the synchronic structure, to use Levinas's term). Heidegger's notions of temporality and historicity, which focus on Dasein's "connectedness of life" between birth and death, on its becoming, are considered from the perspective of linearity, even though it is a finite and not infinite linearity. In focusing on beginning anew and rebirth rather than death and finitude, Levinas's view of time offers an approach that overcomes the linear view of time found even in interpretations that exceed the Aristotelian traditional conception of time as an infinite succession of nows.

Moreover, the metaphorical language of (re)birth and resurrection used by Levinas is associated with the maternal, as Kristeva asserts in the context of her discussion of monumental time, "One is reminded of the various myths of resurrection which, in all religious beliefs, perpetuate the vestige of an anterior or concomitant maternal cult."[39]

Grounding infinite time on recommencement and resurrection appears to offer a circular view of time—one that is unbound, with no beginning or end. However, Levinas is not speaking of an infinite, circular, repetitive structure of time. For him time is constituted by the interruption of the other; time is infinite because through the relation with the other, when the other interrupts the subject's temporality, the finite person has another chance and can always begin anew. So in a certain sense, Levinas agrees with Heidegger who understands the time associated with the human structure of existence to be finite since it is based on the temporality and historicity of the individual. But for Levinas it is the infinite dimension of time that is the primordial, more original, aspect of time. Therefore, Levinas's view of time as grounded in fecundity is not linear and not cyclical, not masculine and not feminine, and at the same time it is linear and cyclical, masculine and feminine.[40] Perhaps Levinas's view of fecund time can be even considered as an answer to Kristeva's call for reconciling circular, feminine time with linear, masculine time.

In focusing on particular events, I attempted to avoid as much as possible the abstraction, thematization, and conceptualization of Levinas's view of time, and tried to follow the phenomenological tradition by maintaining a concrete context for understanding it. Levinas himself believes the other is a concrete person, as Sandra Rosenthal explains, "The face of the Other to which one is exposed is not 'an other' in general, but an individual, specific concrete being with individual needs, a 'concrete other.'"[41] Although an objection may be raised as to whether these cases I have described are not merely singular events in which the other's time is intersected with the subject's present and renews it, these events belong to the structure that underlies time.

But how do these intersubjective relations constitute time? To whom does this time belong? More importantly—is Levinas successful in describing time as intersubjective, as in between the subject and the other? These questions still demand a reply. Levinas's attempt to go beyond the egological interpretation of time, and his claim that time is formed through the subject's relation with the other, implies a view that regards time as neither belonging to the subject nor to the other person. Fecund time requires the encounter with the other person, since it is the alterity of the other that provides the otherness, or difference, necessary for the constitution of time. Without the alterity of the other, without the interruption of the subject's temporality by the time of the other, there is no time but merely the present. This present should not necessarily be understood in terms of the linear present connecting the past with the future, but can be seen as the egological time that involves the temporality or duration of the subject. Or, as I will suggest in the following chapter, we may think of the present also in terms of what Levinas calls synchronic time. Only when the subject encounters the other, and the other's possibilities open new fates before the subject, is the subject given a future, and time is constituted. This future does not entirely belong to the subject, since it is the other's fate and possibilities, nor does it entirely belong to the other, since it is the subject who experiences these possibilities as the renewal of its future. From this perspective, we can think of fecund time as involving a future, which is neither the subject's nor the other's, but is in between them.

However, when pressing the issue in the attempt to further determine what sort of time is fecund time, we cannot but notice that this view of time does not entirely fulfill the promise of intersubjectivity. It seems that to some extent fecund time still belongs to the subject. Even though fecund time cannot be formed without the relation with the other, the function of the other is still to give the *subject* a future. Although Levinas's aim is precisely to go beyond the individual and focus on the *relationship* with the other, to some degree Irigaray is correct in accusing Levinas of describing the son as existing for the father and not for himself.[42] On the one hand, it is not the case that Levinas discusses fecundity from the viewpoint of the subject, or that he considers the child as merely the means for the father's infinite time (as immortality clearly functions in Diotima's speech). In fecund time Levinas focuses on the relation, the difference, between the subject and the other. But on the other hand, the emphasis in fecund time is on the renewal of the subject's possibilities, and in this sense

Irigaray's criticism is justified. The possibilities of the other person renew the *subject's* future, and allow the *subject* new beginnings. But even though the alterity required for the appearance of a new moment, which constitutes time, is provided by the other, and although fecund time focuses on the subject's relation with the other, this view of time does not entirely go beyond the time of the subject.

Surely, fecund time differs from Bergson's duration, which is the time of the individual's consciousness, and from Heidegger's temporality, which is grounded on Dasein's singular, unique, existence. But in *Totality and Infinity* even Levinas's different approach to the question of the infinity of time appears to be embedded in the perspective of the subject. Focusing on the individual entails that for Heidegger, and implicitly for Bergson as well, egological time is finite, whereas for Levinas, who focuses on the constitution of time through the relation with the other, time is infinite. But in his analysis of the infinity of time disclosed in fecundity Levinas does not entirely go past the viewpoint of the subject. Although the structure of fecund time requires the encounter with the other, its role is to free the *subject* from its present, and it is the possibilities of the *subject* which are renewed again and again. Hence, in a way, fecund time is still confined to the logic of egological time that Levinas aims at overcoming. Consequently, even though fecund time does reveal an attempt to go beyond the egological perspective, it still is not an adequate description of intersubjective time, a time that is neither public nor egological.

Perhaps the failure to entirely surpass egological time is grounded on what Derrida has criticized Levinas for—his inability to completely abandon ontological language in *Totality and Infinity*. Levinas does not entirely forsake the ego's perspective, and the tendency to incorporate the other in the same. Derrida's criticism of Levinas's use of ontological terminology in *Totality and Infinity* is often seen as influencing Levinas's approach in *Otherwise than Being* and his other late texts.[43] In many ways, in his late texts Levinas is still preoccupied with the same concerns, but he addresses them by applying a new terminology and viewpoint. Therefore, when discussing the view of diachronic time, which Levinas introduces in his late texts, an imperative question will be whether this view of time is more successful in overcoming egological time and offers a more radical approach to the question of intersubjective time.

FOUR

Intersubjective Time
Diachrony

In his later thought Levinas abandons his view of fecundity and provides a different point of view for understanding time. In texts such as *Otherwise than Being* and "Diachrony and Representation" he discusses time in terms of the opposition between diachrony and synchrony. Although this approach to the question of time is unlike understanding time in terms of fecundity, the two perspectives are different attempts at offering a view of time that exceeds the perspective of the individual. To borrow the metaphor of the repeating movement of the crashing waves at the beach, which Derrida uses to describe Levinas's thinking in *Totality and Infinity,* and Richard Bernstein extends to Levinas's thinking in general,[1] diachronic time is a returning movement of fecund time; it is the same movement against the same shore, but with enriched and deeper insistence. The ideas we find in Levinas's discussion of fecundity—that time is intersubjective and is constituted through the interruption of my time by the time of the other person—are repeated and intensified in his later thought. Hence, even though in fecundity the focus is on the future and in diachrony the primary emphasis is given to the immemorial past (but also to the pure future), what Levinas calls diachronic time can be seen as an amplification of fecund time. This is not because diachronic time is fecund time or vice versa, but in diachronic time, Levinas deepens his claim that time is constituted via the subject's relation with the other.

In *Otherwise than Being* Levinas states, "In the diachrony...one can suspect there is the interval that separates the same from the other" (*OB* 24). That is, diachronic time is the unbridgeable difference or interval that separates the subject's temporality from the other's. It is the movement and evolution of moments, in which each moment is separate and cannot be included in the same. This we find in the occasion of responsibility for the other (10–11), which shows itself in response to the other, that is, in language. To understand Levinas's account of time in his later thought, we must explicate the meaning of diachronic time as the intersubjective lapse in between the subject and the other person and explicate how it is created through the response to and responsibility for the other revealed in proximity and substitution, which in everyday life are most evident in speech, dialogues, and conversations. After considering how diachronic time is constituted, as well as the relation between *dia*chronic time and *dia*logue, we can surmise if diachronic time provides a better description of intersubjective time than Levinas's previous analogy of fecundity.

DIACHRONIC TIME

Like the structuralist tradition, the term "diachrony" is used by Levinas in opposition to "synchrony."[2] The word "diachrony" originates from the Greek prefix *dia*, which means through or across, and *chronos*, which means time. So diachrony means through time, as opposed to synchrony, which means at the same time. But Levinas assigns diachrony a different meaning than given by structuralists, such as Ferdinand de Saussure and his followers, for whom diachrony is the change in the meaning of words *through* time. Levinas employs *dia* in a different context. John Llewelyn explains that for Levinas diachrony indicates that the time of the other person cuts through (*dia*) every moment of my time.[3] In other words, through the interruption of my temporality by the temporality of the other, a new dimension of time is formed—diachronic time. In synchronic time the past and future become present, are *re*-presented, through memories and anticipations, respectively, whereas diachronic time refers to the disintegration of time, the time in which the past and future are not integrated in the present, are not represented. Levinas describes diachronic time as an "obligation for the other that I never contracted—in which I have never signed my obligation, for never to man's knowledge have I struck a contract with another—that a writ was passed. Something already concluded appears in my relation with another. It is there that I run up against the immemorial" (*GCM* 96). Hence, diachronic time is the not representable, immemorial obligation and responsibility for the other, which manifests itself in language and dialogue. Levinas admits that in the context of diachronic time he has not developed the theme of the future as broadly as that of the immemorial past, and explains this claiming, "The future is blocked from the outset; it is unknown from the outset, and consequently, toward it time is always diachrony" (96). But as he says in the same context, the future can be anticipated, even if "the anticipation of the future is very short." Through anticipation, the future—like memory in the case of the past—becomes present, is represented. Nevertheless, even though Levinas does not develop the idea of the future at the same depth as the immemorial past, he describes diachrony as a time "stronger than re-presentation, against any memory and any anticipation" (96), and in this sense diachrony involves not only the immemorial past but also the pure and absolute future.[4]

Similar to the dichotomy Bergson constructs between duration and spatial time and the opposition Heidegger forms between temporality and public time, Levinas appears to postulate his own distinction—a distinction between synchronic time and diachronic time. Parallel to Bergson's claim that real time is concealed by spatial time, and to Heidegger's view that temporality is covered by the vulgar, everyday time, for Levinas "the diachrony of time is synchronized into a time that is recallable, and becomes a theme" (*OB* 37). Jacques Dewitte offers to distinguish between diachronic time and synchronic time by applying the terms "circularity" and "linearity." He suggests that synchronic time is circular since the subject keeps returning to the present, whereas diachronic time is linear, since it involves an open future and past.[5] Synchronic time is similar to Levinas's view in his early writings (e.g., *Time and the Other, Existence and Existents*) in which the subject is confined to the present and keeps returning to it, similar to Nietzsche's eternal return. In this sense Dewitte is correct in calling it circular. However, circularity does not exclude movement, and the point Levinas is emphasizing is that without a new moment given by the other, the motion required for going beyond its present and acquiring time is absent. However, Dewitte's claim that diachronic time is linear is misleading. Although diachronic time conveys the idea that time is a movement that extends beyond the subject's own time (the present), linearity alludes to the synchronic structure that refers to time as a combination of the past, present, and future. This approach to time defies Levinas's ambition to go beyond the traditional views of time.

Despite the priority Levinas gives to diachronic time, and his view that time is primarily diachronic, he is aware of the tendency to synchronize it, thus concealing its diachronic aspect.

From the ego to the interlocutor there is a temporality other than the one that allows the ego to be assembled into the presence of the said and the written, a temporality that is concrete in this "from-me-to-the-other," which at once congeals into the abstraction of the synchronous in the synthesis of the "I think" that grasps it thematically (*TO* 103).

Diachronic time is not a container; it is not an inclusive domain that unites the same and the other, and thus enables communication. In this sense Levinas goes against the tradition, which views time as public and common to all. But he also rejects the Bergsonian and Heideggerian approaches wherein time is tied to the individual. Levinas considers diachronic time as intersubjective, as the dimension in between the same and the other. Therefore, contrary to Bergson and Heidegger, the realm of communication (including the saying and the said) does not take place in the spatial, public, vulgar time, but rather constitutes the veritable, primordial, diachronic time.

Simon Critchley associates Levinas's synchronic time with Bergson's spatial time and Heidegger's vulgar, Aristotelian time, on the one hand; on the other hand, he correlates Levinas's diachronic time with

Bergson's duration and Heidegger's temporality.[6] Like duration for Bergson and temporality for Heidegger, diachronic time for Levinas is the profound way to understand time. And like duration and temporality, diachronic time is covered over by an unoriginal, derivative understanding of time. But despite this apparent correlation between the views of time offered by Levinas and his predecessors, he actually begins where Bergson and Heidegger left off. The real or authentic views of time offered by Bergson and Heidegger, respectively, are from Levinas's perspective the interpretations of time that we should exceed. What Levinas calls synchronic time is, like Bergson's duration and Heidegger's temporality, egological. Synchronic time is the time of the said, the time of the present, the time of the thinking consciousness that gathers the past and the future into the present and tries to make all of time its own time. It is the time of the now that in French is *main-tenant*, hand-holding, which captures the correlation Levinas forms between the present and the act of grasping, that is the absorption of otherness in the same (cf. *GCM* 138, 209n2). Hence, although Bergson and Heidegger go beyond the traditional view of linear time as made of a series of infinite moments, they are still presenting views confined to what Levinas calls synchronic time. For Bergson and Heidegger, the meaning of time is embedded in the individual's future possibilities and the reassembling of the past into the present. Retrieving memories means the past is brought into the present, and the anticipation of possibilities means bringing the future into the present. Bergson's duration involves one's memories and anticipations, and Heidegger's temporality is grounded on the individual's being-ahead-of-itself-already-in-the-world-with-other-beings, and for this reason Bergson and Heidegger can only consider time as synchrony and not as diachrony.[7] Consequently, the view of time that for Bergson and Heidegger is real or authentic is unsatisfactory for Levinas, since it is tied to the assimilation of the other by the same.

However, like Bergson and Heidegger, who did not reject the Aristotelian traditional approach, but showed that it is an inadequate way to approach the issue of time, Levinas is not denying the

Bergsonian-Heideggerian egological view but shows its deficiency. Moreover, although in the thoughts of Bergson and Heidegger spatial/public time covers the real/primordial time, it still plays a role in one's life, since both thinkers are aware of the public aspect of the individual's life. Similarly, synchronic time has a function in Levinas's thought, and he acknowledges that we have different levels or ways for experiencing time. When we consider time in terms of a shared present we experience it at a synchronic level, in which a variety of events occur at the same time. Such an experience of time is necessary for communication. For Levinas "It is only in the said, in the epos of saying, that the diachrony of time is synchronized into a time that is recallable, and becomes a theme" (*OB* 37). That is, synchronized time is required for thematizing a meaning, for assembling a signification, and for conveying content. Only synchronic time is thinkable, since diachronic time is the realm of the immemorial, the irrecuperable, and the unrepresentable, which precedes history and meaning.

But the deeper, more profound level of experiencing time is diachrony. The other is always beyond me and cannot be reduced to the same. My responsibility for the other is prior to the said; therefore, intersubjective time is not synchronic or simultaneous. This idea indicates the exclusion of the individual's time (duration/temporality) from the other's, and at first it may appear similar to the Bergsonian and Heideggerian approach that consider duration or temporality as grounded respectively in the individual's consciousness or existence. But unlike Bergson and Heidegger, Levinas is not focusing on the duration or temporality of the individual. For him the profound experience of time goes beyond the perspective of the individual, resulting in the distinctive characteristics of diachronic time: immemoriality, irrecuperability, and unrepresentability. Already in his early texts Levinas insists that the subject's individual existence is insufficient for the constitution of time. Every ego has its own present, and the alterity required for the formation of time is found in the other person; therefore, time is grounded in the intersection of the individuals' temporalities. To paraphrase Heidegger's claim that Dasein is not *in* time but *is* time, for Levinas the relationship with the other does not occur *in* time, but rather *is* time. In "Diachrony and Representation," Levinas says, "The 'relationship' between the ego and the other is thus asymmetrical, without noematic correlation of any thematizable presence" (*TO* 108). So if we tie the notion of the asymmetrical relation between the subject and the other to the idea of diachronic time, we may claim that although the subject has a relationship with the other, they do not share the same present; that is, they are not contemporaries and remain separate from one another. As Paul Ricoeur says in an essay on Levinas, "The neighbor is not my contemporary; otherwise we should return to synchrony."[8] Similarly Richard Cohen claims that the core of Levinas's theory of time is the fact that "the other person encountered face-to-face is not the subject's contemporary. The I and the you do not meet one another 'at the same time.'"[9] But if this is the case, are we doomed to be enchained to the present? Does Levinas's view allow a relationship between the subject and the other?

This question can be rephrased from the perspective of the discussion of time: if the subject and the other are not contemporaries, if they do not meet one another "at the same time," in which dimension do they meet? Alon Kantor in a different context makes an observation that may be helpful for addressing this issue. He says that the question of simultaneity should not be understood in terms of formal logic, as it is for Aristotle who considers contradictions from a temporal perspective — the same attribute cannot at the same time belong and not belong to the same subject in the same respect. But rather, "at the same time" can be seen as a question of diachronic thought.[10] This different approach to the idea of simultaneity opens up a way to settle the apparent contradiction concerning the temporal dimension of the interaction between the same and other and explain how the same and the other can enter a relationship if they are not contemporaries. If we follow Kantor's suggestion and renounce the perspective confined to formal logic, then we are not necessarily faced with a contradiction. Even though the same and the other are not synchronic, they can still meet on the diachronic level. In claiming that we are noncontemporaries, Levinas is not referring to clock time. We use clock time to set meetings with other people. Surely Levinas is not denying this. But like Bergson and Heidegger before him, Levinas is offering a view of time that is prior to and more original than the time of dates and clocks. Therefore, from Levinas's perspective, a diachronic encounter means that the same and other are noncontemporaries in the sense that they do not share the same present, because this would entail their fusion and assimilation under one order or structure. Moreover, diachronic time is constituted through the responsible relation between the subject and the other.

For Levinas, encountering the other does not involve representation, but rather separation, as the other remains an independent, exterior duration or temporality. Levinas's thought reveals a way to think of a dimension in which two different temporalities can meet without being simultaneous, without one being reduced to the other, and without being united under one category or structure. So although the same and the other are engaged in a nonsynchronic, nonsimultaneous relation, it is still a relation. Levinas opens up a way of thinking in which the same and the other are at the same time absolutely not in relation with one another, and in relation with one another. According to the common understanding of what it means to be in a relation, the same and the other are not in relation with one another, since the other is always exterior to the same, cannot be taken in by it, cannot know it. If we adopt this traditional understanding of a relation involving knowledge, it may seem that a relationship is impossible, since the same can never know, understand, or grasp the other.

However, according to Levinas this relation that prevents the other from being assimilated in the same, this "encounter with the other is my responsibility for him" (*EN* 103). The possibility of the same and the other entering a relationship is by responsibility, proximity, and substitution, which are the relations that constitute intersubjective time. As Levinas states in "Diachrony and Representation," "Responsibility for the Other signifies an original and concrete temporality" (*TO* 104). Hence through my infinite, asymmetrical responsibility, diachronic time is created. In other words, Levinasian time is constituted through the obligation to be responsive to the other; time is revealed as diachronic in the event of my responsibility for the other person. Levinas explains, "The diachrony of a past that does not gather into representation is at the bottom of the concreteness of the time that is the time of my responsibility for the Other" (112). A little further in the text, Levinas states, "Responsibility for the Other, responding to the Other's death, vows itself to an alterity that is no longer within the province of re-presentation. This way of being avowed—or this devotion—is time. It remains a relationship to the other as other, and not a reduction of the other to the same" (115).

The intersubjective relation is the foundation for the formation of time, and therefore, the ethical relations of responsibility, proximity, and substitution are the basis of time. In everyday life responsibility, proximity, and substitution manifest themselves in language, leading Levinas to present a unique view of language and communication, which is closely tied with ethics. Furthermore, the responsible relation with the other is revealed in being approached, being summoned, and then in responding to the other. In this context it is important to clarify that when referring to forms of communication such as dialogue and conversation I am following Levinas in using the terms in a broad sense that includes not only the verbal aspect of language, but also its ethical meaning of welcome, response, and responsibility.

THE TEMPORALITY OF DIALOGUE

On the face of it, dialogue fills the gap between the subject and another person, and this may imply that dialogue has a spatial dimension. However, dialogue is better understood as a temporal event in between the subject and the other involving the flow of words and gestures. In Diotima's speech, *eros,* which is neither god nor human, plays the role of an interpreter, which enables humans and gods to preserve their language and still be able to converse. This view of *eros* as the dimension in between gods and humans, opens up a way to think of Levinasian time not as a public, spatial, inclusive domain that unites the same and the other under one structure or order, but as a difference in between the same and the other that enables them to maintain their separateness, their unique language, and still be able to communicate. The Levinasian idea that "the relation between the same and the other is primordially enacted as conversation" (*TI* 39), is developed in Levinas's later thought and is the basis for his view of diachronic, intersubjective time.

One perspective for showing the temporal aspect of dialogue is by examining the relation between time and the saying and the said. The said is the medium of simultaneity and synchrony in which time is represented in language—the past and future are re-presented (become present). The said is the time of historiography and narration, of "the simultaneity of the successive in a theme" (*OB* 36). The saying, on the other hand, is the relation with alterity, the realm of diachrony in which time is not assembled in the present—is not reduced to the structure of being. This is manifested in the relation between responsibility and the dimension of the immemorial past and absolute future. The immemorial past is never present—as Levinas explains in "From the One to the Other":

> It is, on the contrary, a past that cannot be reduced to the present that seems to signify in the ethical antecedence of responsibility-for-another-person, without reference to my identity guaranteed its right. Here I am, in this rejected responsibility thrown back toward someone who has never been either my fault or my concern, toward someone who has never been in my power, or in my freedom, toward someone who doesn't come into my memory. An ethical significance of a past which concerns me, which "has to do with" me, which is "my business" outside all reminiscence, all retention, all representation, all reference to a recalled present. A significance in ethics of a pure past irreducible to my present, and thus, of an originating past. An originating significance of an immemorial past, in terms of responsibility for the other man. My unintentional participation in the history of humanity, in the past of others which has nothing to do with me. (*EN* 150)

The subject is responsible for the past of others that is not its own, that was never its present, that it cannot represent. As Levinas notes elsewhere, "The obligation toward the other [is] prior to all contract (a reference to a past that has never been present!) and about dying for the other (a reference to a future that will never be present)" (*EN* 233).[11] Responsibility consists in obeying the contract before it is formulated. The subject is obligated to an immemorial commitment—a contract, which it cannot remember committing to, as if it were formulated before every possible present. It is not a response embedded in an act of freedom, but a response to a past, which is not its own. Furthermore, the responsible subject is compelled to answer not only for what others have done before it was born, but also for what others will do after its death—"There is in the Other a meaning and an obligation that obliges me beyond my death!" (*TO* 115). The subject is responsible for the other to the point of dying for the other, and this for Levinas is the meaning of a future that is beyond what happens to me, beyond my anticipations and protentions that are to-come (*à-venir*) (114–16). In terms of temporality this can be described as an extension of the responsible subject over a span of time that begins before its birth and does not end with its death.[12] And as already discussed in chapter three, this reveals one way for considering Levinas's claim that the principle of time is infinity rather than finitude.

Hence, the saying is the time of responsibility for the other, which is a time without beginning (*OB* 51), since responsibility is not a choice but a calling prior to any choice I make that comes before all memorable time. It is also a time with no end, since my responsibility goes beyond the finitude of my life—I am responsible also for events and occurrences that follow my death and will never be my present. But the diachronic time of the saying is translated into the synchronic time of the said; the pure future that will never be present and the immemorial time that was never present are translated into the "recuperable time, the recoverable time, the lost time that can be found again" (36). In the said the past and future become present, and as a result time is congealed. Consequently, if movement is an essential characteristic of time, then the said is the "remission or detent of time" (36). That is, the thematizing of the saying to the said, the ascribing of meaning "coagulate[s] the flow of time into a 'something' "; it fixes the said in the present, re-presents it, and thus extracts from the saying "the labile character of time" (37).

The difference between the said and the saying in relation to time perhaps will become clearer by applying Bergson's distinction between duration and spatial time. For Bergson, duration reveals a perspective that allows us to focus on difference and heterogeneity, and consequently go beyond the spatial viewpoint of concepts and essences. Similarly, for Levinas, the saying avoids the essences, which "fill the said" (*OB* 9). In focusing on themes and concepts the said expresses a spatial perspective in which the heterogeneous movement of the ethical saying is translated into fixed, static concepts. That is, the movement, the unthematizeable and singular aspect of the saying is covered over by the spatial perspective of the said, and consequently real time is concealed as well, leaving accessible only the shadow of time. As an example, we may think of the process of composing music. The composer first plays or hears the music, and then translates the movement, the temporal dimension of music, into the static, congealed form of musical notes on a page. Similarly, prior to the verbal, thematized, conceptual language of the said is the saying, my responsibility for the other. But like the composer's need to translate his or her music to the static dimension of writing in order to preserve and communicate the opus, the movement of the saying is synchronized and assembled into the present and "represents even the time of responsibility for the other" (51). Yet even when synchronized and thematized, the trace of the saying is not erased from the said—even when saying "Hello," the welcome and exposure of the saying is evident. This disruption of the said by the saying, the friction between movement and immobility found in everyday encounters with the other person that is manifested in speech, dialogue, and conversation reveals the time constituted through relaxation and tension.[13]

The relation between time and dialogue becomes evident in the temporal structure of dialogue. In dialogue every reply is the beginning of a new question or comment, entailing a continuous heterogenic movement. As I have already suggested, the pure said combined of concepts, themes, and verbal statements has a spatial structure, and the temporal structure of the saying is translated into the said. But dialogue involves both the saying and the said. Although dialogue appears to be no more than the communication of statements and themes, it has a trace of the saying. Moreover, the saying is the condition of the communicated content of dialogue, since ethics is the condition of language. Hence, the correlation of the said, the spatial aspect of language, with the voice, tone, welcome, and summoning of the saying, conveys the movement and change of dialogue, which reveals a temporal structure. But often a dialogue is written down, and as a result, is translated from the temporal to the spatial. This is the case, for example, in newspaper articles, which convert the temporal movement of oral dialogue to the spatial order of writing. The reporter's conversation with her interviewee, which originally is characterized as temporal, is thematized and synchronized through the reporter's observations, and the temporal ethical relation between two people is translated into the spatial realm of writing.

Although presented to us in written form, and thus spatial, Plato's dialogues can serve as an illustration of the temporal structure of dialogue. This may seem to be a curious example, since Levinas claims, "In the writing the saying does indeed become a pure said, a simultaneousness of the saying and of its conditions" (*OB* 170–71). Surely the translation of the saying to the said can be regarded as necessary because "in the logos said, and written, it survives the death of the interlocutors that state it, and assures the continuity of culture" (169)—unless Plato's dialogues were available in writing they would have been lost. But the survival of texts does not necessarily entail a constant, unchanging, spatial, eternal dimension but can imply a temporal structure. As in the case of most texts, Plato's dialogues invite us to enter a dialogue with the dialogue, with the text, the author, and with the scholars and interpreters of Plato's texts. Levinas himself admits that books are "interrupted, and call for other books and in the end are interpreted in a saying distinct from the said" (171). Therefore, through the different levels of dialogue we break out of the apparently static, spatial structure of the said of written texts. By exchanging ideas with the text and among ourselves, we incite movement, change, and becoming, which provide the ground for a continuing creation and a regeneration of views, and such a motion is particularly noticeable in dialogue.

But although the said of dialogue, at least to some extent, is temporal, more important is the temporal structure of the saying. Recorded dialogues, although available to us as written texts, also exhibit the structure of an oral exchange revealing different voices that disclose the saying, the ethical approach to the other, which cannot be thematized or conceptualized.[14] Unlike the said that is grounded in essences, concepts, themes, ideas, theories, and models, which convey a spatial perspective, the saying presents a temporal structure, since it focuses on heterogeneity, on that which remains uncaptured and singular. This understanding of conversation as a temporal dimension rather than a spatial structure constituted of categories and concepts opens up another angle for approaching the wonder raised by what may seem to be Levinas's claim that language offers a common ground for the same and the other, and that it unites them. That is, the temporal structure of dialogue allows us to escape the unification of the same and the other under one order, which the spatial structure cannot avoid. Written dialogue can also reveal the aspect of the in between relevant to Levinas's thought. Neither 'pure' writing nor 'pure' speech, such dialogue could be understood as in between the written and the spoken—as neither pure said nor pure saying. The inability to classify these texts as written or spoken, saying or said, complies with Levinas's demand to escape the tendency to categorize, totalize, and conceptualize—or from Bergson's perspective, spatialize—our relation with the other, and consider dialogues as constituting the diachronic time in between the same and the other.

It may be helpful to compare time again to a piece of music since, like speech, music is temporal. The temporal experience of the dialogue escapes the unification of the same and the other under a certain category, which may take place within the spatial structure. In conversation each person maintains its singularity, its voice, but when its voice meets another voice a contrapunctus (counterpoint) is formed.

The comparison of diachronic time to music is particularly interesting because Bergson and Husserl form their own analogies between music and time. For Bergson the melting of notes of music into one another serves as an illustration for duration's organic wholeness that synthesizes the past and present states; similar to the constant change of a melody with the addition of every new note, the individual is altered with every new experience (*TFW* 100, 106, 111). Husserl compares the flow of time involving retention and protention to the flow of music, showing that when we listen to a piece of music we simultaneously retain the memory of the note just played, hear the note currently played, and anticipate the next note in the sequence.[15] Although Bergson and Husserl have noticed the temporal dimension of music and the heterogeneity and movement of a melody, they are confined to synchronic time, to the perspective of the totality of the musical piece and to the consciousness that represents this piece through retention and anticipation. They do not take under consideration the dialogue and tension between the different instruments and voices. Music is formed by the interruption of notes, instruments, and voices into one another and the tension and relaxation formed by the dialogue between the different elements of the musical piece create a temporal movement. As in the musical contrapunctus, in conversation, the different voices (melodies) meet in such a way that they establish a new dimension that is grounded in the different voices, but is not affiliated with one or the other—it is a dimension that does not belong to one of the voices but is in between them. Like music, time is an ethical (harmonic) relationship that retains the individuality and singularity of the voice of a person (melody).[16]

DIALOGUE AND TIME

The relation between the subject and the other person, which involves not only verbal dialogue, but is grounded in the language of the saying, in response and responsibility, opens up a way to clarify Levinas's view of intersubjective time. Time is the relation of nonindifference revealed in the ethical relation of responsibility. But how does the relation of responsibility and obligation constitute time? In *God, Death, and Time* Levinas writes, "Time is at once this Other-within-the-Same and that Other who cannot be together with the Same; it cannot be synchronous. Time would thus be a disquieting [*inquiétude*] of the Same by the Other, without the Same ever being able to comprehend or encompass the Other" (*GDT* 19). In *Otherwise than Being* Levinas explains, "This being torn up from oneself in the core of one's unity, this absolute noncoinciding, this diachrony of the instant, signifies in the form of one-penetrated-by-the-other" (*OB* 49). Time is formed through the interruption of the same by the other, and this disturbance of the same provides the alterity necessary for the constitution of time. This disruption is revealed in the ethical relation between the subject and the other person, in which the same and the other remain separate, noncontemporaries. Although the other encountered face-to-face does not share the ego's present, diachronic time is the occasion in which the time of the other intersects with and disrupts the ego's time. Without assembling the other's past into the ego's present, this disruption provides a new moment, which is the alterity required for the constitution of time. But in what sense does the interruption of the same by the other create time? How does the ethical intersubjective relation of conversation, dialogue, speech, and response create this interruption? And why call this time? These questions remain vague in Levinas's writings, but deserve our attention if we wish to appreciate his view of intersubjective time.

Levinas's notion of proximity is helpful for the purpose of addressing these questions. Prima facie, proximity is a spatial term referring to nearness or closeness in place, order, or relation. When I move closer to an object, the gap between myself and the object diminishes until it disappears with my touching of the object. Such a spatial view of proximity requires the possibility to compare the same and the other (I am here and the other is there), and consequently demands the same and other to take part in the same order (space/place). But Levinas conceives the proximity to the other "outside ontological categories" (*OB* 15), and refrains from considering it in terms of limits and boundaries. He removes the spatial meaning from proximity, as he explicitly states, "The relationship of proximity cannot be reduced to any modality of distance or geometrical contiguity, nor to the simple 'representation' of a neighbor" (100–01). This is clearly a corrective to his account of time in *Totality and Infinity*, where he repeatedly reveals a dependence upon spatial terms. Throughout the earlier text, Levinas depicts the subject in a spatial location—a dwelling, habitation, or home (*TI* 152–57)—and describes the relation between the self and other as a "distance" between shores (64) and a "dimension of height" (75, 86, 215, 220, 251).[17] In contrast, in *Otherwise than Being*, proximity is not to be understood as a spatial interval between the subject and the other.

Proximity is approach, contact, neighborhood; it "is already an assignation, an extremely urgent assignation—an obligation, anachronously prior to any commitment" (101). That is, "in proximity a subject is implicated in a way not reducible to the spatial sense" (81), but rather the subject enters an ethical relation when meeting the other, addressing the other, facing the other. Even if we touch the skin of the other, that is, are in proximity and contact with the other person, we always remain separate. Instead of thinking of proximity as a spatial situation in which I am in point X and the other is in point Y, and assess the distance between us as proximity, or even consider proximity as a movement in space that brings me closer to the other, Levinas suggests we think of proximity as an ethical approach involving the saying, the response to and responsibility for the other. It is an ethical nearness and contact that avoids the integration of the same and other. Unlike a spatial proximity that may end in the merging of two entities, in their contemporaneous encounter, the ethical proximity demands openness to the other, but also ensures the distance and nonsynchronic relation between the subject and the other person. This ethical movement toward the other is infinite. "The closer you get to the other, the greater your responsibility towards him becomes" (*BV* 32) —both in the sense of more and more responsibilities (nonfinite), and in the sense that one can never be responsible enough for the other (intrinsic infinity). As Robert Gibbs notices, for Levinas "ethics notes that the more I draw near the further away I am. . . . As I step closer, my obligations grow. . . . This infinition of my responsibility occurs in nearness to the Other."[18] As a consequence, since for Levinas time is grounded in the infinite ethical movement toward the other, he is claiming that time is also infinite.

Proximity does not imply the diminishing of distance, but rather the upholding of the unbridgeable separation between the subject and the other. Hence, even though it is inevitable but to describe proximity by using a spatial vocabulary (such as bridging and separation, drawing near and coming closer), Levinas's notion of proximity implies a temporal relation. In characterizing proximity as "restlessness, null side, outside the place of rest" (*OB* 82), and applying terms of movement rather than considering it as a state or repose, we are presented with a view that regards proximity as temporal. But proximity is not temporal because it enters "into the common time of clocks, which make meetings possible" (89)—this would entail a synchronic or spatial view of time, one that regards time as uniting the same and the other within one order (clock time). Rather, proximity reveals a temporal structure in the sense that it escapes the unification of the same and other under one structure, and allows separateness and singularity by avoiding simultaneity, essences, similarities, and categories. However, the relevance of proximity for understanding time goes beyond the claim that proximity exposes a nonsynchronic, nonspatial, temporal structure grounded in the subject's relation with the other, for it is through the relations of proximity, responsibility, and substitution, which are uncovered in speech and dialogue, that diachronic time is constituted.

In proximity the subject is concerned with another individual and is interrupted by the infinite responsibility for the other. Therefore in proximity we do not experience tranquility and rest, but a disturbance and interruption (*OB* 89), and consequently, "proximity is a difference, a non-coinciding, an arrhythmia in time, a diachrony" (166). Hence, in proximity the synchronic, tranquil, rememberable time of the subject is disturbed by the time of the other, and diachronic time is created. In diachrony there is no common present, for it involves the past that cannot be caught up with and the future that is unimaginable. Unlike synchronic time that focuses on the continuous temporal movement of the individual's life and existence, diachronic time is "putting the identical out of phase with itself" (34; cf. 28).

But how does this disturbance, out of phasing, discontinuity, or arrhythmia occur? The answer lies in the view that the difference that separates the same from the other in diachrony "lasts from a question to a response" (*OB* 24). Hence, the interruption that reveals diachronic time is created through dialogue, through the subject's response to and responsibility for another. For the purpose of revealing that time is constituted via the relation with the other we must focus not only on the said of dialogue, but also on the saying—on proximity, substitution, and responsibility. Levinas's thought reveals the event of contact with the other as opening a diachronic lapse of time between the nonsynchronic temporalities of the interlocutors. The interlocutors are not merely bodies that occupy space, but more importantly they are noncategorizable, nonconceptual, singular, independent temporalities, and their ethical relation involving the various aspects of dialogue constitutes a new level of time, diachronic time.

Both diachrony and dialogue begin with the Greek prefix *dia*, which means "through" or "between." For Levinas the *dia* of dialogue is an I saying, "You" (*GCM* 147). When I say, "You," I am disrupted by you, revealing the interruption of the same by the alterity of the other. Dialogue is also the flow between question and response, between the saying and the said, between wordlessness and wordiness, between passivity and imperialism, between singularity and essentialism. Diachrony indicates for Levinas that although the time of the other person is nonsynchronic with my time, it runs through every moment of my time, it interrupts and postpones my time, forming an ethical understanding of time. This can be summed up to say that even though the same and the other are nonsynchronic, the words as well as the ethical nonverbal aspects of openness, attentiveness, listening, and responsibility, which flow through and between the interlocutors in conversations, allow them to form a temporal, singular, ungraspable relationship, which constitutes diachronic time. But it is yet to be clarified why this ethical relation constitutes diachronic time. Why should we call the relation involving speech, proximity, and substitution time?

Revisiting Levinas's relation with Blanchot may be helpful for addressing these concerns.[19] Blanchot's responsibility for Levinas, disclosed in the action of substitution for Levinas, is an event of an original communication and dialogue that lies "behind the *de facto* communication" (*OB* 119). Hence, substitution, the manifestation of "Here I am," reveals a nonverbal dialogue, a saying, which is the basis for the verbal dialogue that surely has accompanied Blanchot's act of risking his life and freedom for Levinas. In other words, Blanchot's deed displays a communication with Levinas that involves more than the verbal said. Through such a movement from one to the other, which is more than the motion of words, time is constituted.

The idea that time is a motion that involves alterity and change is already found in Aristotle's definition of time ("a number of change in respect of before and after"), as well as in the views of Bergson and Heidegger, who find difference, movement, and otherness crucial for the formation of time. But for Levinas the motion that grounds diachronic time is an ethical movement toward the alterity of the other. This movement is formed through substitution, proximity, and responsibility, involving ethical actions and dialogues that demand an encounter with another—I substitute myself in the place of the other, I am in proximity with the other, and I am responsible for the other. These actions reveal the getting out of phase, the disengagement from one's identity, from oneself, which for Levinas is the definition of diachronic time (*OB* 28). Getting out of phase occurs in such ethical manifestations of responsibility when the subject goes beyond its own time and temporality, beyond its own past and future, beyond its history and hopes, beyond synchronic time. Such ethical situations manifest the interruption that creates a moment of time that does not have a memorable past or an anticipated future and does not belong to any individual—it is neither the time of the same, nor the time of the other, but a movement of dialogue, attention, and ethical gestures in between them.

But is time constituted only in the event of the ethical response taking place in an extreme moment of crisis, or is this view of time relevant also to everyday encounters? The interruption and getting out of phase that constitute diachronic time seems more obvious in events in which the commitment to the other clearly demonstrates the ethics of "Here I am," such as Blanchot's substitution for Levinas, or Harry Ramos's decision to stay with a stranger named Victor instead of saving himself from the burning World Trade Center Building on September 11, 2001.[20] However, by limiting diachronic time to such occasions we are presented with a narrow structure of time, excluding ordinary relations. Levinas admits that diachronic time appears "in the extraordinary and everyday event of my responsibility for the faults or misfortunes of others, in my responsibility that answers for the freedom of another" (*OB* 10). But Levinas's thought does not limit responsibility, proximity, and substitution to radical occasions but recognizes the ethical relation to the other in trivial, daily events such as saying, "After you, sir," "Hello," and "Here I am" (117, 114; cf. *IR* 211–12; *EI* 89). These everyday phrases of communication reveal the extraordinary. We rarely respond like Blanchot's reaction to Levinas's situation and place the freedom of the other prior to our own freedom, or take upon ourselves a responsibility similar to Harry Ramos's commitment of "Here I am" when staying with Victor instead of saving himself from the burning World Trade Center. But as Jill Robbins insightfully observes, "In the speaking relation with the Other, Levinas glimpses transcendence."[21] That is, speaking to the other—saying, "After you, sir" when opening the door, greeting someone with "Hello" when entering the elevator, or answering, "Here I am" when my son calls out—is the imprint of ethical responsibility in everyday occasions, the trace of the extraordinary in the ordinary. Therefore, time is constituted not only in the uncommon situations in which the infinite, radical responsibility for the other is evident, but also in everyday, ordinary encounters when we face and speak to another person.

For example, not long ago I was waiting for the bus that would take me home. I was particularly absorbed in my thoughts after receiving a series of bad news when a beggar in the background solicited the crowd for money. I looked away. Turning my face from the other may seem to be a non-Levinasian response to the call of the other; even in describing him as a beggar I am categorizing him, labeling him, and placing him within a social context, which defies Levinas's view of the face as the singular and ungraspable. But for Levinas being a subject means to respond to the other, and "every attitude in regard to the human is greeting—if only in the refusal of greeting" (*BPW* 7). So even my seemingly nonresponse of ignoring the solicitor was a response. In everyday situations we cannot always be responsible for all the others and cannot live up to the Levinasian ethical utopian standards of responsibility for the other. For example, in Levinas's view the best way to encounter the other is not to notice his or her eye color (*EI* 85), but we do notice the facial characteristics of the person we are talking to.

Nonetheless, we can still learn from Levinas to divert our focus from ourselves to the other, just as it happened when an elderly woman (again a description, a categorization) addressed me after the beggar solicited for money. Before she spoke I had not noticed her sitting beside me. She was for me an unnoticed face in the crowd, but when she addressed me, saying, "He [the beggar] should get a job," she got my attention, and I listened. Contrary to the beggar who never addressed *me*, never invited me into a conversation, but just threw into the air the general, nonsingular words begging for money, the woman exposed herself in conversation allowing me a glimpse of her singularity, her individuality. The act of begging triggered her to tell me her story, and I turned my face toward her in attention. In the first time in 15 years she visited her daughter, who lives only a two-hour drive from her. Unfortunately she sprained her ankle, and not only was in pain during the entire visit, but she was also struggling to keep her pain concealed. I met the woman, whose only daughter was soon to leave with her family to live abroad, in the central bus station after she got off one bus and was waiting for the bus that would take her home. When the bus finally arrived she did not get on it. She remained sitting, lifting her bad foot on the metal rail, waiting for her husband, who took the opportunity of the stop in a big city to go to the market. The moment caught me in a vulnerable state that allowed me to open myself to her and listen. In conversation with the other the ego leaves itself, and opens itself to an ethical relation with the other, and through the confluences with the other a dimension that is neither the ego's nor the other's is formed. Such an encounter, even with a total stranger, opens us to the possibility of leaving ourselves and listening to the other and creates a momentary, fleeting, and even fortuitous event in between the self and the stranger.

I met this woman in a central bus station—a stop in between two movements, a place that is neither the destination nor the origin, which belongs to no one and to everyone. But between the woman and myself, as between any two people, there is not only a spatial distance, but a temporal one as well. We are not synchronous; we do not exist at the same time. Each person has his or her own temporality or duration, but through proximity what seems impossible becomes possible. The apparently unbridgeable difference is actually a new dimension that involves the turning of one's face to the Other, the words spoken, the attention given, the gestures and facial reactions manifested. In this context it is interesting to note that the Hebrew language alludes to the relation between time and ethics, to which Levinas points. The Hebrew words for available (זמין *zamin*), willing (מזומן *mezuman*), invite (להזמין *le'hazmin*), and summon (לזמן *le'zamen*) all originate from the root z'm'n, which is the same grammatical root of the Hebrew word for time, *zman* (זמן).[22] By facing me and speaking to me, the woman not only extended herself to me, but she invited me into conversation and summoned me. As Robert Gibbs suggests, "My first responsibility arises in listening to another person, not in speaking to her,"[23] and I was willing to leave myself, become available and listen to her, not comprehend or absorb her. The encounter with the women left its trace on me, but not in the memory of the encounter or the details of the said. I have already forgotten the categorical characteristics of the women (the color of her eyes), and the memories of the specific words uttered have faded. But the encounter marked me in a way that I am unable to conceptualize. I recognize that it is not only the content of the said that has influenced me. Yet, I am unable to rationalize and explain the source of and reason for the affect this encounter had on me. Every attempt to analyze this conversation will require the use of concepts, and as a result the temporal and singular aspect might be lost and covered over by the spatial and theoretical viewpoint. Diachronic time is experienced and cannot be explained by adopting an exterior and theoretical point of view. The exterior viewpoint implies a totalizing structure under which the subject and the other are united, and this betrays the diachronic perspective.

The interruption of my time by the time of the woman may seem ordinary compared to the cases of disruption we find in Blanchot's relation with Levinas or when Harry Ramos met Victor. But even though there is nothing extraordinary about this encounter, in approaching me, the woman who was in need to tell her story summoned me, demanded my response, and by responding, by facing her, I reacted according to the Levinasian "Here I am," and by doing so my time was penetrated and disturbed by the other. The motion of the diachronic time in between us had begun with the woman's approach, with her singling me out (there were other people waiting for the bus) and summoning me. When speaking to me, I turned my face to her, and as Richard Sugarman puts it, diachrony "begins when the other turns toward or away from me."[24] Already with the movement of facing the elderly woman, my temporality was interrupted by her temporality. When approaching me, the stream of my inner time had been put out of phase. That is, proximity "temporalizes itself, but with a diachronic temporality, outside, beyond or above, the time recuperable by reminiscence, in which consciousness abides and converses, and in which being and entities show themselves in experience" (*OB* 85). By interrupting my thoughts with her story, my temporality was penetrated by the woman, leading me to leave myself and become disengaged from my identity. When speaking to me she interrupted my preoccupation with my memories, hopes, and anticipations, and she might have even obstructed or delayed my intentions (such as reading a book or getting a soda from the machine)—my temporal movement had been suspended by my reaction to her demand, causing an arrhythmia in my egological time. Similar to the penetration of one musical sound by another forming a new independent sound, the diachronic time constituted in dialogue does not belong to the subject or to the other, but is in between them. By interrupting my temporality, my synchronic time, a new moment of time is created constituting the diachronic dimension.

Levinas characterizes time as the motion that should be understood in terms of relaxation and tension (*OB* 29). Hence, the movement forming diachronic time is revealed not only in the motion of the words constructing the content of the dialogue, but more importantly, it is created by the tension and relaxation experienced with the disturbance of the face of the other and the postponement between the demand for response and our actual response. This tension is not my tension or the other's tension, but a tension between us that is dissipated with my response or nonresponse. The delay between the calling of another person and my response form a tension, which is followed by relaxation when the tension is eased with the anticipated response. Consequently, even when ignoring the call of the other, as I had ignored the solicitation of the beggar, time is formed. It means that time is created in every encounter with the other, even in cases in which the ethical saying of "Here I am" is concealed. The reaching out of a person to another is the stretching out of time.

Similar to fecund time, diachronic time is the dimension formed when the subject is interrupted by the alterity of the other. This disruption is characterized in *Otherwise than Being* as the other-in-the-same (*OB* 114), which elsewhere Levinas explicates, "The *in* does not signify an assimilation: the Other disturbs or awakens the Same; the Other troubles the Same, or inspires the Same, or the Same desires the Other, or awaits him (does time's duration not come from this patient awaiting?)" (*GCM* 80). The model of the ethical relation with the other remains the relation with the child, but the relation of disruption illustrated in *Totality and Infinity* by the father-son relation of fecundity is replaced in his later thought with the relation of maternity.[25] Motherhood begins by the growing, residing of otherness within the subject; it is manifested in the offering of "the bread out of one's mouth to nourish the hunger of another with one's own fasting" (*OB* 56). Levinas uses the maternal as the model of ethical responsibility involving substitution and proximity: "In maternity what signifies is a responsibility for others, to the point of substitution for others and suffering both from the effect of persecution and from the persecuting itself in which the persecutor sinks. Maternity, which is the bearing par excellence, bears even responsibility for the persecuting by the persecutor" (75). Diachronic time formed via proximity and substitution can be seen as maternal time.

Just as Levinas's choice of adopting the paternal metaphor for describing fecundity (in *Totality and Infinity*) should be seen as a model revealing a saying purged from sexual assumptions, which is also the case with the metaphor of the maternal. As Stella Sandford correctly observes, maternity is a universal model, and even though the model for ethical responsibility is in a sense feminine, it is a model that can be assumed by the male as well.[26] So in *Totality and Infinity*, the model of eros is replaced by fecundity (the paternal structure), and in *Otherwise than Being*, the model of fecundity is replaced by maternity. But we should not think of maternal time as "the gift of time," as Lisa Guenther suggests.[27] Giving life and time to the child alludes to a view restricted to the synchronic perspective for reasons similar to those leading me to claim that fecundity does not entirely overcome the synchronic approach to time. The maternal structure is diachronic; it is the model of substitution, of the interruption manifested in "Here I am." Consequently, maternity is associated with diachronic time, and it is the maternal metaphor, which provides the mature description of intersubjective time that is an improvement of fecund time.

Despite its attempt to exceed egological time, fecund time does not reflect a view entirely independent of the subject. By taking upon him or herself the possibilities and fate of the other, the subject's possibilities and future are extended, so in a sense, fecundity is confined to synchronic time. Nevertheless, already in Levinas's interpretation of fecund time the temporality of the subject is disrupted. Indeed, the idea of interruption first revealed in fecund time is intensified and pushed to an extreme in diachronic time. The diachronic description of time offers a way of understanding the interruption of the same by the other as creating time that is beyond the individual's singular existence—it is an interpretation of time that does not belong to the same or to the other. The diachronic view considers time as constituted by the temporal motion of words and ethical gestures involving responsibility, proximity, and substitution that move continuously between myself and the other forming an infinite temporal lapse in between us. So although Levinas does not dismiss the experience of synchronic time, for him diachronic time is the primary experience of time and from this experience the meaning and significance of synchronic time is derived.

FIVE

From Ethical Time to Political Time

The view of intersubjective time offered by Levinas can be considered as a way to satisfy the discontent with the Bergsonian-Heideggerian egological, synchronic time. This is particularly relevant to diachronic time, which is successful in going beyond the limited viewpoint of the individual. But does Levinas actually succeed in presenting a view that bridges the gap we inherit from Bergson and Heidegger? Does not even Levinas's interpretation of diachronic time leave us still dissatisfied to some extent? Bergson and Heidegger are confined to the egological perspective of time, and for the most part consider our relations with other people as occurring within the order of public time. Levinas corrects this by understanding time precisely as intersubjective, as constituted through the relationship between the other and the self. But this raises the concern as to whether a view of time grounded in the face-to-face encounter, in my responsible relation with another individual, provides a satisfactory approach; or is it again a limited view, one that does not involve the community of people? The purpose of this chapter is to extend and enrich Levinas's view of time, and present an original interpretation that recognizes time as constituted through our human existence but also acknowledges its collective aspect.

THE QUESTION OF COMMUNAL TIME

The ethical relations described in *Totality and Infinity* as a face-to-face encounter, and in *Otherwise than Being* as involving proximity and substitution, focus on the subject's relation with a singular other. But we should keep in mind that "next to the one who is an other to me, is 'another other' to me" (*EN* 229). The human society is not a society of two, but is a complex network of people and relations so that the consequences of one's acts always to some extent go beyond one's intentions. Levinas recognizes this difficulty and for this reason he introduces the idea of the third party, *le tiers*.[1] This idea appears already in texts that precede *Totality and Infinity*, such as "The Ego and the Totality" (1954), but it is developed in his late texts and interviews. My responsibility for the concrete other is not limited to this particular individual, but neither is it a general categorical imperative. Rather, the other I encounter here and now is the disclosure of the possibility of additional unique others. The third person, like the other, is "a neighbor, a face, an unreachable alterity" (*IR* 214), so I am tied in an obligation to a variety of others for whom I am infinitely responsible. "Starting from this third person, is the proximity of human plurality," but this raises a problem: "Who in this plurality comes first?" (*TO* 106). If I listen to the third, I am at the risk of doing wrong to the second one. Levinas admits that within the multiplicity of humanity it is impossible to establish a face-to-face ethical relation of incomparable individuals, unique to unique, and he believes this is the role of the state (*IR* 193–94). So it seems that since in a society the individuals are comparable, we are forced to leave the realm of ethics and return to the realm of ontology, which Levinas aims at overcoming. This implies that in the collective society, alterity is covered over. Yet, for Levinas "the saying as contact is the spirit of society" (*OB* 160); the situation of equality between the different members of a society is founded upon the original structure of asymmetry and nonreciprocity. But here we are faced with the difficulty of describing the relation between the political and the ethical—of sketching the move from ethics to politics, from the other to the community, from asymmetry to equality.[2] We are faced with the question whether such a transition requires abandoning Levinas's ethical demand of alterity, of difference.

This difficulty affects the possibility of expanding intersubjective time to a collective view of time. Given the absence of the idea of the third party from Levinas's discussion of time, indicates that Levinas ignores the essentiality of the move toward a collective, political time. Another problem involves the role of contemporaneous time in his thought. It may seem that like Bergson and Heidegger before him, Levinas considers collective time as a degradation of a more profound and original experience of time. Levinas claims, "The contemporaneousness of the multiple is tied about the diachrony of two" (*OB* 159). This suggests that for Levinas the collective time involving the entire community is grounded in the more original, diachronic time. Here we are reminded of Bergson's view that spatial time is the shadow of duration, and of Heidegger's claim that the everyday vulgar time, including the time of natural processes, receives its significance from temporality. Similarly, for Levinas the elements that involve the constitution of diachronic time—nonsimultaneity, proximity, substitution—which entail inequality (e.g., I am more responsible than the other, the other and myself are not contemporaries), are the basis of the equality and of the contemporaneousness of collective time relevant to politics, justice, and the state.

This may indicate that the time of justice and politics is in fact the simultaneous time involving dates and clocks, and its meaning depends on diachronic time. If that is the case, then Levinas appears to accept the Bergsonian-Heideggerian assumption that collective time is founded on the structure of a more original time, and he leaves no room for a view of political time that is not dominated by the totalizing ontological structure of the same. Even though Levinas is interested in forming a connection between time and the assembling of individuals into a community, claiming already in *Existence and Existents,* "Is not sociality more than the source of our representation of time: is it not time itself?" (*EE* 93), he actually concentrates on the social relation with one singular other. Levinas refrains from offering an explicit and detailed link between the diachronic structure of time and society, which following Richard Sugarman's suggestion, can be named "polychrony."[3] Although Levinas's interpretation of time goes beyond the solitary individual, it is still limited to the relation between one person and another and does not take into account the third party. Hence, even though Levinas's view of intersubjective time is compelling, it results in a dissatisfaction similar to the one produced by the thought of Bergson and Heidegger. Although Levinas's view of time is innovative and pushes the discussion of time beyond the egological views, he does not develop a view of collective time that considers our communal human existence as providing the meaning for our temporal existence. However, a fully developed view of time that preserves the relation between time and human existence should acknowledge that a crucial aspect of our human life involves communal forms of existence. Therefore, we are faced with the pressing question: is the time of justice and politics necessarily the everyday time of dates and clocks, which receives its meaning from and depends on diachronic time; or, is there a way to describe time as a collective event that is not public and synchronic?

Levinas considers the conjunction of politics and ethics as intrinsically possible, and he suggests that fraternity, the motto of the republic and the basis of the political community, is detected in the nonindifference and responsibility for the other (*OS* 123, 125). This opens up a political dimension that is not grounded in equality, but rather regards human fraternity as preserving Levinas's ethical requirement of irrecusable, nontransferable responsibility for the other, and thus preserving the demand of alterity, uniqueness, and incomparability. However as Levinas explicitly claims, this cannot be guaranteed by the state, but requires "a vocation *outside* the state, disposing, in a political society of a kind of extra-territoriality, like that of prophecy in the face of political powers of the Old Testament, a vigilance totally different from political intelligence, a lucidity not limited to yielding before the formalism of universality, but upholding justice itself in its limitations" (123). We must, then, locate a nonsynchronic, collective, temporal dimension that is outside the state and preserves alterity and difference.

Even though Levinas does not take the explicit step toward a view of collective time produced by our social encounters, his thought may provide the basis for developing a view of time that is grounded in our collective existence but is not the public, everyday time of clocks and dates. An implicit allusion to such a possibility is found in one of Levinas's talmudic readings where he analyzes an ancient, communal ceremony in which the holy Shewbread (*lechem hapanim*) is moved from the marble table to the gold table. Levinas makes two points that are relevant to my discussion. First he ties this ceremony with the political dimension, which for Levinas means first and foremost "thinking of men's hunger" (*BV* 18). Second, he regards the ceremony as revealing that the principle of change is elevation. This elevation is "a duration which never wears out, a duration which is an opening out. Higher and higher irreversibly. Is this not an interpretation of profound temporality, or of the diachrony of time? The striving of the holy toward the holier, the 'more' already working at the heart of the 'less'" (21). Perhaps then, a collective nonsynchronic time is revealed in the context of holy communal liturgies in which the working of transcendence, of the 'more' in the 'less' is experienced, and responsibility for the other is manifested.

Critchley notices that in Levinas's thought the passage to the collective, communal dimension is a passage to the prophetic world, "the commonness of the divine father in a community of brothers."[4] But for Levinas (according to Critchley's reading) God is not the God of ontotheology but "is" an empty space, an absence at the heart of the community. That is, transcendence enters politics by anchoring the community in the trace of God, *illeity*.[5] So, to begin addressing the issue of collective time, I will turn to the notion of *illeity*, a "more" working at the heart of the "less," which reveals a different approach to the third. Toward the end of *Otherwise than Being* Levinas refers to *illeity* saying, "This 'thirdness' is different from that of the third man, it is the third party that interrupts the face to face of a welcome of the other man, interrupts the proximity or approach of the neighbor, it is the third man with which justice begins" (*OB* 150). In his article "The Trace of the Other" Levinas explains that "*illeity* is not a 'less than being' by comparison with the world in which a face enters; it is the whole enormity, the inordinateness, the infinity of the absolutely other, which eludes treatment by ontology."[6] Unlike the third party that brings us back to the realm of ontology, *illeity* seems to present a new relation that opens up a way to the political, social situation of reciprocity that is different from the political realm of justice created by the third party. We are now faced with a number of questions. Does the symmetrical, reciprocal relation of a political life engendered by *illeity* entail the reduction of alterity? Is the political time, which is developed from the reciprocal relation that binds the community through the trace of *illeity,* synchronic? Does political time unite the individuals under a totalizing structure that expunges alterity, or does it open up a unique view of collective time that preserves alterity?

Based on his reading of "The Trace of the Other" and the section entitled "Witness and Prophecy" in *Otherwise than Being,* Howard Caygill suggests that *illeity* presents a relation with the third that is not below the relation with the other but is beyond it. Unlike the notion of *le tiers, illeity* is not the order that represents the state or justice in which alterity is reduced.[7] Rather, as Levinas explicitly states, "*Illeity* is the origin of the alterity of being."[8] In *Otherwise than Being* Levinas claims, "'Thanks to God' I am another for the others. God is not involved as an alleged interlocutor: the reciprocal relationship binds me to the other man in the trace of transcendence, in illeity" (*OB* 158). It is because of God that I am treated by others as an other. It is *illeity,* the trace of transcendence—or to return to the Cartesian model, it is the interruption of the finite by the infinite—that directs me toward the reciprocal political relation with the other; the force of responsibility that underlies society comes from the trace of *illeity.* The trace of *illeity,* of God, ties together the individuals of the community, thus enabling the move from the ethical moment to the political life of equality. But unlike the order of justice in which I and the other are comparable, are contemporaries that exist within the same synchronic structure, in the community bound by the trace of *illeity,* alterity is not reduced, thus preventing the community from becoming a totality. According to Caygill, considering *illeity* as a different perspective for understanding the relation with the third opens up in Levinas's thought a way to justice, which is additional to the justice that falls from the ethical relation with the other to representation.

It is the justice of prophetic politics that exceeds representation as well as the relation with the other. Bettina Bergo suggests that prophetism as the universalization of ethics (of responsibility for the other) interrupts ordinary life (the political realm).[9] Both Bergo and Caygill relate prophetism with the role of the biblical prophets. Critchley interprets the prophet as "the person who puts the community under the word of God, who binds the community and makes a community."[10] Prophets, such as Isaiah, also took upon themselves the role of disturbing the monarchical institution in order to correct its political course by appeal to God. Similarly, Levinas's view of prophetic politics is grounded in disruption; the justice of prophetic politics is not reconciliation but interruption, which even interrupts the relation of proximity with the other. Therefore, such a justice does not form a structure, a totality, but is the trace inscribed in me: the law that orients the interruption that constitutes justice is the inscription of the trace. Consequently, Caygill suggests that prophetic politics opens the possibility for a notion of justice as perpetual interruption, of the self by the other and of the other by the third (see *OB* 150).[11]

Caygill's instructive interpretation of prophetic politics and his interpretation of *illeity* directs us toward a view of collective time, which maintains Levinas's basic demand of preserving the alterity of the individual and supports his view that time is created by interruption. It opens up a way to consider Levinas's thought as leaving room for making the move from time as constituted via one's relation with the singular other to a view of collective time, which is grounded in our existence as a community of people. Caygill's interpretation of *illeity* suggests we think of alterity without relying on asymmetry; consequently, by allowing a sense of equality without forming a totalizing structure, a new pathway for thinking of political time is opened up. Levinas himself forms a relation between *illeity* and time when considering *illeity* as the trace of the immemorial responsibility for the other.[12] Although this connection is confined to the intersubjective perspective, perhaps the notion of *illeity* can enable us to go beyond the limited view of intersubjective time and deepen Levinas's original claim that time is constituted via social relationships.

One possible example in concrete experience in which collective time is revealed as a continual interruption, of the self by the other and of the other by the third, is a communal cultic experience, such as Judaic prayer. David Hartman, rabbi and philosopher of contemporary Judaism, regards the experience of Judaic prayer as the "continuation of the prophetic encounter" in the sense that it "casts the individual into social action."[13] Considering how the trace of *illeity* appears in the experience of Judaic prayer enables the constitution of a social time in between the different individuals, which does not submerge them under one totalizing order. Linking the notion of *illeity* with collective experiences such as Jewish rituals and communal prayer allows extending Levinas's view of intersubjective time into a communal, political time. Prayer is not necessarily the only experience that can reveal a nonsynchronic collective time. In the context of a different discussion, Robert Gibbs considers the holy Jewish texts as binding individuals to each other and commanding us to responsibility for others; according to Gibbs, these texts disrupt me, oblige me, and forge an allegiance to the other person.[14] The collective experiences (prayer and reading Jewish texts, for example) that ground this new interpretation of time correlate with Levinas's view of dialogue and speech. Like dialogue, these collective experiences involve not only words and communicated content, but are also grounded in responsibility, substitution, and proximity, in which interruption prevents the unification of the same and other under a totalizing order.

While preserving Levinas's basic structure of intersubjective time as revealed in speech and dialogue, we can apply his perspective to public prayer and its role in the constitution of communal time. Returning to the metaphor of a musical piece suggested in the previous chapter, prayer presents a temporal movement that reminds us of the one we find in music. Richard Cohen makes a similar comparison, writing: "Prayer and ritual are peculiar, then, in that the sense they make is not exhausted by a sense that can be communicated universally. In this they resemble a song, whose sense is not exhausted by the discursive meaning of the sentences enunciated, but also involves such non-linguistic dimensions as melody, harmony, intonation, and rhyme."[15] As in a musical piece, in prayer there is a tension between the individual voices and the chorus, forming a motion constituting time. Each voice preserves its uniqueness, its alterity, but through the disruption of one voice by the others a new contrapuntal, temporal dimension is formed. This dimension does not unite the different individuals under one order or structure, but rather, it reveals a way to overcome the limitations of Levinas's intersubjective time and present the justifications for understanding communal experiences as constituting a form of collective time grounded in human existence. For Levinas the prayer of Israel supports even the Judaism that no longer wishes to be religious (*DF* 271). A generous reading suggests we may push the idea of the time of prayer beyond Judaism, allowing us to consider it as a model for a new understanding of political time, which is relevant to a variety of collective structures of existence.

PRAYER, RESPONSIBILITY, AND TIME

Levinas does not form an explicit connection between prayer and a nonsynchronic structure of time,[16] but he does dedicate discussions to the topic of prayer. In his early essay "Education and Prayer," Levinas examines the idea of collective prayer, claiming that in prayer the individual renews its link to the community, and the dispersion of Israel becomes a unity (*DF* 270). This claim may seem to contradict Levinas's fundamental ethical requirement of avoiding the assimilation of the other in the same. But instead of considering this as a paradox to be settled, I suggest we think of prayer as a temporal experience in between the individuals forming a community. The experience of communal prayer is a lapse of time that opens up a view of collective political time, which is absent from Levinas's philosophical writings. But before examining the temporal dimension of prayer and the way it can offer a model for political time, first the relation between prayer and ethics should be discussed.[17]

In his essay "The Name of God according to a Few Talmudic Texts," Levinas says, "Rituals, invocations and . . . the responsibility for the other man: according to the Rabbis of the Talmud, these constitute a proximity that is closer than that of thematization" (*BV* 123). Here Levinas associates ritual and prayer with proximity, with the saying, rather than seeing these experiences as the thematization of the said. The ethical aspect of prayer is also found in his late text, "Prayer without Demand," where Levinas claims, "Prayer means that instead of seeking one's own salvation, one secures that of others. True prayer is never for oneself, never 'for one's needs.'" He continues, "How could any individual allude to his egoistic needs in his prayer, and so compromise the pure dis-interestedness of the holocaust?" (*LR* 233). Likewise, according to Levinas's reading of the book of the Lithuanian Rabbi Hayyim Volozhiner, *Nefesh ha'Hayyim* (The Soul of Life), pious prayer makes no demands for oneself; it is selfless. Prayer does not affirm one's own selfish ego(ism) or one's natural *conatus essendi,* but reveals and verifies the ethical responsibility for the other (*ITN* 130). A more robust way to put it is to follow Levinas's claim in "The Transcendence of Words": "By offering a word, the subject putting himself forward lays himself open and, in a sense, prays" (149). So prayer is more than a confirmation of one's responsibility for the other; to some degree, addressing and speaking to the other is prayer. Hence, even though we tend to consider prayer as a personal plea addressed to God, for Levinas, prayer is a generous offering (substitution) of oneself for the other—not only for the other person, but for God as well.[18]

However, although prayer can be seen as a manifestation of the ethics of the saying, a significant part of Levinas's discussion of prayer is dedicated to the said—to the question *what* the worshipper can pray for. If we consider demand as an entreaty, then a demanding prayer is a request with content (*what* I am requesting for). So even a selfless prayer that asks nothing for oneself is still a prayer with demand if it makes a request for the other. On the other hand, prayer *without* demand can mean that no plea, entreaty, or demand is made whatsoever. It is prayer for the sake of prayer. According to Levinas, even a prayer, such as the Hannah's prayer for a son (1 Sam. 1:10, 12, 26, 27), which makes a personal demand, is "far from being a demand addressed to God, prayer consists in the 'elevation, surrender and *adherence* of the soul to heights.' The soul rises up, just as the smoke from sacrifice does" (*LR* 232–33). For Levinas, even when a demand is made in prayer, the significance of prayer lies beyond the literal said. As quoted earlier in this chapter, in a different context Levinas claims that the irreversible movement of elevation reveals "the diachrony of time" (*BV* 21), the interruption of the more in the less, of the said by the saying.

To continue exploring the idea of prayer without demand it may be helpful to look at the view of prayer offered by the Israeli philosopher, Yeshayahu Leibowitz. Leibowitz distinguishes between two excluding forms of prayer. One type is, like Hannah's prayer, a human-psychological phenomenon, which serves the individual itself. Entirely different is the obligatory and fixed preestablished public prayer that continued communal worship by replacing the sacrifices of the temple after its destruction. This form of prayer is not initiated by the individual but is cast upon the worshipper and is not intended for the fulfillment of one's needs. Consequently, this type of prayer considers prayer as an expression of worship and not as an attempt to intervene within the divine order.[19] In other words, it is a prayer without demand. But from a Levinasian perspective the significance of a prayer without demand is not merely following the *Halakha*, the Jewish religious law, but its meaning is derived from the setting aside of the said, the content of the prayer, thus revealing the significance of prayer in the saying, in the ethical responsibility for the other. As Levinas states, "The ethical must intervene. Man, and man's prayer are essential. In this way, prayer, which is called in Hebrew 'the service of the heart' or even 'the work of the heart' (once again such an expression is not simply a metaphor) refers, in the true sense of the term, to the task of edifying the worlds, or 'repairing the ruins of creation'. For the self (*moi*), prayer means that, instead of seeking one's own salvation, one secures that of others" (*LR* 233). Consequently prayer is an experience that even does not require the comprehension of the uttered words (which often is the case). This way of understanding prayer allows us to shift our focus from the said of prayer, "the words carefully chosen" (232), to the saying, the infinite ethical responsibility for the other, in which prayer is grounded in and depends on.

But in focusing on the individual who prays for the other, Levinas reveals a view according to which prayer is confined to the limited perspective of intersubjectivity. It describes a diachronic relation between the individual and an other. Regardless of whether this other addressed to or prayed for, is a singular individual, a community, the universe, or God, it is always conceived as one homogeneous unit. So how can the ethical experience of prayer bring about a collective, political temporality? For the purpose of addressing this query, I suggest we first turn to the explicit connection Franz Rosenzweig forms between cultic experiences, such as prayer, and collective time. The influence of the philosophy of Rosenzweig on Levinas's thinking has been acknowledged by Levinas himself. In the preface to *Totality and Infinity* he refers to Rosenzweig's magnum opus, *The Star of Redemption*, saying it is "a work too often present in this book to be cited" (*TI* 28). Indeed, unlike thinkers such as Plato, Descartes, Kant, Hegel, Bergson, Husserl, Heidegger, and Buber, who are mentioned numerous times in *Totality and Infinity* and in *Otherwise than Being*, this is the only explicit reference of Rosenzweig in Levinas's two major philosophical works.

Similar to Levinas's view, for Rosenzweig the proper prayer is the prayer that is not addressed to personal fate. But contrary to Levinas, who focuses on infinity, for Rosenzweig proper prayer is the prayer of the congregation directed beyond every individual toward eternity (*SR* 294). Like Nietzsche's notion of the eternal return and Kierkegaard's notion of repetition, Rosenzweig's concept of redemption is grounded in a seemingly impossible link between the excluding categories of time and eternity, permanence and motion, unchanging and changing. Nevertheless, to some extent this relation is possible since Rosenzweig, like Nietzsche and Kierkegaard before him, does not regard eternity in the traditional sense. Although time and eternity are different ontological categories, they are not excluding categories, and for Rosenzweig eternity is not the realm traditionally conceived as beyond the boundaries of time. Although the human and the world are temporal, and this aspect cannot be overcome, eternity can enter time. Peter Eli Gordon describes this as "an eternal way of being within the temporal horizon."[20] This does not mean that the temporal dimension becomes eternal, but that it takes on some features of eternity.[21] Rosenzweig claims, "What eternity does is to make the moment everlasting" (*SR* 258). "Eternity is a future, which without ceasing to be future, is nonetheless present" (224). This means that eternity is both future and present: "It is a tomorrow that could as well be today" (224). The relation between eternity and time can be seen as the return of the same instant causing an immobilization of the present within the flow of time. But how does a temporal human being experience an unchanging anticipation of redemption? That is, how can we experience eternity, the repetition of an unchanging moment, within the temporal finite dimension of human life?

Here Rosenzweig's answer differs from the one offered by Kierkegaard (and to some degree by Nietzsche as well). Kierkegaard focuses on the internal repetition experienced by the individual who acquires the movement of infinite resignation; whereas for Rosenzweig eternity cannot be experienced as an individual but only as a community. Rosenzweig claims, "The prayer of the congregation is addressed not to the personal fate but to the Eternal. ... This prayer looks beyond anything individual to the Universal and to it alone" (*SR* 294). As discrete individuals our existence is fleeting, but as a community performing repetitious rituals directed at God, eternity can be experienced as redemption. The entry of eternity into time is attained by collective experiences, such as liturgical prayer. In prayer we "ceaselessly repeat" (265); prayer is not a new moment but the return of the same moment. Like the hour that begins the moment it ends, through the cycles of liturgy repeated again and again, the same recurs, and the eternal is invited into the day, the week, the year (292). But eternity is not merely a continuous return of the same. In liturgy eternity is anticipated by living the repetition of the sacred cycles bringing about an earthly redemption. For example, when reciting the preestablished text of the daily morning service, *Shacharit* (from *Shachar,* the Hebrew word for "morning light"), the Jew returns to the previous day, the day before that, and so forth. The same experience is relived again and again circularly forming a Nietzschean eternal return in which the linear time of the individual is intersected with the eternal moment of society. However, not only prayer but also other forms of repetitive cultural rites, such as reading the Torah and eating together (particularly the Passover *seder*), invite eternity into the individual's temporality, into the finite linear time, which begins with birth and ends with death.

Robert Gibbs compellingly suggests that we understand the entry of eternity into time as interruption.[22] The timeless, the constant, the unchanging, disrupts the ephemeral, the changing, the moving. Mundane life is disrupted by the performance of the sacred ritual. For example, when it is time to recite *Shacharit,* the worshipper is forbidden from engaging in any daily experience (work, eating, etc.) and must first pray. The interruption occurs when the worshipper arrests the daily tasks and performs the service. Observant Jews stop their mundane activities of reading the newspaper, eating breakfast, or engaging in conversation in order to recite the prayer. Similarly, Muslims are bound to perform the *Salaah,* the fixed ritual of the Islamic prayer. When it is time for one of the five obligatory prayers, no matter what they are doing or where they are, Muslims stop their daily actions, get down to the ground, and lie prostrate facing Mecca. As a result, the prayer that is the eternal recurrence of the same disrupts the continuous, linear movement. The cycles of cultic prayer "prepare time to accept eternity, and eternity, by finding acceptance in time, itself becomes—like time" (*SR* 292). The eternal moment of liturgy enters the linear time of history. Rosenzweig emphasizes that eternity is experienced or anticipated as a community and not as an individual, because the individual experiences the celestial periods in the changes of age and in the linearity of conception and birth (291). The time the cult prepares for the visit of eternity is not the time of the individual—it is neither mine, nor yours, nor God's, but is a collective time (292). This communal experience directed toward God that brings eternity into time, into life, is the "act of redemption" (225). That is, the collective rhythm of the day, week, and year revealed in liturgy marks eternity in time.

The different individuals are united by a common point of reference—God. So in performing cultic rituals directed toward God, such as prayer, the discrete individuals form a community. But it is not only the mutual point of reference, which unites the individuals to form a community, but also liturgy's nature of collective experience—on *Sabbath*, the seventh day of the week, all Jews are commanded to rest; Jews all around the world conduct the Passover *seder* or begin and end reading the Torah on the same day. Consequently, for Rosenzweig time is a social structure, and the community is formed in the structuring of time. That is, by performing the rituals determined by the cosmological orbit at the same time, the individuals are united into a community. Hence, contrary to Bergson and Heidegger, who consider public time as a degradation of real or authentic time, for Rosenzweig public time brings redemption as a community *in* the world rather than in the sense of an individual separated from the world.

ILLEITY, PRAYER, TIME

Rosenzweig's thoughts on time seem to originate from human experiences and intersubjectivity. In "The New Thinking," Rosenzweig states that in "the future there reigns the language of the chorus, for even the individual grasps the future only when he can say We."[23] According to Rosenzweig time is experienced not as an individual but as a community that chants together. Further in this text Rosenzweig describes a view of time that may even remind us of the view Levinas presents. He writes, "Speech is bound to time, nourished by time, [and] it neither can nor wants to abandon this ground of nourishment; it does not know beforehand where it will emerge; it lets itself be given its cues from others; it actually lives by another's life, whether that other is the one who listens to a story, or is a respondent in a dialogue, or the participant in a chorus."[24] Similar to Levinas, Rosenzweig identifies a relation between speech and time, but he describes a reverse relation. As seen in the previous chapter, for Levinas time emerges from the intersubjective, ethical relation of speaking to the other, whereas for Rosenzweig speech is nourished by time. Similarly, in *The Star of Redemption* Rosenzweig argues that the community is united by taking part in the same rituals at the same time, and therefore claims that the community is grounded in the structure of time. Therefore, although Rosenzweig appears to suggest a new way for describing the relation between time and community, in focusing on the cosmic orbit of earth, which is independent of human existence, his view ultimately does not overcome the cosmological, traditional view.

However, in continuing the move initiated by Levinas, and considering time to be constituted via social relations, we can reconsider the connection Rosenzweig forms between liturgy and time and his idea that collective prayer assembles the different individuals into a community. As a reinterpretation of Rosenzweig's link between the cultic prayer of the congregation and time, perhaps what he considers as the invitation of the eternal into the temporal actually forms a new interpretation of time—a collective view of time that is not cosmological time, but is a dimension in between the different individuals. This is revealed by replacing the trace of eternity in time found in Rosenzweig's thought with Levinas's notion of the trace of *illeity* in the temporal existence of the individuals. Levinas himself alludes to a relation between time and *illeity* saying, "While being designates a community, without any possible dissidence, of the totality of fate and the undephasable contemporaneousness of cognition or comprehension (even historical) to which the time tied in the present lends itself, in the trace of *illeity*, in the enigma, the synchronism falls out of tune, the totality is transcended in another time. This extravagant movement of going beyond being or transcendence toward an immemorial antiquity we call the idea of infinity" (*CPP* 71). Here Levinas suggests that the trace of *illeity* breaks up the simultaneity of synchronic time allowing the formation of a nonsynchronic, noncontemporaneous time. The context of this link between time and *illeity* appears to be rooted in the difference between, the nonsynchronicity of the same and the other, from which Levinas develops his view of intersubjective time. However, by considering the trace of *illeity* as the alterity required for the formation of collective, political time that does not succumb to the totalizing structure of time, collective experiences like prayer can serve as a model for a new mode of time in which the individual transcends its own singular and finite temporal existence and moves toward a communal temporal existence without the elimination of alterity.

Introducing the trace of *illeity* into Levinas's view of time allows for considering collective experiences as activities or occurrences, which bind individuals into a temporal communal relation that does not form a holistic structure in which the different individuals are integrated to form a unified community. However, such a view of community goes against the view that Peter Eli Gordon attributes to Rosenzweig. According to Gordon's interpretation, for Rosenzweig community is not "a collectivity of distinct beings united through dialogue," but "a kind of collective singularity."[25] Gordon finds a stark contrast between Levinas's focus on the alterity of the other and Rosenzweig's focus on community, since according to his interpretation, the community in Rosenzweig's thought is not a collective of discrete individuals, but is a united singular totality, which Gordon names holism.[26] This may entail the impossibility of carrying out the objective of extending Levinas's view of time into a collective political structure that emerges from the Levinasian demand of alterity. However, a nonholistic, nontotalizing structure of political time becomes possible if we connect the trace of *illeity* with the experience of prayer. The trace of *illeity*, of God, of the immemorial past, interrupts the temporality of the individual, but contrary to the time formed due to the interruption caused by a dialogue with one concrete individual, the time constituted by the interruption of *illeity* is the movement in between a community of individuals. The trace of *illeity* inscribed not only in me but in every individual of the community has the paradoxical role of uniting the individuals and preserving their alterity through interruption. The trace of the immemorial covenant is the trace of alterity inscribed in every Jewish individual, which interrupts the individual's temporality. This disruption of the immemorial past constitutes a collective temporal dimension in which the different individuals are not united under a totalizing order.

Jewish prayer is a concrete manifestation of the trace of *illeity*. At the end of the morning service (*Shacharit*) there are six past experiences that the worshipper is commanded to remember every day. The first one is to remember the day of leaving Egypt. The second one is to remember the Divine revelation at Mount Sinai. This does not mean remembering what one has read in the Torah, but it refers to remembering an experience that occurred before one's lifetime. These experiences are an example of the immemorial past, a past that is ours and yet is immemorable. In "The Pact" Levinas says that the pact first made at Mount Sinai is revealed and repeated when studying the Torah (*BV* 79), and in "Model of the West" Levinas claims that "liturgy and study are merged" (25). This alludes to the social role that prayer assumes in Levinas's thought, which is emphasized when in the following sentences Levinas relates the twice-daily recitation of the prayer *Shema* with submission to the Law. Similarly, in discussing Judaic prayer, Hartman claims that the essence of prayer is drawn from the covenantal encounter at Mount Sinai, and that "prayer casts the individual into social action."[27] At Mount Sinai the Israelites not only encounter God and enter a covenant with Him, but by receiving the Ten Commandments, they become a nation, and prayer is an expression of this collective, covenantal experience. Referring to Deuteronomy 27, in which an anticipated ceremony of the covenant is described, Levinas states, "It is through this covenant that the society of Israel is instituted by legislation and the Torah" (70). In this chapter from Deuteronomy are listed interdicts, which although coinciding only on a few points of the Ten Commandments, Levinas correctly notes represent the essential principles of the pact. These interdicts include ethical obligations to one's parents, neighbor, to the weak (the blind, the orphan, and the widow), the stranger, and consequently they are, the founding principles of society (72). The ceremony of the pact, including the reply, "Amen" to every recited interdict, is an example of early collective rituals, which are later replaced by covenantal prayer.

Prayer is an expression, a trace, of the covenant. As Hartman explains, "The community as a whole enters into the covenant of *mitzvah*, and in the prayer experience the individual Jew gives expression to his or her covenantal communal consciousness."[28] According to Hartman, the early rabbinic traditions in which the community recited the Ten Commandments and the *Shema*[29] suggests that the recital of the *Shema* was meant to be a reliving of the covenantal moment at Sinai, and even though the recital of the Ten Commandments was discontinued, the significance of the *Shema* as the reassertion of the Sinai covenant was never lost.[30] According to Levinas, "It is through the regular return of these sovereign moments—the crown of the Torah being added to the crown of liturgy—that the dispersion of time is brought back together and retied into permanence" (*BV* 25). Here, Levinas thinks of liturgical experiences such as prayer as uniting the individuals dispersed through space and time under a synchronic order of as permanence. However, thinking of prayer in the context of the immemorial past of the covenant depicts prayer as a concrete manifestation of the trace of *illeity* that involves an immemorial obligation, which unites the individuals into a community through disruption rather than through unification.

This disruption of the subject by the trace of a shared immemorial past (the covenant) is grounded in responsibility and avoids the annihilation of alterity even though the asymmetrical relation is abandoned. Not only do we find in Levinas's thought an association between prayer and responsibility, but he also appears to remain within the intersubjective structure. Forming a link between responsibility and the interruption caused by the trace of *illeity* in the context of communal prayer opens up a pathway toward political time. In Levinas's essay "The Name of God according to a Few Talmudic Texts," we find an allusion to a link between *illeity* and responsibility: "*Illeity*, in an extremely specific way, is excluded from being, but orders it in relation to a responsibility, in relation to its pure passivity, a pure 'susceptibility': an obligation to answer preceding any questioning which would recall a prior commitment, extending beyond any question, any problem and any representation, and where obedience precedes the order that has furtively infiltrated the soul that obeys" (*BV* 128). In the following paragraph Levinas refers to the connection he forms between language and responsibility indicating that the trace of *illeity* is revealed in everyday situations involving language and discourse. Like speech, prayer not only demonstrates the said but manifests the saying of proximity, and from Levinas's perspective, prayer can be seen as a mode of addressing others responsibly. But unlike the inter-subjective context of Levinas's discussion of dialogue, prayer involves a collective model. In essence Jewish prayer is communal prayer, and the German-Israeli Jewish educator and religious philosopher Ernst Simon lists aspects and features that give Jewish prayer its specific and distinctive character of collectivity. First, although Jews can and do pray in solitude, they are expected to do so at the same time the community worships. Also, many Jewish prayers require the presence of *minyan,* of ten male adults, and every *minyan* represents the prayer of the entire Jewish community. Second, Jewish communal prayer is and must be formulated prayer. Prayer for the Jew is the fulfillment of an essential commandment — *kiyum mitzvah* — which requires praying at specified times and in accordance with the specific order of a preestablished text. And third, Jewish prayer employs a multitude of external symbols for internal meanings — the *talit,* the *shofar,* and Sabbath candles, for example. Although other religions also use symbols, in Judaism ritual is a way of life, designed to sanctify every act and stage of one's life, to evoke a constant awareness of God's presence, and to relate the Jew to the covenant, to the past of his or her people as an ever-renewed contemporary experience.[31]

The covenant is not only the immemorial past of the Jewish people, but expresses an attitude of commitment. Hartman explains that prayer is not a quietism or relinquishment of responsibility, but rather prayer is consummated only in moral action.[32] This commitment and responsibility can be found in the Israelites' reply of *Naase VeNishma* ("We will do and we will listen") when receiving the Torah at Mount Sinai (Exod. 24:7). The obligation of committing oneself, before even knowing what it is I am committing myself to, corresponds to the commitment, "Here I am." Similar to the obligation, "Here I am," *Naase VeNishma* is directed not only at God but involves also a commitment to the others of the community. This is in accord with Levinas's view of the covenant; he says, "*kol Yisrael areivim ze lazeh*, 'Everyone in Israel is answerable for everyone else,' signifies: all adherents to the divine Law, all men who are truly men, are responsible for one another" (*BV* 85). The covenant establishes "living links with all those who adopt the Law: everyone finds himself responsible for everyone else; in every act of the covenant more than six hundred thousand personal acts of responsibility are outlined" (84; cf. *DF* 84). At Mount Sinai for the first time the individuals stood as a community before God, and consequently the event can be seen as anticipating the responsible, covenantal, communal rituals such as prayer. When receiving the Torah the people of Israel did not merely accept a set of rules, but from Levinas's perspective accepting the Torah is becoming ethically obligated to the other. The Torah was not given to individuals but to a community; the community is a crucial part of the life of worship, and only a community together can follow the Torah or become ethical.

Public Judaic prayer can serve as a form of experience that like Levinas's view of dialogue and speech involves not only words and communicated content, but is a response, closeness, or interaction in which the alterity of the other is not compromised. In prayer the community is tied together in an immemorial covenant of responsibility. As Hartman points out, prayer has features of commitment to the community, and reflects the same pattern of the prophetic experience. The prophetic experience does not isolate the prophet from the community but demands his social and political action. Similarly, "in Judaic prayer one never prays for oneself alone, but always begins by praying on behalf of the community with a prayer whose style is heal *us*, redeem *us*, restore Thy *people* to Jerusalem."[33] Although every individual prays for the community, this does not form an intersubjective structure between the individual and a homogeneous other—the community. When the covenantal community prays together, each for the other, we are presented with a collective structure. Surely, public prayer does not manifest a Levinasian ethical intersubjective asymmetrical relation, but reveals a symmetrical relation of equality relevant to politics. Yet the interruption caused in public prayer by the trace of *illeity* avoids the unification of the individuals under a totalizing structure. In covenantal prayer the individuals are not united by their responsibility for the community or by the covenant, but the trace of *illeity* disrupts the temporality of each individual forming a nontotalizing dimension of collective time. This opens up a way to preserve and enrich Levinas's understanding that time is in between us (*entre nous*) and constituted by disruption. It enables us to extend the Levinasian view of time by going beyond the viewpoint of the subject's relation with another singular person, and think of the time in between us as the time in between the individuals of a community of people.

Consequently, Judaic prayer provides a useful model for offering a collective view of time that does not succumb to the totalizing structure of the cosmological time of dates and clocks, and it supports Levinas's original claim that time is constituted via social relationships of response and responsibility that preserve alterity. In addition to the idea that the disruption of the individual's temporality forms a dimension of time in between the individuals, the constitution of collective time can be considered by focusing on the variety of tensions involving collective prayer, which create the movement and change required for the formation of time. This movement for the most part originates from the tension between the individual and the community found in the framework of communal prayer. Hartman notices such a tension saying, "Although for the individual Jew the covenantal community mediates the hearing of the *mitzvoth,* nevertheless prayer and the *Shema* must be appropriated in a way that expresses the individual's particular sensibility and human situation."[34] Prayer is more than the recitation of a preestablished text but is a personal affair. The Jewish philosopher and theologian Abraham Joshua Heschel characterizes it as "an enterprise of the individual self, as a personal engagement, as an intimate, confidential act."[35] Although communal prayer is a formulated prayer, it requires the complete attention of the individual, and according to the rabbinic approach, personal supplication can be brought into the fixed framework of prayer.[36] The Talmud permits individuals to bring into the fixed prayers (*tefilat 18*) their own unique requests.[37] This is not only—as Levinas claims—in the circumstances where Israel as whole is in danger, when its people are persecuted (*LR* 233), but the Talmud is clear that a unique request can be made in personal cases relating to a sick member of the family or to one's livelihood.[38] Hartman notices two distinct legitimizations of prayer in the Babylonian Talmud (*Berakhot*, 26b)— "prayers were instituted by the patriarchs" and "prayer was instituted to replace the daily sacrifices." According to Hartman's interpretation, these "exemplify the combination of the individual and communal dimensions in Judaic prayer"; the patriarchal experience mirrors the role of the individual in prayer, whereas the memory of the sacrifices reveals the function of the community.[39]

The practice of public prayer can be seen as a tension between the interior experience of praying and the ecstatic experience that leads the individual to transcend itself, to go beyond its own existence and the natural predisposition of the *conatus essendi*. It is a tension between the praying, contemplating individual and the unity of the congregation. The tension between the individual and the collective aspects of prayer can be described also as a tension between the repetitive nature of the covenantal prayer and the unique experience of the individual that is never repeated. On the one hand the individual recites day after day the same text recited by the entire covenantal community; but on the other hand, every experience is unique. As Heraclitus claimed, we can never enter the same river twice. These tensions do not require settling. They not only present an essential aspect of Judaic public worship, but they create the alterity and disruption necessary for the constitution of a nontotalizing collective time.

Another way to describe these tensions is by returning to the tension between the saying and the said, and to the relation of these two aspects of language to time. This distinction also reveals how collective covenantal Judaic prayer is a collective, nonstructural experience of time. Covenantal public prayer is made of words and has a fixed language and format. It is recited by the entire community at specific times that are determined by the cosmological orbit, and often the prayers are recited in chorus when the entire community is gathered at the same place in the same time. In this respect public prayer has features of the said, which even though it has a multivocal temporal dimension similar to the temporal aspect found in the said of intersubjective dialogue, for the most part it manifests the synchronic totalizing structure of time. But in covenantal prayer the said is disrupted by the saying, politics by ethics, totality by infinity. The fixed language and format of public prayer is disrupted by the ethical obligation of the saying. The saying and the said in prayer is not unlike Gibbs's observation of exegesis: the fixity of the written verse incites me to comment on it.[40] Even though Judaic public prayers are fixed and recited according to cosmological time, their synchronic, thematized aspects are disrupted by their nonsynchronic, nontotalizing, temporal dimension of responsibility when one takes upon oneself the commitment that prayer brings with it. Public covenantal prayer reveals the saying as the time of responsibility for others, as an obligation to an immemorial covenant. Covenantal prayer originates from a calling prior to any choice I make that comes before all memorable time. It manifests a response to an immemorial past (the covenant), which was never present for the individual worshipper. But covenantal prayer also ties the individual to a future that will never be its present. The worshipper is responsible for events that have occurred before his or her birth and for events that follow his or her death, and for this reason, covenantal prayer reveals an infinite time with no beginning or end.

Further, it is from the collective nonsynchronic experience of time grounded in Judaic collective prayer that other experiences of time—cosmological, egological—are derived. Levinas claims that "all other relation is dominated by the relation with God through the ritual act that has been commanded. This relation is not measured by the uprightness of knowledge, as if it were approximation. It is thought and lived in Judaism as the greatest proximity, as a total adherence, prior in some way, to all initial act of adhesion" (*BV* 118). In the ethical relation with the other we find the trace of God. God inspires us to be ethical; that is, "inspiration's original mode is not in listening to a Muse dictating songs, but in obedience to the Most-High as an ethical relation to the Other" (147–48). But by linking the relation with God with rituals, Levinas's statement here opens a pathway to a different, perhaps richer, argument. The relation with God, with *illeity*, constitutes through liturgy the temporal relation between the different individuals in a community. This relation with *illeity* opens up a way to consider the intersubjective, ethical, diachronic relation with a singular other as grounded in a collective liturgical relation inspired and directed by God.

The experience of public Judaic prayer can overcome the limitations of Levinas's intersubjective time and present the justifications for understanding communal prayer as constituting a form of collective time. Perhaps, in focusing on Judaic prayer the description of collective-political time may seem limited. But Jewish culture provides a model of political time, because Levinas himself develops concrete views of collectivity and politics mainly in his discussions of Judaism. This is not to limit the collective view of time, nor argue that a collective, nonsynchronic view of time is derived only from the experience of Judaic prayer. Indeed, Levinas locates a universal significance in the unique experience of the Jewish people. In the context of his discussion of the ceremony of the repetition of the covenant described in Deuteronomy 27 and Joshua 8, Levinas writes, "Universality is thus born, in some way, from a society, which, moreover, is entirely visible to its members assembled on two mounts, visible as if on a stage. Right from the beginning, the society which aspires to intimacy between twelve tribes looking at one another, this society of a community, is already present to the whole humanity, or opens on to the whole humanity" (*BV* 75). The particular experience of Judaic covenantal prayer serves a universal model from which other forms of collective relations can be developed to include other everyday gatherings.

From Cronos to Moses
Bringing Together Levinas's Views of Time

This book has depicted Levinas's view of time as continuing the views presented by Bergson and Heidegger while going beyond them. I have discussed the various perspectives Levinas undertakes in his approach to the question of time, arguing that a coherent and consistent structure of time can be extracted from his thought. Even though Levinas's writings at different periods reveal a number of interpretations of time, his early views in *Existence and Existents* and in *Time and the Other*, his views in *Totality and Infinity*, and his later views in *Otherwise than Being* and "Diachrony and Representation" are consistent. The refusal of the present emphasized in fecund time and diachronic time is already found in Levinas's discussion of the instant in his early writings. Levinas's views of fecund time and diachronic time are two different attempts to describe a view of intersubjective time. Despite the difference between the two, they share the same goal of going beyond synchronic time, beyond the time of the present, and beyond the time of the individual. The idea that time is created through the disruption of the same by the other, which we find in the view of fecund time, is strengthened in Levinas's interpretation of time as diachronic. But even though his innovative view that time is intersubjective overcomes the dissatisfaction with the egological interpretations offered by Bergson and Heidegger, it is a limited view. In interpreting time as formed between the subject and a singular other at a specific situation, Levinas ignores the aspect of time that is relevant to complex networks that characterize human society.

Nevertheless, communal experiences such as public prayer, if introduced into Levinas's discussion of time, might open up a way to go beyond his interpretation and present a unique view of time relevant to the structure of collective existence.

CRONOS

The development of Levinas's unique view of time emerges from his aspiration to break away from the hegemony of the philosophy of the present. It is an attempt to escape "the Greek language of intelligibility and presence" (DEL 20). Yet while Levinas's view of time is influenced by the Greek tradition, a Hebrew source of inspiration should be recognized as well. Alfred Tauber offers an insightful interpretation showing that the foundation of Levinas's ethics is the traditional Jewish understanding of time.[1] However, my argument is different. Levinas's interpretation of time develops not only from the Greek tradition, but is influenced by the Jewish heritage as well. Moreover, although not explicitly argued by Levinas, perhaps it is precisely the influence of the Jewish scriptures that enables Levinas to distance himself from the Greek, philosophical views of time.

In contrast to the trace of the Jewish tradition in Levinas's interpretation of time, the Greek myth of Cronos devouring his children reveals the view of synchronic time, which Levinas is striving to go beyond. According to the myth, the Greek Titan Cronos devoured his children (the dynasty of the Olympian gods) in order to overcome his fate: to be dethroned by one of his children (Zeus). Although written differently, Chronos, god of time, and Cronos, father of Zeus, are usually identified. The similarity of the two names (even homophony in English) may point to an etymological relation, tying the devouring god with the view of time as destructive and all-consuming.[2] For Levinas, Cronos is a symbol of the totalizing of Western philosophy in which all otherness is consumed by the same and time is dominated by the present (cf. *TI* 58; *AT* 10). In "Hommage à Bergson" Levinas alludes to this myth as well. He suggests that similar to Jupiter's (Zeus) attack by Saturn (Cronos), it presents the scientific view of time that is confronted by Bergson.[3] According to the scientific view, time is irreversible: it is a movement in which an existence comes into being, endures, and perishes. This traditional view privileges the present, since only the present exists. If we understand time (chronos) as the origin of the Titan's name, Cronos, then the legend symbolizes how time ravages and destroys all that it creates. And unlike Zeus, who escaped Cronos, mere mortals cannot evade the clutches of time. This not only conforms to the traditional view of time as independent of human existence, but it is also in accordance with the view that time is grounded in the individual's human existence. As a mortal being my existence is finite, and so is my time. Such a view of time is affiliated with egological interpretations, which regard time as founded on the subject's finite existence. These interpretations are characterized by Levinas as synchronic time, since they consider time in reference to the present, which presides over the future and the past. In other words, from Levinas's perspective, the egological views of time are synchronic, because the individual gathers the past and the future into the present. Hence, from Levinas's point of view, not only is the traditional Aristotelian interpretation of time synchronic, but the temporal views of Bergson, Husserl, and Heidegger are also confined to the present.

The view that time is not confined to the solitary individual can be tied to Levinas's endeavor to go beyond an approach that considers time in terms of the present, since, as seen in chapter 2, there is a correlation between the solitary subject and the present. In this sense we can tie his interpretation of the present in his earlier thought (*Existence and Existents, Time and the Other*) to his attempt to overcome the synchronic view of time in his later thought (*Otherwise than Being*, "Diachrony and Representation"). Levinas's objection to the understanding of time as synchronic, as dominated by the present, corresponds to his effort to provide a view of time that is not restricted to the perspective of the individual. He points to a correlation between understanding time as reduced to the present of the individual, and the absorption of the other by the same. In "Diachrony and Representation" he writes:

> To comprehend the alteration of presence in the past and future
> would be a matter of reducing and bringing back the past and future
> to presence—that is, re-presenting them. And, seemingly, it would
> be a matter of understanding all alterity, which is brought together,
> welcomed, and synchronized in the presence at the interior of the I
> think, and which then is assumed in the identity of the Ego—it is a
> matter of understanding this alterity assumed by the thought of the
> identical—as its own and, then still, of leading its other back to the
> same. (*TO* 99)

The inclination to gather the future and the past into the present (to
re-present them) is only one aspect of the ego's tendency to assimilate
the other into itself. Consequently, the overcoming of the synchronic
view of time requires the overcoming of the tendency to absorb the
other into the same.

This connection between the incorporation of the other in the same
and the gathering of the past and future into the present is exhibited
in the Greek myth of Cronos devouring his children. Cronos symbolizes the present, the same, the ego; his act of devouring his children,
the other, in order to avoid his destiny, eventually leads to the formation of his history. So the present act of devouring is shaped by the
history it has inherited. In other words, the prophecy about Cronos's
future destiny of which he learned in the *past* is realized in his *present*
through his act of devouring. To use Levinas's terminology, the past
and the future are re-presented—the memory of the prophecy about
the predicted (anticipated) dethroning is gathered in the present act
of devouring—and this is equivalent to the assimilation, or digestion,
of the other by the same. In this myth the incorporation of the other
into the subject is literal, but Levinas is confronting precisely this
assimilation of alterity by the same, as well as the gathering of the past
and future into the present. The violent, cannibalistic description of
this absorption of the other as illustrated in Goya's painting conveys
the challenge that Levinas undertakes. Unlike other famous depic-
tions by artists such as Rubens, which carefully illustrate the story in
detail, in Goya's image there is no context of the legend, but instead a
stripped-down scene. The sickle of Cronos, as well as other attributes
of the devouring god, are depicted throughout the pictorial tradition

but are absent from Goya's painting.[4] On the one hand, then, we are familiar with the scene from a well-known legend, while on the other, all specific details are removed. This corresponds with Levinas's view that the other is a specific, concrete, singular person that is part of an identifiable scene, and the relation between the other and the same should be understood in the ethical context that is relevant to every one of us, but cannot be defined according to totalizing concepts and categories. Like the picture the other is a concrete person with a specific history, but at the same time, everyone is an other and the picture is a stripped-down scene.

This ancient legend describes a father-son relation grounded in enmity and jealousy. One of the children of Cronos is expected to dethrone him, leading Cronos to regard his offspring as a menace, as truncating his possibilities. The father-son rivalry is a motif found elsewhere in the Greek myths. Cronos himself posed a threat to his father, Uranus, which ended with the castration of the father. And in the well-known story of Oedipus, Laius left Oedipus to die in the wilderness in order to evade the prophecy that his son would kill him and so prevent his son from terminating his possibilities. This view of father-son rivalry has further penetrated Western culture with Freud's psychoanalytical analysis of what he named the Oedipus complex, which even has popular contemporary manifestations.[5]

ABRAHAM

Levinas's notion of fecundity reveals a father-son relation, which opposes the hostility dominating the Western-Greek tradition. According to Levinas, the son (the other) does not limit the future possibilities of the father (the same), but rather, it is the other way around: the other extends the possibilities and the future of the subject into the future (*TI* 267). Further, it is only through the relation with the other that time is constituted, or else the subject would remain confined to the present. Time is infinite because the father through his relation with the son, has another chance, and as such can always begin anew. Such an approach to father-son relations, which is

Saturn (Cronos) Devouring One of His Children, 1820–1823. Francisco de Goya y Lucientes (1746–1828). Oil on canvas (146 × 83). Madrid, Prado Museum.

the basis of Levinas's interpretation of fecund time, is consistent with the saying from the Talmud, "Of everyone a man is jealous, except his son and disciple."[6] Even though Levinas does not explicitly recognize the Jewish experience as the source of inspiration of his notion of fecundity, his view of fecund time echoes the biblical father-son model. The father-son relations found in the Torah oppose the rivalry found in the Greek sources. Unlike the Greek tradition, the basic biblical enmity is often between siblings, as presented in the stories of Cain and Abel, Jacob and Esau, Joseph and his brothers, and so on. It is true that there are a number of biblical stories that illustrate father-son hostility. One example is the rebellion of Absalom against the monarchy of his father, King David, but in this story it is the son who acts against his father (2 Sam. 15–19). Similarly, the hostility between Saul and Jonathan does not originate in the father's jealousy of his son, but in Jonathan's defense of David, who is seen by Saul as a threat to the dynasty (1 Sam. 20:30–32). Moreover, this father-son relationship is restored when Saul and Jonathan fought together and died together for the same cause (1 Sam. 31:1–9). One should not ignore these examples of father-son rivalry, but the enmity we witness in these stories is different from the conflict we find in Greek mythology, in which a recurring theme is the father's fear that the son will limit his possibilities.

One biblical story that reveals the Levinasian father-son relation is the tale of Abraham, the founding father of the Jewish nation. In the story of the binding of Isaac, the *Akedah*, Abraham is described as willing to sacrifice his son, but not for reasons similar to those leading Cronos to devour his children or Laius to expose Oedipus. There is an essential difference between Abraham and the paternal figures in the Greek mythology. For Abraham, the sacrifice of the son is required for the extension of his possibilities, as in the Greek myths. But whereas Cronos and Laius focus on their ownmost possibilities of gaining and maintaining their own power as individuals, Abraham obeys God's command in order to keep his covenant with God that promises the extension of his possibilities not as an individual but as the founder of a nation. Abraham is therefore not concerned with the limitation of his own possibilities. The Greek figures act according to the natural instinct of self-preservation, Spinoza's *conatus essendi,* whereas Abraham's actions reveal the Levinasian demand to suspend this natural right. From Levinas's perspective, accepting the other's right to exist takes precedence over my own, and the individual cannot find meaning within his or her own existence. Abraham embraces the ethical order and acts out of responsibility to Isaac. In a passage that comes before the story of the binding of Isaac, we read:

> And when Abram was ninety years old and nine, the LORD appeared to Abram, and said unto him, I am the Almighty God; walk before me, and be thou perfect. And I will make my covenant between me and thee, and will multiply thee exceedingly. And Abram fell on his face: and God talked with him, saying, As for me, behold, my covenant is with thee, and thou shalt be a father of many nations. Neither shall thy name any more be called Abram, but thy name shall be Abraham; for a father of many nations have I made thee. And I will make thee exceeding fruitful, and I will make nations of thee, and kings shall come out of thee. And I will establish my covenant between me and thee and thy seed after thee in their generations for an everlasting covenant, to be a God unto thee, and to thy seed after thee. And I will give unto thee, and to thy seed after thee, the land wherein thou art a stranger, all the land of Canaan, for an everlasting possession; and I will be their God. (Gen. 17:1–8 KJV)

As in the Greek myths there is a prophecy: not one that warns the father from his children, but one that promises Abraham, the first of the three founding fathers of the Jewish nation, that nations will be created and kings will arise from his descendants. This relation between Abraham and his offspring resonates with Levinas's view of fecund time. Through his progeny, Abraham is presented with a future that is beyond his present, beyond his time. Abraham will never live to see the nation of Israel, he will never see Canaan become Israel, and he will not be at Mount Sinai when the Torah and the laws are given to the Children of Israel; yet these events are *his* future. The promise made to Abraham both is and is not his future: what is impossible for Abraham becomes possible through his offspring. As seen in Abraham's relation with his descendants, through the son's life and the possibilities open before him, the father's life and future are extended — a new fate and future become available.

Levinas does not explicitly discuss the relevance of the Torah to his philosophical discussion of time. In fact, he seems to make a more overt move in the opposite direction, and draw on his philosophical view of time in his interpretations of the Talmud, as in the case of his examination of remembrance in his reading of tractate *Berakhot* (*ITN* 81–82, 87). As noticed by Catherine Chalier, Levinas crosses the border here from Jewish thought to philosophy. She points at the influence of Levinas's view of time in giving meaning to the prohibition found in this tractate against using Abraham's old name. At the same time, she claims, the talmudic commentaries may have inspired his thoughts about time, but in making this claim she is referring to diachronic time.[7] It is interesting that the commandment to call Abram Abraham, interpreted in this tractate, appears in the passage referring to the promise made to Abraham quoted above. However, Levinas does not introduce his idea of fecund time into his discussion of this tractate and limits his analysis to the perspective of diachronic time. This may be the case because, by focusing only on the talmudic commentaries discussing Abram's change of name without referring to the entire context of this commandment, there is no relevant reason for introducing the idea of fecund time. But disregarding the notion of fecundity in this context raises a question as to whether Levinas is fully aware of the similarity between his view of fecundity and the description of father-son relations found in the Jewish scriptures.

MOSES

The Torah's perspective in other aspects of Levinas's view of time can also be observed through the story of the biblical prophet and leader, Moses. Like the story of Abraham, the story of Moses manifests a profoundly different line of approach to father-son relations that stands in contrast with the Greek tradition. But before discussing the tale of Moses as illuminating Levinas's view of time, it is interesting first to refer to Freud's Moses as an interpretation that has the opposite outcome. Freud argues that Moses was not a Hebrew but an Egyptian, monotheistic priest who became the leader of a Semitic tribe of slaves, which ultimately turned on him and murdered him.[8] The way Freud tells the story, Moses has similar characteristics to Greek tales, such as the myth of Oedipus, in which the son kills his father. Additionally, as Freud notes, Moses, like other heroes in many Greek myths, was condemned to death by the "father" (the Pharaoh) because of the threat the Israelites posed to Pharaoh's possibilities (though in the biblical story, Pharaoh's edict called for the death of every newborn Hebrew male). Against Pharaoh's command, baby Moses is saved, raised by a foster family (in Pharaoh's palace), and eventually grows to become the threat the "father" feared.[9] Despite these similarities, the story of Moses after the flight from Egypt, particularly the moment before his death, can be considered from the perspective of Levinas's view of time.

The Levinasian father-son model is conveyed in the story of Moses' relation with the Israelites, whom he leads out of Egypt. Throughout their journey in the desert, Moses assumes the role of a father to the Israelites, the Children of Israel. He provides them water and nourishment, leads them, educates them, judges them, punishes them, enhances their pride and self-confidence (by assuring them that they are the chosen people), and defends their behavior before God. Furthermore, Moses is considered a father figure in the Jewish tradition even in the present day. In many senses he is the founder of the Jewish religion, he is the lawgiver, and the prototype of the prophets. Moses' relationship with his people is a relation with a son who is both other and the same: Moses both is and is not his people. The Israelites are part of the father but are also separate from and independent of him.

However, despite the significant role Moses had in leading the Israelites out of Egypt toward Canaan, he was punished, never to enter the Promised Land. This event can be considered from Levinas's view of time, focusing on its connection with responsibility. The moment preceding the death of Moses is described in Deuteronomy 34:

> And Moses went up from the plains of Moab unto the mountain of Nebo, to the top of Pisgah, that is over against Jericho. And the LORD showed him all the land of Gilead, unto Dan, and all Naphtali, and the land of Ephraim, and Manasseh, and all the land of Judah, unto the utmost sea, and the south, and the plain of the valley of Jericho, the city of palm trees, unto Zoar. And the LORD said unto him, This is the land which I swear unto Abraham, unto Isaac, and unto Jacob, saying, I will give it unto thy seed: I have caused thee to see it with thine eyes, but thou shalt not go over thither. So Moses the servant of the LORD died there in the land of Moab, according to the word of the LORD. (Deut. 34:1–5 KJV)

This scene is usually considered as a manifestation of a missed opportunity. Moses will not live to take part in the fulfillment of the promise to enter Israel and can only watch it from afar. Nebo has become a symbol of the tragedy of the human fate involving the anticipation of an event that will never occur. However, from a Levinasian perspective, even though Moses never entered the Promised Land, this possibility is still available to him through his people who do enter, and in this context his future is extended. The Israelites provide their father a new beginning, a future that goes beyond Moses' anticipated present: what is impossible for Moses becomes possible through his sons and daughters. Also the ideas of the pure future that cannot be anticipated, and the absolute, immemorial past that is not susceptible to the work of recollection is apparent in this scene. In seeing the Promised Land, future and past horizons are revealed to Moses. As a metaphor for the pure future, entering Canaan will not become his present. As a metaphor for the immemorial past, the promise made to the three forefathers was never Moses' present. This belongs to the time of the other, which will never be re-presented. In this sense the time of the other interrupts the time of Moses, but this interruption does not occur in synchronic time but constitutes diachronic time.

Levinas hints at the relevance of this episode for his view of time when stating in "The Trace of the Other" that the agent renounces "being the contemporary of its outcome, to act without entering the promised land."[10] Without assembling the immemorial past and the pure future into Moses' present, this disruption provides Moses with a new moment, a future and a past, which are the alterity required for the constitution of time.

The explicit reason for Moses' punishment never to enter the Promised Land is an occasion in which Moses shows disbelief in God (Num. 20:1–14). After hearing the complaints of the Israelites that they have no water to drink, God instructs Moses (and Aaron) to assemble the people and *speak* to the rock in front of them in order to bring forth water. But instead, Moses *strikes* the rock twice with his rod, and water comes out. Acting instead of speaking is interpreted by God as conveying doubt and lack of faith, and Moses is punished. Even if we add to this a deeper reason that explains the punishment—Moses took credit for the miracle and did not attribute it to God[11]—it still seems that he has been punished too harshly. Moses challenges God a lot more openly and much more seriously than in this incident, with both word and deed. The severity of the punishment in relation to the sin has troubled the rabbinic tradition, and various explanations have been offered. One set of interpretations suggests that Moses is banned from the Promised Land because at first he refused to liberate the Israelites from the Egyptians, and as Jerald Blidstein nicely puts it, in these interpretations the punishment suits the sin—if Moses won't lead the Israelites *out* of Egypt, then he won't lead them *into* the Promised Land; if he does not trust God, God will not trust him.[12]

A second set of interpretations focuses on Moses' affinity to the generation he has led out of Egypt. Moses is not able or allowed to disconnect himself from the "generation of the wilderness," and like them he is sentenced to die in the desert. These interpretations tie Moses' fate with the fate of the generation that took part in the sin of the spies. At the threshold of the Promised Land, Moses sends twelve spies to explore, but only Joshua and Caleb are in favor of entering and possessing it. The Children of Israel are convinced by the evil report provided by the ten remaining spies, and "murmured against Moses and against Aaron and the whole congregation said unto them, Would God that we had died in the land of Egypt or would God we had died in this wilderness. And wherefore hath the

LORD brought us unto this land, to fall by the sword, that our wives and our children should be a prey? Were it not better for us to return into Egypt?" (Num. 14:2–3 KJV). God is furious, and he expresses his intent to annihilate the people and create another nation through Moses. Moses in return argues against God's decision by presenting a rational argument. Eventually, God does not consume the entire people, but neither does he grant full forgiveness. God punishes the ten spies to die in a plague, and the desert generation is condemned to wander in the wilderness for forty years and never to enter the Promised Land. In this context, some interpretations consider Moses one of the sinners, and others concentrate on his moral obligation to lead this generation till its end. A third set of interpretations concentrates on Moses' willingness to die for his people, which is most explicit in the context of the golden calf incident. These readings suggest that Moses is willing to give up his life before he enters the Promised Land in order to assure the survival of his people. Blidstein concludes that Moses does not die for the people or die in their place, and that his death is not one of atonement. He maintains that these interpretations disassociate Moses' willingness to die and the sins of the people, and that Moses acts for the sinners by praying that they will repent.[13]

The last two sets of traditional interpretations, in which Moses is considered responsible for his people, can be tied with a Levinasian reading, which opens up a different way to explain the harshness of the punishment. Moses' punishment is especially disproportionate to the offense when compared to the misdemeanor of the golden calf incident. In creating the golden calf and worshipping it, the Israelites turn away from what God has commanded them. God expresses his decision to consume the people and make from Moses a great nation. But Moses pleads to God, "Oh, this people have sinned a great sin, and have made them gods of gold. Yet now, if thou wilt forgive their sin; and if not, blot me, I pray thee, out of thy book which thou hast written" (Exod. 31:31–32 KJV). Some rabbis take from the incident of the golden calf that Moses gave his life for Israel. A Levinasian reading suggests Moses is punished severely because he substitutes himself for the Israelites, but not for the purpose of atonement. In this incident, which occurs before that of the spies, Moses does not merely convince God to renounce his decision to annihilate the entire congregation, but takes responsibility for them. Moses substitutes himself for the community of the Israelites, and they enter the Promised Land and eventually become a nation, whereas Moses remains to die outside alone on the mountain of Nebo, buried without human presence, in an unknown location.[14]

For Levinas, "The other engages you in a situation where you are obligated without culpability" (*IR* 216). Responsibility is not a choice one makes but a calling that comes from alterity before all memorable time. Like the chosenness of the Jewish people, we are chosen. It is not a privilege, but an obligation to respond to and be responsible for the other. This idea, which Levinas summarizes by quoting from Dostoyevsky's *The Brothers Karamazov*, "We are all responsible for all men before all, and I more than all the others" (*EI* 101; cf. *OB* 146; *LR* 182; *TO* 108), is already found in the Torah. For example, in the incident of Korah's revolt described in Numbers 16, Korah, Dathan, and Abi'ram sinned when they rebelled against Moses and Aaron, complaining that the two made themselves a sovereign over them, and have led the children of Israel out of Egypt to die in the desert. God's response is to consume the entire congregation (except for Moses and Aaron), but Moses pleads to God: "Shall one man sin, and wilt thou be wroth with all the congregation?" (Num. 16:22 KJV). In the end not the entire congregation is consumed, but only the three rebels and their families. The Talmud discusses the question of the responsibility of the whole family for the actions of one of its members, leading to the famous saying, "*kol Yisrael areivim ze bazeh.*"[15] The Hebrew word *areivim* means guarantor, but the phrase actually states that as a Jew, I am responsible for the other Jew. Although this saying implies a reciprocal relation which contradicts Levinas's demand of asymmetry, it illustrates and inspires Levinas's view that each one of us is responsible to and for the other (*LR* 225–26).

Moses' responsibility for the other is manifested in accepting the possibilities of the Israelites as his own. In *Totality and Infinity* responsibility is located in the concrete encounter with the transcendent other, and a connection can be made between responsibility and fecund time. The responsibility for the other is manifested in accepting the other's possibilities as mine, and fecund time is precisely the view in which time (mainly the future) is constituted in considering the other's possibilities as my own. When Moses takes upon himself the fate of the Israelites and dies in the desert in their place, time is constituted. In this sense, the time of a nation is created.

Moses is responsible also for the past of others that is not his own, that was never his present, and that he cannot re-present. It is not a response embedded in an act of freedom, but a response to a past which is not its own, which was never present to it. In the moment before he dies for the other, Moses mentions the promise made to Abraham, Isaac, and Jacob. He is referring to the contract in which the generations, who will come out of the three forefathers, will prosper and be given the Promised Land. Moses is obligated to an immemorial commitment to the patriarchs. This reveals the Levinasian idea that the responsible subject is compelled to answer not only for what others have done before it was born, but also for what others will do after its death. The subject is responsible for the other to the point of dying for the other, and this for Levinas is the meaning of a future, which is beyond what happens to me, beyond my anticipations and protentions that are to come.

In Levinas's late thought, the notions of substitution and proximity are described through the metaphor of motherhood, and Moses' infinite responsibility for the Israelites complies not only with the paternal model of fecundity but with the maternal model of substitution as well. In the context of the assertion that I am ethically responsible for the stranger, Levinas refers to Numbers 11:12 (*OB* 91). In this episode the people of Israel are already fatigued from travelling in the desert toward the Promised Land, and although Moses (with the help of God) provides them plenty of manna for their nutrition, they are tired of the tasteless, dry manna and long for the meat, fish, cucumbers, watermelons, onions, and garlic they remember eating in Egypt. Their complaining leads Moses to his own protest:

And Moses said unto the LORD, Wherefore hast thou afflicted thy servant? And wherefore have I not found favor in thy sight, that thou layest the burden of all this people upon me? Have I conceived all this people? Have I begotten them, that thou shouldest say unto me, Carry them in thy bosom, as a nursing father beareth the sucking child, unto the land which thou swearest unto their fathers? Whence should I have flesh to give unto all this people? For they weep unto me, saying, Give us flesh, that we may eat. And if thou deal thus with me, kill me, I pray thee, out of hand, if I have found favor in thy sight; and let me not see my wretchedness. (Num. 11:11–15 KJV)

Moses is complaining that these are not his children, he has not conceived them, and he is unable to nurse and nurture them all. Here the nurse bearing the nursling is not the mother, not even a female wet nurse, but Moses. Moses is required to take upon himself not only the role of a father, but also functions as their nurse, their nurturer—the mother that is ethically, infinitely responsible for the child.[16] Moses, the nursing father, unites the apparently opposing metaphors of maternity and paternity alluding to the possibility of considering fecund time and diachronic time, which are respectively grounded in the paternal and maternal metaphors, as coherent.

The tale of Moses is relevant also for considering Levinas's view of subjectivity. For Levinas, insofar as consciousness is restricted to the present and is outside the structure of time, the self is not formed. Only when time is introduced, is the structure of the self fully formed. In *Totality and Infinity* Levinas writes, "To be conscious is precisely to have time" (*TI* 166).[17] In the traditional sense, time is relevant for the question of subjectivity, since the subject underlies certain acts and experiences. That is, traditionally the subject presupposes a stable and persistent substratum that is at the base of every change and experience.[18] In contrast, Bergson teaches us to divert our focus from preservation to formation. And in Heidegger's thought, Dasein at every given moment is the unity of a future, which makes present in the process of having been. From Levinas's viewpoint this process involves a re-presentation of the future and the past. But unlike Bergson and Heidegger, for Levinas the relation with the past and future, necessary for the formation of the self, is exterior—it is a relation of the present established by an individual with a past and a future that it cannot re-present or contain. This relation is revealed in the subject's responsibility for the other. Being responsible for the other is constitutive of the self—the subject is founded on the structure of for-the-other. Like the structure of time, the subject cannot be formed in isolation from the other, but is revealed in the superiority of the other over the same. The Levinasian self is not constituted in consciousness but is formed through being ethically responsible to and for the other—in the proximity, obligation, and obsession for the other.

In summary, the story of Moses reveals the Levinasian idea that we are responsible for the other before any choice we make. This does not mean that Moses did not freely choose to replace the Israelites, and take upon himself their punishment, but his unique self is based on his responsibility for the other person. His choices are made within the structure of his responsibility for the other, the Israelites, and his self is constituted not by making free choices but by the effect of his choices on the Israelites. "The prophet who demands justice is chosen not by others; he is chosen because he was the first to hear the call" (*IR* 163). The infinite responsibility for the other is revealed in the chosenness of the Jewish people to bear responsibility for the world, and Moses is a manifestation of a single person taking upon himself the burden of being responsible for an entire nation. However, Moses is a unique subject not only because he is chosen to answer for the Israelites, and cannot refuse this chosenness. The true meaning of Moses' subjectivity consists in his devotion and subjection to his people. The stories involving Moses do not concentrate on his consciousness or include descriptions of his inner life—his thoughts and aspirations—and nor do they express attempts to describe his own possibilities. The narrative of Moses' story does not focus on Moses as an individual I, but on his responsibility, obligation, and obsession for the Israelites. Even the moment of his death, which from Heidegger's perspective is one's ownmost possibility, is not a moment of mineness (*Jemeiningkeit*), nor a moment of inner reflection, or summing up of his life. But the meaning of this moment is derived from Moses' responsibility to and for the Israelites and through the immemorial contract. In this moment the present of Moses is interrupted by the future and past of the other, and diachronic time as well as Moses' subjectivity are constituted.

THE PROMISE OF THE PROMISED LAND

When Moses overlooks the Promised Land from Mount Nebo, Israel is promised, but what happens when Israel becomes present?[19] The scene can serve as the background for considering Levinas's relation with the state of Israel. From a promise, an ideal, a pure future, Israel becomes a reality, an actual present—a state. But in becoming a state is the promise fulfilled? In a letter Levinas wrote to his friend and colleague Maurice Blanchot, we notice Levinas's ambivalence toward the founding of the state of Israel. This letter, written only a week after the declaration of the establishment of the state of Israel, reveals a mixture of Levinas's reservations regarding the rebirth of Israel and his excitement by this overwhelming occasion.[20] Levinas later develops and discusses the primary, crude feelings expressed in this note in his writings on Judaism. In his essay "From the Rise of Nihilism to the Carnal Jew" Levinas seems to identify a tension between the promise and its fulfillment, writing, "Besides the Israel that is interpreted spiritually, where there is obvious equation between Israel and the Universal, there exists an Israel of Fact, a particular reality that traversed history as a victim" (*DF* 223). Howard Caygill notices a distinction Levinas makes between two histories of Israel: the universal and the holy. As part of the universal history, Israel is a nation-state that participates in the history of other nation-states; but Israel is more than any nation-state, and its holy history is that of an ethical mission.[21] Simon Critchley describes the double function of the state of Israel in Levinas's thought "as an ideal where ethical responsibility would be incarnated in social justice, and as a really existing state where justice is endlessly compromised by violence."[22] Bettina Bergo locates Levinas's paradoxical approach to Israel in terms of messianism—Israel is both a messianic state and an antimessianic site.[23]

Levinas's ambivalence toward the State of Israel is found also in a personal observation he makes: "The satisfaction we can experience when, like a tourist, we can see a Jewish uniform or a Jewish stamp, is certainly one of our lesser delights. But it is difficult to resist" (216). As a persecuted diasporic Jew, Levinas cannot resist the satisfaction and delight he experiences when coming across symbols of the State of Israel, but at the same time, mundane symbols such as stamps and uniforms prove that the Holy Land assumes profane forms. The State of Israel is, in a way, just like any other state.

It is possible that the tension between fact and ideal, between the universal history and holy history, which we find in Levinas's approach to Israel, is grounded in the traditional approach to the history of Israel. As an example, consider the history of the city of Jerusalem. Ideally, Jerusalem is the city of peace, as its name is interpreted by an early Midrash.[24] But in reality Jerusalem rarely, if at all, lives up to its name. Jerusalem was destroyed by the Babylonians and Romans, fought over by the Crusaders and Muslims, and today it is the crux of the conflict between Israelis and Palestinians. This dual aspect of Jerusalem is also manifested in the future tense of the liturgy "next year in Jerusalem."[25] Speaking of next year rather than this year, of the future rather than the present, reveals that Jerusalem is not only a very real city, but also a prayer, a hope, an ideal, a pure future.

We can further consider Levinas's approach to the State of Israel, and address the possibility that for Levinas Israel should have preserved its diachronic dimension as an immemorial past and a pure future, in terms of the relation between Diaspora[26] and diachrony. Is Israel's past ours or is it an immemorial past? Is the diachronic dimension of the Promised Land covered over by the synchronic dimension of the presence of Israel? Does the diasporic spreading through space and time constitute diachronic time, whereas the diminishing of the diasporic situation by the gathering of the Jews in the melting pot of Israel present a synchronic perspective that assimilates otherness in the same? These questions lead us to the political dimension and can be seen as presenting another angle for raising the problem of the transition from ethics to politics, of the passage from asymmetry to equality.

Diachronic time may appear to be particularly relevant to the diasporic existence, whereas the experience of Jews existing as a unified community in the State of Israel actually manifests a synchronic experience of time. Exile is an interruption of the continuous Jewish life that can be regarded as an interruption that constitutes diachrony by avoiding the assimilation of the Jewish people under the order of totality (e.g., the state, the same time and place). In the Diaspora the laws of Judaism are interrupted by the laws of the state, whereas the State of Israel, Levinas claims, "offers the opportunity to carry out the social laws of Judaism" (*DF* 218). The lack of disruption may lead us to consider the State of Israel as a synchronic unity. Not only does the individual Jew become assimilated in the State of Israel, but when assuming the structure of a state, Israel itself becomes assimilated in the synchronic history involving other states.[27] Levinas seems to criticize the State of Israel for behaving like any other state, when he states, "The eschatological dream was substituted by the seduction of tourism, and eighteen years after the creation of the State of Israel, glossy brochures still feed their readers an implausible and invariable visual diet of athletic girls striding joyfully towards the rising sun" (222). The danger that Levinas seems to be concerned with is that in behaving like any other state, Israel is assimilated in synchronic history. Caygill writes similarly in his interesting interpretation of the relation between the State of Israel and the Jews of the Diaspora. According to Caygill, in Levinas's thought the Jews of the Diaspora serve as a form of prophetic control upon the State of Israel in struggling for human rights and studying the Jewish tradition. The Jews of the Diaspora take upon themselves the role of the biblical prophet intervening in the name of justice in the actions of the state.[28]

But perhaps even the diachronic event of the Diaspora is covered over by synchrony. Levinas comments, "After the captivity of Babylon, such prayer restored the continuity of the Jewish life, which has been interrupted by exile" (*LR* 232). Levinas seems to suggest that the diachronic situation of the Diaspora is overcome by prayer: through prayer the diachronic Diaspora becomes synchronic. Surely, public prayer has a unifying, synchronic dimension of the said: reciting the same text at the same public cosmological time along with all other worshippers. The experience of prayer brings together the dispersed individuals and forms a synchronic order. However, covenantal Judaic prayer can be considered to constitute a collective experience of time that preserves alterity and avoids the structure of totality. In the experience of public prayer, the temporal existence of the individual is disrupted by the trace of *illeity.* Consequently, not only is it that prayer does not necessarily form a synchronic structure, but the diasporic situation is not a prerequisite of a collective, nonsynchronic temporal experience. Public prayer resists the unification of the individuals and opens a pathway to a nonsynchronic experience of political time. In covenantal prayer the trace of *illeity* breaks up the simultaneity of synchronic time, allowing the formation of a nonsynchronic, noncontemporaneous time; the individuals are not united by their responsibility for the community or by the covenant, but the trace of *illeity* disrupts the temporality of each individual forming a nontotalizing dimension of collective time.

This view complies with Levinas's argument that Judaism involves an ineffaceable moment of isolation and distancing that "is not simply the fruit of exile and the ghetto, but probably a fundamental withdrawal into the self in the awareness of a surplus of responsibility towards humanity. It is a strange and uncomfortable privilege, a peculiar inequality which compels obligations towards others while not demanding such obligations in return" (*BV* 198). That is, Judaism is protected from assimilation through its infinite responsibility for the other. Similarly, in Judaic prayer the responsibility for the other disrupts the temporality of the individual, but in the case of prayer, the disruption creates a collective, nonsynchronic moment.

Although I have suggested that when assuming the form of a state, Israel is assimilated in synchronic time, when focusing on the ideal aspect of the State of Israel, Israel can be seen as a disruption of history. For Levinas, "The state of Israel has become the place where man is sacrificed, where he is uprooted from his recent past for the sake of an ancient and prophetic past" (*DF* 164). The Jews immigrating to Israel have sacrificed their memorable history, the culture of their homeland. Their temporality has been disrupted by the immemorial covenantal past, thus forming a political dimension of equality that is grounded in infinite responsibility for the other, for the Jewish community and for the State of Israel. The question is whether this interruption creates a diachronic dimension. Levinas writes, "The State of Israel, whatever the ephemeral political philosophy of its greatest workers, is not for us a state like any other. It has a density and depth that greatly surpass its scope and its political possibilities; it is like a protest against the world" (250). The State of Israel is a protest against the world, and is not like any other state. We may consider this in the context of the foundation of the State of Israel. Does Israel, which was founded after the trauma that has disrupted the lives of the European community, interrupt the world, its synchronic history, and create a diachronic moment of difference? For Levinas, "The state of Israel is the first opportunity to move into history by bringing about a just world.... The sacrifices and works which the realization of this justice invites men to make give body once more to the spirit that animated the prophets and the Talmud" (164). That is, the State of Israel interrupts history by bringing a just world of prophetism "in the image of Abraham interceding on behalf of Sodom" (260; cf. Gen. 18:20–33). In Levinas's view, "It is for the whole humanity that Judaism came into the world" (176), and Israel is the first one responsible. Being chosen involves a surplus of obligation, and "this is what is represented by the Jewish concept of Israel and the sense that it is a chosen people" (177). Israel can be seen as a manifestation of the infinite responsibility for the other, which according to Levinas constitutes diachronic time. Levinas asks, "Can we see, in this possibility given to humanity—that of being responsible for the other—the foremost meaning of Israel's historical existence?... Or should we understand this reversal of the self (*moi*) into the for-the-other as the Judaic endowment of all men?" (*LR* 231). By linking the responsibility for the other with Judaism and with Israel, Levinas suggests that politics and ethics are rejoined: "It is not because the Holy Land takes the form of a state that it brings the Reign of the Messiah any closer, but because the men who inhabit it try to resist the temptations of politics; because this State, proclaimed in the aftermath of Auschwitz, embraces the teachings of the prophets; because it produces abnegation and self sacrifice" (*DF* 263).

Yet we cannot overlook the fact that the founding of Israel is also a disruption of the non-Jewish community of people living in Israel prior to its constitution. If diachrony is grounded in responsibility for the other, then the violence that characterizes the life in Israel seriously questions the possibility of considering Israel as uniting ethics and politics. This not only includes the Israeli-Palestinian conflict, but also other extremely violent events that are part of Israel's reality. As examples, we can consider Israel's attitude toward foreign workers and their children, the violence among Israeli youth, the intolerance toward new immigrants, and even the verbal violence that spreads through the Israeli society from its leaders to its children. Such a violent reality fails to manifest a joining of politics with ethics, and it does not fulfill Levinas's prophecy that "only a Jewish culture called upon to develop out of a new life in Israel might put end—for Jews above all, but also for nations—to the persistent misunderstanding" (*BV* 201). Perhaps the State of Israel is the end of the assimilation of Jews, as Levinas suggests in the following sentence, but we are faced with a question: Does Israel, as a Jewish state, prevent the assimilation of its non-Jewish others—Muslim Arabs, Christian Arabs, Druzes, and Circassians—and allow them to preserve their alterity? The problem of assimilation is intrinsic to Levinas's view of ethics as first philosophy, and if the State of Israel is unable to avoid the assimilation of its others, we are faced with the problem concerning Israel's ability to assume an ethical role. Levinas himself has admitted that in many ways the State of Israel is just like any other state, and as a result Israel is assimilated in the synchronic history of all other states. In this sense the State of Israel is not a fulfillment of the promise of the Promised Land, which for Levinas is the promise of a just, ethical community, responsible for the other. The promise of the Promised Land revealed to Moses from Mount Nebo remains an absolute, pure, nonrepresentable, messianic future.

The examination of the biblical events of Abraham and Moses in relation to Levinas's thought illuminates and brings together the key themes of Levinas's interpretation of time—fecundity, diachrony, maternity, paternity, the pure future, the immemorial past—as well as their relation to Levinas's ideas of responsibility, substitution, and subjectivity. The scene describing the moment preceding the death of Moses organizes these themes in a way that provides a concrete example for drawing together the apparently inconsistent views of time found in Levinas's different writings. Fecundity and diachrony, which can be affiliated respectively with paternity and maternity, are the two models by which the constitution of time via the subject's relation with the other is revealed. The figure of Moses unites these different moments, thus providing an example for reconstructing Levinas's different views of time. The stories of Abraham and Moses are not unique examples of the father-son relation, but they convey the general approach to such relations in the Jewish Scriptures (although, as aforementioned, there are exceptions), which is contrasted with the hostile and destructive father-son relations portrayed throughout the Western tradition (Greek myths, Freud's psychoanalytical views, and even contemporary fiction). The diachronic model of time is inspired by the scriptures as well. The radical past is the Covenant to which every Jew is obligated without remembering ever committing to it. The pure, absolute, messianic future, which will never be present, reminds us of promises that remain in the future, such as the promises made to Abraham and Moses, as well as the prayer every Jew (not only the diasporic Jew) prays: next year in Jerusalem.

NOTES

Notes to Introduction

1. A partial list of titles in which aspects of Levinas's view of time are discussed include the following: Bergo, "Levinas's Weak Messianism"; Chanter, *Time, Death and the Feminine;* Ciaramelli, "Un temps achevé?"; Cohen, "Responsible Time"; Delhom, "Le temps de la patience"; Olivier, "L'être et le temps"; Legros, "L'expérience originaire du temps"; Sugarman, "Emmanuel Levinas"; Tauber, "Outside the Subject"; Vassilicos, "The Time of Images"; Wygoda, "Time in the Philosophy of Levinas."

2. I thank the anonymous reader of Duquesne University Press for this valuable reference, and for suggesting its relevance for my own project.

3. It may be argued that Levinas is ambiguous regarding the nature of the relation between time and intersubjectivity. At times he states explicitly that "time is constituted by my relation with the Other" (*EE* 96), "time...is the very relationship of the subject with the Other" (*TO* 39), "the condition of time lies in the relationship between humans" (79), "devotion [to the Other] is time" (115), and "time start[s] from the face of the Other" (120). These allusions seem to suggest that time is caused by intersubjective relations. Yet, Levinas also appears to present a different relation between time and intersubjectivity, suggesting that the relation with the Other signifies time, or that time is the relation with the Other: "Time, on the contrary, in its dia-chrony, would signify relationship that does not comprise the Other's alterity....Time...as the relationship to *that* which...would not allow itself to be assimilated by experience....Time signifies this *always* of noncoincidence, but also the *always* of the relationship" (31–32). Despite this ambiguity I will use the term "constitute" throughout my discussion, but one should be aware of this discrepancy in Levinas's writings.

4. One might object that if this thesis is valid for everyone other than me, then all human beings are equally obligated, and this leaves us within the realm of reciprocity. However, as Adriaan Peperzak insightfully claims, this objection is made from a perspective that is exterior to the relation of the other and me, and from this totalizing perspective, everyone is at the same time a master and a slave. But according to Levinas, we should consider this situation from the perspective of *my* unique experience in which *I* am responsible for any other, and not regard it as a universal imperative. Moreover, the view that there is a fundamental equality between myself and all other people is the result of a reflective comparison; it follows the revelation of a more original asymmetry. Cf. Peperzak, *To the Other,* 27–28; Peperzak, "The One for the Other," 448. A similar issue is addressed in Dewitte, "Un beau risque à courir," 64–76.

5. Sartre, *Being and Nothingness*, 623.

6. Gibbs, *Why Ethics?*, 35–37.

7. Critchley, *The Ethics of Deconstruction*, 7.

8. Derrida, "At This Very Moment," 23.

9. For a linguistic explanation of the Hebrew word *hineni* see Putnam, "Levinas and Judaism," 37–38.

10. Ibid., 38.

11. Katz, "For Love Is as Strong," 129.

12. "Loving the Torah more than God" means for Levinas that ethics comes before God. This is also the title of an article in *Difficult Freedom*.

13. Katz, *Levinas, Judaism, and the Feminine*, 108–25.

14. The Hebrew reads: "ויאמר אברהם אלוהים יראה לו השה לעולה בני וילכו שניהם יחדיו." The King James translation revised the word ordering according to the English style: "And Abraham said, My son, God will provide himself a lamb for a burnt offering: so they went both of them together." This literal translation loses the basis for the Midrash.

15. The quotations of the Midrash Rabbah follow the translation by Harry Freedman and Maurice Simon. Another explanation focuses on the Hebrew word for lamb—"seh." In Greek, the word for "you"—"σε"—is "seh," like the Hebrew word for lamb. So it is as if the Bible refers to the Greek, and we understand the Hebrew word for lamb as actually meaning the Greek word "you," leading us to read this sentence as: God will provide himself *you* ("she," "σε") for burnt offering, my son. The phrase in Hebrew: "אלוהים יראה לו אתה (σε) לעולה בני." See Albeck, *Midrash Genesis Rabbah* 56, 599 (in Hebrew). I thank Ya'acov (Gerald) Blidstein for referring me to this interpretation.

16. Kook, *Olat Raiyah*, 88–89 (in Hebrew).

17. The Midrash asks, "Can one bind a man thirty-seven years old [another version: 26 years old] without his consent?" (Gen. Rabbah 56:8).

18. The full sentence is: "Get thee out of thy country, and from thy kindred, and from thy father's house, unto a land that I will shew thee" (Gen. 12:1 KJV).

19. For an illuminating and rich philosophical discussion of the question of ethical response to texts see Gibbs, *Why Ethics?*, esp. 66–129.

Notes to Chapter 1

1. Cohen, *Elevations*, 133.

2. Most discussions of Levinas's interpretation of time are formed against the thought of Heidegger and Husserl. For the relation with Heidegger see Chanter, *Time, Death, and the Feminine;* Ciaramelli, "Le déformalisation du temps"; Cohen, *Levinasian Meditations*, 57–79; Manning, *Interpreting Otherwise than Heidegger;* Pawliszyn, "A Temporality of Dasein." For the relation with Husserl see Bernet, "L'autre du temps"; Bovo, "Le temps, cette altérité intime"; Conesa, "Urimpression husserliana"; Legros, "L'expérience originaire du temps." For

an example of recent articles dedicated to the relation between the thought of Bergson and Levinas see Warren, "Miracles of Creation"; Vieillard-Baron, "Levinas et Bergson."

3. Scott, "The 'Concept of Time,'" 199.

4. Deleuze, *Bergsonism*, 38.

5. Bergson, *Introduction to Metaphysics*, 45–46.

6. Ibid., 137.

7. It should be emphasized that these sets of dualism—inner and outer, concrete and abstract, fixed and living—do not correspond with the body-mind dualism, it is not an opposition between understanding ourselves as body and understanding ourselves as mind. For Bergson both inner and outer self-understanding refer to consciousness. However, despite Bergson's comprehension of the self as merely the conscious state of mind, I refer to the self as a whole, as one unit that includes both body and mind—the temporal self lives in space as in time.

8. A similar claim is presented in Matthews, "Bergson's Concept of a Person," 133.

9. Zahavi, "Life, Thinking and Phenomenology," 129–30.

10. Deleuze, *Bergsonism*, 78.

11. Warren, "Miracles of Creation," 191.

12. Lacey, *Bergson*, 197.

13. Blattner, "Temporality," 323. For a thoughtful and lucid discussion of the different aspects of Heidegger's view of time see also Blattner, *Heidegger's Temporal Idealism*.

14. Scott, "The 'Concept of Time,'" 189.

15. Vieillard-Baron, "Levinas et Bergson," 473.

16. Tina Chanter discusses this point by focusing on four ideas found in Heidegger's thought: the concept of the world, the distinction between inauthentic and authentic, the *who* of Dasein, and the notion of death (Chanter, *Time, Death, and the Feminine*, 96–107). Chanter also provides a reference to a similar point made in Fynsk, *Heidegger*, 28.

17. Theodore R. Schatzki summarizes four basic ways other Daseins bear on the existence of the individual Dasein: (a) one encounters them out of the world (such as encountering those for whom a finished good is intended when holding the product); (b) one acts toward them; (c) one shares with them the (public) world in which one lives; (d) worldhood is largely the same for all involved (Schatzki, "Early Heidegger on Sociality," 234–36).

18. Heidegger, *Basic Problems of Phenomenology*, 267.

19. Heidegger, *Concept of Time*, 17.

20. Heidegger, *Basic Problems of Phenomenology*, 262.

21. Blattner, *Heidegger's Temporal Idealism*, 130.

22. Kockelmans, *Heidegger's Being and Time*, 251.

23. The German word *Geschichte* means both "story" and "history," as does the French word *histoire*.

24. Beistegui, *Heidegger and the Political,* 13.

25. Ibid., 18.

26. Nancy, "Being-with of Being-there," 4.

27. For example see the detailed discussions offered by Fritsche, *Historical Destiny and National Socialism;* Guignon, "History and Commitment"; Wolin, *Politics of Being;* Salem-Weisman, "Heidegger's Dasein." For books focusing on the relation between Heidegger's thought and the political see Fried, *Heidegger's Polemos;* Beistegui, *Heidegger and the Political;* Thomson, *Heidegger on Ontotheology,* esp. chap. 3; Vogel, *Fragile "We";* Wolin, *Heidegger's Children,* esp. chap. 7.

28. For a discussion of the relation between destiny and historicity from the perspective of Heidegger's discussion of Dasein's response to its repeatable possibilities see Birmingham, "Time of the Political."

29. Guignon, "History and Commitment," 138; Guignon, "History of Being," 397.

30. Fritsche, *Historical Destiny and National Socialism,* 49, 132, 269n3.

31. Vogel, *Fragile "We,"* 53.

32. Blitz, *Heidegger's* Being and Time, 206.

33. Up until his discussion of leaping-in (*einspringen*) and leaping-ahead (*vorausspringen*), both of which involve individuals integrating themselves in the lives of others, Heidegger's portrayal of human relations highlights indifference for the other Daseins. Unlike leaping-in, in which the individual Dasein dominates others by taking care away from them, leaping-ahead is described as awakening another Dasein to the possibility of authentic existence, or at least letting the other Dasein exist in its ownmost potentiality of being. For a discussion of leaping-ahead and leaping-in see Vogel, *Fragile "We,"* 69–102. It should be noted that, as the author himself admits, this discussion "does not faithfully represent Heidegger's intentions" (7, 9).

34. Wolin, *Politics of Being,* 61.

35. Wingenbach, "Liberating Responsibility," 44.

36. Guignon, "History and Commitment in the Early Heidegger," 141.

37. Wolin, *Politics of Being,* 61.

38. Villa, *Arendt and Heidegger,* 218.

39. For an exhaustive discussion of time in Heidegger's thought after *Being and Time* that focuses primarily on the *Augenblick,* the moment of vision, see McNeill, *Time of Life,* 139–43.

40. A great deal has been written on the relation between Heidegger's philosophy and Nazism. I will not address this issue, but will limit my discussion to the question whether we can extract from Heidegger's later texts an authentic, intertemporal collective relation between the individuals of a community. For treatments of the relation between Heidegger, his philosophy, and Nazism see for example: Bernstein, *New Constellation,* 77–141; Blitz, *Heidegger's* Being and Time, 210–22; Caputo, *Demythologizing Heidegger,* 101–17; Lyotard, *Heidegger and "the Jews,"* 51–82; Sluga, *Heidegger's Crisis;* Rockmore, *On Heidegger's*

Nazism; Ward, *Heidegger's Political Thinking.* Ward's book offers a reading of Heidegger's texts for the purpose of examining Heidegger's political thinking (rather than his political engagement).

41. See, for example, Heidegger's notorious statement about the "inner truth and greatness" of National Socialism (Heidegger, *An Introduction to Metaphysics,* 166); his rectoral address on "The Self-Assertion of German Universities" (Neske and Kettering, *Martin Heidegger and National Socialism,* 5–13); his thinking of the relation between the people and history (*Contributions to Philosophy,* 29–30, 34–38, 66–69, 224–25, 279–80); his 1934 lectures on "Logik" (*LGC* 69–89); and his work on Hölderlin's poetry. See also Bernstein's close and illuminating reading of Heidegger's essay "The Question Concerning Technology," which ties it to Heidegger's silence about the Holocaust and the atrocities of the Nazis (Bernstein, *New Constellation,* 77–141).

42. Wolin, *Politics of Being,* 97, 112.

43. See an elaborate discussion of this issue in Beistegui, *Heidegger and the Political,* 45–47, 100–05.

44. Korab-Karpowicz, "Heidegger's Hidden Path," 307. See also Dallmayr, *Other Heidegger,* 125.

45. Wolin, *Politics of Being,* 107.

46. Fried, *Heidegger's Polemos,* 179.

47. Villa, *Arendt and Heidegger,* 223.

48. Heidegger, "Hölderlin and the Essence," 56.

49. Ibid., 57.

50. McNeill, *Time of Life,* 95–96.

51. Wolin, *Heidegger's Children,* 196.

52. For a discussion of Heidegger's political thinking from the perspective of his engagement with Hölderlin's poetry see Ward, *Heidegger's Political Thinking,* 205–59.

53. Heidegger, *Hölderlin's Hymns,* 49–51.

54. Ibid., 50.

55. Ibid., 51.

56. Nancy, "The Being-with of Being-there," 4.

57. An insinuation to such a "with" that complies with the intertemporal dimension I am referring to, Nancy finds in Heidegger's thinking of love analyzed in his letters to Hannah Arendt (Ibid., 14).

Notes to Chapter 2

1. Manning, *Interpreting Otherwise than Heidegger,* 7.

2. Chanter, *Time, Death, and the Feminine,* 1.

3. *EI* 27–28; DEL 13; Levinas, *Carnets de Captivité,* 217–19.

4. For articles that discuss the relation between the thought of Levinas and Bergson's philosophy see Cohen, "Responsible Time," 39–53; Durie, "Wandering among Shadows," 371–92; Warren, "Miracles of Creation," 174–200; Vieillard-Baron, "Levinas et Bergson," 455–78.

5. Durie, "Wandering among Shadows," 392.

6. Critchley, *Ethics-Politics-Subjectivity,* 51–62.

7. From a Levinasian perspective Husserl's view of time also privileges the present. See Bernet, "L'autre du temps," 148–51. Legros, "L'expérience originaire du temps," 84–85.

8. Wyschogrod, *Emmanuel Levinas,* 64–65.

9. Wygoda, "Time in the Philosophy of Levinas," 296–97.

10. Aristotle, *Physics,* 218a3, 7.

11. Aristotle's claim that the now is not part of time is the result of his view of the now as without duration—as the limit between past and future—whereas time is continuous. However, there are also passages in which Aristotle appears to claim that the now has duration, since he compares it to the unit of number (see for example *Physics,* 219b38–20a4). So Aristotle is applying two alternate models for understanding time—the continuous model and the discrete model—which share the property of computing lengths of time intervals.

12. Aristotle, *Physics,* 219b9.

13. Ibid., 218a3.

14. Ciaramelli, "Le déformalisation du temps," 25.

15. Eli Schonfeld forms an interesting analogy between the Cartesian God and the Levinasian other. In terms of continuous creation, God or the other are at the origin of temporality (Schonfeld, "Philosophical Present and Responsible Present," 198–201.

16. Not all thinkers believe that change is necessary for the constitution of time, and thinkers such as Newton and more recently, Sydney Shoemaker, consider the possibility of time without change.

17. As discussed by Elena Bovo, also for Husserl the idea of time is tied with alterity (Bovo, "Le temps, cette altérité intime," 7–20, esp. 9–11).

18. Aristotle, *Physics,* 220a24.

19. Ibid., 223a29.

20. Ross, *Aristotle's Physics,* 64–65.

21. Vieillard-Baron, "Levinas et Bergson," 472.

22. Richard Cohen makes the same point in *Elevations,* 147. Jung Lee criticizes Levinas and says, "Ironically, in his attempt to preserve the alterity of the Other, Levinas unwittingly diminishes, if not altogether effaces, the alterity, the infinity of the self" (Lee, "Neither Totality nor Infinity," 260). The Levinas of *Totality and Infinity* might reply that his point is precisely that there is no genuine alterity within the self, since within the self everything—knowledge, recognition, and so forth—is gathered into the same. Only the other person cannot be absorbed into the same, and remains beyond it. In this sense, when the same meets the other, it encounters an alterity it can never contain or know.

23. Bovo, "Le temps, cette altérité intime," 8, 16, 18; Legros, "L'expérience originaire du temps," 77–97, esp. 77, 82.

24. Bovo, "Le temps, cette altérité intime," 9.

25. Lawlor, *The Challenge of Bergsonism,* 81–82.

26. For an elaborate discussion of Levinas's view of death in comparison to Heidegger's view see Cohen, *Levinasian Meditations,* 57–79.

27. Peperzak, *To the Other,* 134.

28. Olivier, "L'être et le temps," 355.

29. Cohen, *Elevations,* 150; Cohen, *Levinasian Meditations,* 67.

30. Manning, *Interpreting Otherwise than Heidegger,* 72.

31. Cohen, *Elevations,* 141–42.

32. Chanter, *Time, Death, and the Feminine,* 202.

33. Aristotle, *Physics,* 222a28–22b7. Aristotle justifies his position that time is infinite by focusing on two aspects relevant to time. One is the relation between time and change: since time is the number of change — it involves change — and since change is everlasting, time is infinite. Aristotle's reasons for asserting this claim are presented in the first chapter of book 8 (251a8–b10). Here Aristotle's main argument for claiming that change is infinite is that when arguing that there was a first change, one must admit that something capable of producing this change and something capable of bearing it exist. For this to happen either these things must have originated before the change occurs, or they have already existed but without change occurring. In both cases a change earlier than the one discussed is required — either to bring them into being (first case), or to create the conditions for them to act upon each other (second case). The second explanation Aristotle offers for the infinity of time concerns the nature of the *now.* The now ensures that time cannot begin or end, since the now is without duration and thus always both a beginning and an end but not of the same time — it is the beginning of future time and the end of past time — time, therefore, is infinite (*Physics,* 222a28–22b7).

34. This is also true in French (*in-fini*), German (*un-endlich*), and Hebrew (אֵין-סוֹפִי).

35. Levinas, "Trace of the Other," 355.

36. Ciaramelli, "Le déformalisation du temps," 21–37, esp. 22, 36.

37. Critchley, *Very Little...Almost Nothing,* 75.

38. Legros, "L'expérience originaire du temps," 85.

39. Ward, "On Time and Salvation," 166.

40. Delhom, "Le temps de la patience," 45–46.

41. For discussions of messianism and eschatology in Levinas's thought see, for example, Bernasconi, "Different Styles of Eschatology," 3–19; Ward, "On Time and Salvation," 153–71.

42. Ciaramelli, "Un temps achevé," 11–13.

Notes to Chapter 3

1. In an interview Levinas remarks that he barely allows himself to designate the same and the other as a "relation," because a relation rests on the ground of an ensemble, of a totality — it presupposes a universal genus. Instead he suggests the expression "nonindifference" (*IR* 148). This disclaimer should be in mind every time I use the term "relation" when speaking of the same and the other.

2. Stella Sandford refers to Plato's *Symposium* and in particular to Diotima in the context of her discussion of Levinas's notion of maternity (Sandford, "Masculine Mothers," 191–202.

3. Plato, *Symposium*, 206c.

4. The translator William Cobb comments that the term "procreation" usually refers to the father's role in the generation of a child or to the general activity of creating something (Plato, *Symposium*, 75).

5. Plato, *Symposium*, 208b.

6. Cobb insightfully notices in his commentary to the *Symposium* that the delay between Agathon's party and the present report can illustrate the process of immortality as described by Diotima. The speeches, like all of Plato's dialogues, are beautiful "children" left behind by Plato, and contribute to Plato's immortality (Plato, *Symposium*, 62).

7. For some of the growing secondary literature regarding Plato and Levinas, see Allen, *Philosophical Sense of Transcendence;* Hamblet, *The Lesser Good;* Schroeder and Bergo, *Levinas and the Ancients;* Stähler, *Plato and Levinas.*

8. Plato, *Symposium*, 206e.

9. Perpich, "Figurative Language," 107.

10. Chanter, *Time, Death, and the Feminine,* 254.

11. Cohen, *Elevations,* 144.

12. Miller, "Phenomenology, Dialectic, and Time," 229; Perpich, "Figurative Language," 107.

13. In Plato's *Symposium,* Diotima claims that only through creating and leaving behind something new, can a mortal creature approach immortality, since in mortal beings neither the body nor the soul is immortal (207d–08b). Since Socrates' speech in which he repeats Diotima's teachings is seen as conveying Plato's opinion, this denial of human immortality seems inconsistent with the *Republic,* the *Phaedo,* and the *Phaedrus,* which all include arguments for immortality. For discussions of this issue and attempts to reconcile the apparent discrepancies see Bury, *The Symposium of Plato* xliv–xlv; Price, *Love and Friendship in Plato and Aristotle,* 30–35.

14. Plato, *Symposium*, 208e–09c.

15. Irigaray, "Questions to Emmanuel Levinas," 111–12.

16. Plato, *Symposium*, 202a.

17. Ibid., 204b.

18. Ibid., 202d–e.

19. Perpich, "Figurative Language," 107.

20. In my mother's case this is true also due to a concrete fulfillment of her wish. In the process of my registration to a ballet class in Worthington, Ohio, she learned that there was a ballet class for adults at a beginners level. So again, through my possibility of attending a ballet class, she was given the opportunity of realizing her own childhood wish.

21. Fecundity, paternity, and filiality are interrelated terms. The converse of paternity is filiality (*TI* 278)—in paternity fecundity is discussed from the father's perspective, and in filiality it is discussed from the son's perspective.

22. Ainley, Hughes, and Wright, "The Paradox of Morality," 180.

23. Peperzak, *To the Other,* 195.

24. Sandford, "Masculine Mothers," 189.

25. Irigaray, "Questions to Emmanuel Levinas," 110–15.

26. For an elaborate discussion of the relation between Levinas's thought and the feminine see Chanter, *Feminist Interpretations of Emmanuel Levinas.*

27. Levinas wrote four essays on Blanchot collected in *Proper Names.* As Jill Robbins comments, two of Blanchot's books, *The Infinite Conversation* and *The Writing of the Disaster,* are influenced by Levinas's thought (Robbins, *Altered Reading,* 150).

28. For Levinas every other person is an absolute alterity, regardless of his or her particular characteristics (such as religion). In this case, religion and ethnicity help to convert Levinas's philosophical idea into a concrete everyday situation.

29. Chanter, *Time, Death, and the Feminine,* 259.

30. I owe this observation to Hagi Kenaan.

31. Bernet, "L'autre du temps," 158–59.

32. Besides the continuous model, Aristotle also presents a model of discrete time. There are passages in which he compares the now to the unit of number, suggesting that the now has duration (cf. Aristotle, *Physics* 219b38–20a4).

33. For example, the function that measures the weight of clear chicken soup is continuous, and the function that measures the weight of dumplings is discrete, but the function that measures soup with dumplings is discontinuous but not discrete.

34. Aristotle, *Physics,* 222b16–22.

35. In *On Generation and Corruption* (319a20 324a10–15, 327b11, 336a22, 338b5–10), Aristotle considers coming-to-be and passing-away as equally significant. So contrary to the *Physics,* not only is corruption time-related but generation is time-related as well. I believe there is a way to settle this discrepancy between the two texts, but this is beyond the scope of the present discussion.

36. Manning, *Interpreting Otherwise than Heidegger,* 78.

37. Kristeva, "Women's Time," 190–93.

38. See Jardine, "Introduction," 8.

39. Kristeva, "Women's Time," 191.

40. Jacques Dewitte offers a different perspective in connecting the notions of linearity and circularity with Levinas's view of time. He suggests that synchronic time is circular since the subject keeps returning to the present, whereas diachronic time is linear, since it involves an open future and past. (Dewitte, "Un beau risque àcourir," 58).

41. Rosenthal, "A Time for Being Ethical," 194.

42. Irigaray, "Questions to Emmanuel Levinas," 111–12.

43. Derrida, "Violence and Metaphysics," 109–17.

Notes to Chapter 4

1. Derrida, "Violence and Metaphysics," 312n7; Bernstein, "Evil and the Temptation," 252.

2. Unlike the structuralists who favor the perspective of synchrony over diachrony, Levinas focuses on diachrony.

3. Llewelyn, "Levinas and Language," 136.

4. Perhaps Levinas thought that the immemorial past better described diachronic time since we can anticipate the future even if it is not realized, but we cannot remember a past that we have not experienced.

5. Dewitte, "Un beau risque àcourir," 58.

6. Critchley, *Ethics-Politics-Subjectivity*, 155.

7. As suggested by Robert Legros, a similar criticism can be directed at Husserl's interpretation of time (Legros, "L'expérience originaire du temps," 84–85).

8. Ricoeur, "Otherwise," 91.

9. Cohen, *Elevations*, 147.

10. Kantor, "Time of Ethics," 29.

11. In *Otherwise than Being* Levinas speaks of "substitution, responsibility without recallable commitment, without beginning, infinite approach in the proximity of another" (OB 154).

12. Lingis makes a similar point in "The Self in Itself," 533.

13. The tension between movement and immobility can be added to the different sets of tensions according to which I suggested in the introduction to think of the relation between the saying and the said.

14. If we consider the Egyptian myth about the invention of the art of writing, illustrated in the *Phaedrus* by Socrates (274c–75b), we can agree with Theuth's claim that writing enables us to remember and become wiser. Without the structure of writing, Plato's dialogues (and many other enlightening texts) would have probably been lost and forgotten, leaving us ignorant to a certain extent. On the other hand, we can also agree with Thamus's claim that writing inserts forgetfulness into our souls, since it tempts us to rely on external patterns in order to remember, instead of using our own internal capacity, and remembering on our own. Thus, we could assert that our encounter with the written word is not sufficient for wisdom. Therefore, while reading the Platonic dialogues we are reminded that insight does not come through reading and writing alone, but requires also discussion with others, and therefore the verbal exchange is an essential experience for philosophy and life.

15. Husserl, *Phenomenology of Internal Time-Consciousness*, 50–51.

16. Admittedly, Levinas's approach to art is complex. In "Reality and Its Shadow," Levinas argues that art brings irresponsibility (*CPP* 12). Yet, despite Levinas's mistrust of aesthetics, art is not a thematic said, but has the characteristics of saying. The relation to (modern) art is not a relation of knowledge. It presents things in their materiality and not as representations (*EE* 50–51). Like

saying, art is precognitive. It is a disturbance or interruption of the rational discourse. These characteristics of art are similar to the role of ethics in Levinas's thought, so even if Levinas himself does not consider art as the saying without the said, the resemblance between the two should not be ignored. See Bruns, "The Concept of Art" and Robbins, *Altered Reading,* 75–81.

17. I thank Brock Bahler for this enlightening comment.

18. Gibbs, "Jewish Dimensions of Radical Ethics," 16–17. Elsewhere, Levinas states, "The more I face my responsibilities the more I am responsible" (Levinas, "The Trace of the Other," 354).

19. In chapter 3 I suggest this relation as an example for fecund time. Now I return to this story in order to clarify diachronic time.

20. The story of Harry meeting Victor is described in an essay, which offers a Levinasian reading of examples of care, rescue, and sacrifice during the events of September 11, 2001 (Jovanovic and Wood, "Speaking from the Bedrock of Ethics," 322–23).

21. Robbins, "Who Prays," 33.

22. Efraim Meir points out that "time-available" (*zman-zamin*), "willing" (*mezuman*), "inviting" (*le'hazmin*), and summoning (*le'zamen*) originate from the same grammatical root. (Meir, "How to Think Death," 8 (in Hebrew).

23. Gibbs, *Why Ethics,* 29.

24. Sugarman, "Emmanuel Levinas and the Deformalization of Time," 259.

25. For a discussion of the role of maternity in Levinas's later thought, see Sandford, "Masculine Mothers," 180–202.

26. Sandford, "Masculine Mothers," 186.

27. Guenther, "Like a Maternal Body," 133.

Notes to Chapter 5

1. An elaborate discussion of the third party and the problem of relating face-to-face relations to collective structures are beyond the scope of this book, and I am raising this issue in order to make a point concerning Levinas's view of time. For a discussion of the notion of the third see, for example: Bergo, *Levinas between Ethics and Politics,* 177–88; Peperzak, *To the Other,* 166–84; Critchley, *Ethics of Deconstruction,* 225–37; Caygill, *Levinas and the Political,* 131–33. For a discussion of the third person that goes beyond Levinas's notion, see Gibbs, *Why Ethics,* 133–55, 246–57.

2. For a discussion of the problem of the relation of the political to the ethical, see Critchley, "Five Problems," 172–85; Critchley, *Ethics of Deconstruction,* 219–36.

3. Sugarman, "Emmanuel Levinas," 263.

4. Simon Critchley, *Ethics of Deconstruction,* 227–28.

5. Ibid., 228.

6. Levinas, "Trace of the Other," 356.

7. Caygill, *Levinas and the Political,* 146–47.

8. Levinas, "Trace of the Other," 359.

9. Bergo, *Levinas between Ethics and Politics,* 245, 298.

10. Critchley, *Ethics of Deconstruction,* 226.

11. Caygill, *Levinas and the Political,* 129, 148–50; cf. Bergo, *Levinas between Ethics and Politics,* 238–39.

12. *OB* 150; Levinas, "Trace of the Other," 357–58.

13. Hartman, *A Living Covenant,* 138.

14. Gibbs, *Why Ethics,* 115. Gibbs elaborates this idea, suggesting that in interpreting these texts, and interpreting the commentaries on these texts (such as the oral Torah wherein the Torah is interpreted, and contemporary interpretations), and continuing to discuss the holy texts today by readers all around the world, the text becomes an interruption of all its readers — an interruption that binds them together.

15. Cohen, *Ethics, Exegesis and Philosophy,* 342.

16. Levinas does allude to a connection between time and prayer at the beginning of *Otherwise than Being* when he says, "in a prayer in which the worshipper asks that his prayer be heard, the prayer as it were precedes or follows itself" (*OB* 10).

17. For a discussion of ethics and prayer in Levinas's thought see Robbins, "Who Prays," 32–49; Morgan, *Discovering Levinas,* 347–53.

18. "God who, though remaining the One to whom all prayer is addressed, is also the One *for whom* the prayer is said" (*ITN* 130).

19. Leibowitz, "Al Ha-Tfila," 385–90 (in Hebrew).

20. Gordon, *Rosenzweig and Heidegger* 189.

21. Ibid., 190.

22. Gibbs, *Correlations in Rosenzweig and Levinas,* 110.

23. Rosenzweig, *New Thinking,* 86.

24. Ibid., 86. Bracketed text in the original.

25. Gordon, *Rosenzweig and Heidegger,* 199.

26. Ibid., 199–201.

27. Hartman, *Love and Terror,* 177.

28. Hartman, *A Living Covenant,* 167.

29. The *Shema* is an affirmation of Judaism and a declaration of faith in one God. The obligation to recite the *Shema* is separate from the obligation to pray and a Jew is obligated to say *Shema* in the morning and at night.

30. Hartman, *A Living Covenant,* 165.

31. Simon, "On the Meaning of Prayer," 103–04.

32. Hartman, *A Living Covenant,* 138.

33. Hartman, *Love and Terror,* 176.

34. Hartman, *A Living Covenant,* 163.

35. Heschel, "On Prayer," 69. This is in contrast to Yeshayahu Leibowitz's view that the routine of prayer and the absence of personal identification with the content is a requisite for true worship (Leibowitz, "Al Ha-Tfila," 386). For

a discussion of Leibowitz's view of prayer, see Hartman, *A Living Covenant,* 161–64.

36. Ibid., 168.
37. Tractate *Avoda Zara,* folio 8a. See Hartman, *A Living Covenant,* 170.
38. Ibid., folio 8a.
39. Hartman, *A Living Covenant,* 169–70.
40. Gibbs, *Why Ethics,* 116.

Notes to Afterthoughts

1. Tauber, "Outside the Subject," 439–59.
2. "By Saturnus [Kronos] again they denoted that being who maintains the course and revolution of the seasons and periods of time, the deity so designated in Greek, for Saturnus' Greek name is Kronos, which is the same as khronos, a space of time. The Latin designation 'Saturnus' on the other hand is due to the fact that he is 'saturated' or 'satiated with years' (anni); the fable is that he was in the habit of devouring his sons — meaning that Time devours the ages and gorges himself insatiably with the years that are past. Saturnus is bound by Jove [Jupiter] in order that Time's courses might not be unlimited, and that Jove might fetter him by the bonds of the stars" (Cicero, *De Natura Deorum,* 2.24).
3. Levinas, *Carnets de Captivité,* 218.
4. For a discussion of Cronos in the literary and pictorial tradition see: Kalibansky, Erwin, and Fritz, *Saturn and Melancholy.*
5. One example is found in the TV series *Lost.* Two of the leading characters, Benjamin Linus and John Locke (like the philosopher), have complicated relationships with their fathers. Linus, whose mother died giving birth to him, is perceived by his father as the cause of his wife's death. The father does not see Linus as his continuation and extension, but as a limitation, and in this sense Linus curtails his father's possibilities, such as the possibility of living a long life with his wife. In Locke's case, his father does see him as an extension of his life, but in the literal sense as a functional means for prolonging his life: for him, Locke is a living organ donor he can harvest, and he cons Locke into giving him his kidney. When Locke becomes a threat to his father's acts of deceit, the father throws him out of a window with the intention of killing his son, and with him the peril that he will limit his opportunities as a conman. Both sons long for their fathers' appreciation and love, but at the end kill them in order to expand their own options and gain leadership of the community of Island natives called the others.
6. Tractate Sanhedrin, fol. 105b.
7. Chalier, "Levinas and the Talmud," 100–01, 114–15.
8. Freud, *Moses and Monotheism.*
9. Following Otto Rank, Freud presents a number of features common to a large number of myths: the hero belongs to an aristocratic family, his conception is impeded by difficulties, the father is warned of the child's birth,

the father orders the baby to be killed, the child is saved, and when full grown he discovers his history and takes vengeance on his father.

10. Levinas, "The Trace of the Other," 349. I thank David Brezis for referring me to this quotation.

11. See Numbers 20:10 (KJV), where it says, "And Moses and Aaron gathered the congregation together before the rock, and he said unto them, Hear now, ye rebels; must we fetch you water out of this rock?"

12. Blidstein, *Death of Moses,* 32 (in Hebrew).

13. Ibid., 55–59.

14. According to Blidstein the traditional interpretations maintain that Moses was buried by God (Ibid., 171).

15. Tractate *Shevuot,* fol. 39a.

16. For a feminist reading of this episode see: Guenther, "Like a Maternal Body," 119–36.

17. In "Substitution" Levinas admits he has treated subjectivity and consciousness as equivalent, interchangeable, terms (*BPW* 82–83).

18. For an account of the term "'subject'" in the philosophical tradition and its relation to metaphysics see Critchley, *Ethics-Politics-Subjectivity,* 51–59.

19. I am indebted to Simon Critchley for suggesting I address this issue in the context of this biblical episode.

20. Levinas, "Letter to Maurice Blanchot," 645–48.

21. Caygill, *Levinas and the Political,* 160.

22. Critchley, "Five Problems," 175.

23. Bergo, "Levinas's Weak Messianism," 234.

24. Sifré Zuta Leviticus 6:26, ed. Horovitz (2nd edition), 250. An English translation of the specific Midrash can be found in Sperber, *Midrash Yerushalem,* 118.

25. At the conclusion of the Yom Kippur service (the Day of Atonement) and the Passover Seder, the phrase, "Next year in Jerusalem" is recited. Jerusalem here is the ideal, and not merely as a geographical location. One can live in Jerusalem the city but be very distant from "Jerusalem," while another can be on the other side of the world but very close to "Jerusalem."

26. The term "diaspora" is a combination of the Greek words *dia + speirein,* and means "spread through, dispersion."

27. Surely Levinas was not an anti-Zionist, but such a view echoes the criticism of Zionism offered by extreme Orthodox Jews such as Neturei-Karta, a group in Jerusalem who refuse to recognize the existence or authority of the State of Israel because in their view the concept of a sovereign Jewish state is contrary to Jewish Law.

28. Caygill, *Levinas and the Political,* 174–76.

BIBLIOGRAPHY

PRIMARY WORKS

Aristotle. *The Complete Works of Aristotle: The Revised Oxford Translation.* Edited by Jonathan Barnes. Princeton, NJ: Princeton University Press, 1984.

———. *Physics.* Translated by Robin Waterfield. New York: Oxford University Press, 1996.

Bergson, Henri. *Creative Evolution.* Translated by Arthur Mitchell. London: Macmillan, 1911.

———. *An Introduction to Metaphysics.* Translated by T. E. Hulme. London: Macmillan, 1913.

———. *Time and Free Will: An Essay on the Immediate Data of Consciousness.* Translated by F. L. Pogson. Mineola, NY: Dover, 2001.

———. *Two Sources of Morality and Religion.* Translated by Ashley Audra and Cloudesely Brereton. Garden City, NY: Doubleday Anchor Books, 1935.

Derrida, Jacques. "At This Very Moment in This Work Here I Am." Translated by Ruben Berezdivin, in Bernasconi and Critchley, *Re-reading Levinas,* 11–48.

———. "Violence and Metaphysics." In *Writing and Difference.* Translated by Alan Bass, 79–153. Chicago: The University of Chicago Press, 1978.

Freud, Sigmund. *Moses and Monotheism.* Translated by Katherine Jones. New York: Vintage Books, 1967.

Heidegger, Martin. *The Basic Problems of Phenomenology.* Translated by Albert Hofstadter. Bloomington: Indiana University Press, 1982.

———. *Being and Time.* Translated by Joan Stambaugh. Albany: State University of New York Press, 1996.

———. *The Concept of Time.* Translated by William McNeill. Cambridge, MA: Blackwell, 2001.

———. *Contributions to Philosophy.* Translated by Parvis Emad and Kenneth Maly. Bloomington: Indiana University Press, 1989.

———. "Hölderlin and the Essence of Poetry." In *Elucidations of Hölderlin's Poetry*, translated by Keith Hoeller, 51–66. Amherst, NY: Humanity Books, 2000.

———. *Hölderlin's Hymns: Germania and the Rhine*. Frankfurt: Vittorio Klostermann, 1980.

———. *An Introduction to Metaphysics*. Translated by Ralph Manheim. New Haven: Yale University Press, 1959.

———. *Logic as the Question Concerning the Essence of Language*. Translated by Wanda Torres Gregory and Yvonne Unna. Albany: State University of New York Press, 2009.

Husserl, Edmund. *The Phenomenology of Internal Time-Consciousness*. Translated by James S. Churchill. Bloomington: Indiana University Press, 1973.

Levinas Emmanuel. *Basic Philosophical Writings*. Edited by Adriaan T. Peperzak, Simon Critchley, and Robert Bernasconi. Bloomington: Indiana University Press, 1996.

———. *Beyond the Verse: Talmudic Readings and Lectures*. Translated by Gary D. Mole. London: Athlone Press, 1994.

———. *Carnets de Captivité: Écrits sur la Captivité Notes Philosophique Diverses*. Paris: Éditions Grasset & Fasquelle, 2009.

———. *Collected Philosophical Papers*. Translated by Alphonso Lingis. Pittsburgh: Duquesne University Press, 1993.

———. "Dialogue with Emmanuel Levinas." Interview translated and conducted by Richard Kearney, in Cohen, *Face to Face with Levinas*, 13–33.

———. *Difficult Freedom*. Translated by Seán Hand. Baltimore: Johns Hopkins University Press, 1990.

———. *Entre Nous: On Thinking-of-the-Other*. Translated by Michael B. Smith and Barbara Harshav. New York: Columbia University Press, 1991.

———. *Ethics and Infinity: Conversations with Philippe Nemo*. Translated by Richard A. Cohen. Pittsburgh: Duquesne University Press, 1985.

———. *Existence and Existents*. Translated by Alphonso Lingis. Pittsburgh: Duquesne University Press, 2003.

———. *God, Death, and Time*. Translated by Bettina Bergo. Stanford: Stanford University Press, 2000.

————. *In the Time of Nations.* Translated by Michael B. Smith. London: Athlone Press, 1994.

————. *Is It Righteous to Be?: Interviews with Emmanuel Levinas.* Edited by Jill Robbins. Stanford: Stanford University Press, 2001.

————. "Letter to Maurice Blanchot on the Creation of the State of Israel." *Critical Inquiry* 36 (2010): 645–48.

————. *The Levinas Reader.* Edited by Seán Hand. Oxford: Blackwell, 1989.

————. *Of God Who Comes to Mind.* Translated by Bettina Bergo. Stanford: Stanford University Press, 1998.

————. *Otherwise than Being or Beyond Essence.* Translated by Alphonso Lingis. Pittsburgh: Duquesne University Press, 2000.

————. *Outside the Subject.* Translated by Michael B. Smith. London: Athlone Press, 1993.

————. *Proper Names.* Translated by Michael B. Smith. Stanford: Stanford University Press, 1996.

————. *Time and the Other.* Translated by Richard A. Cohen. Pittsburgh: Duquesne University Press, 1987.

————. *Totality and Infinity.* Translated by Alphonso Lingis. Pittsburgh: Duquesne University Press, 2000.

————. "The Trace of the Other." In *Deconstruction in Context: Literature and Philosophy,* edited by Mark C. Taylor, 345–59. Chicago: The University of Chicago Press, 1986.

Plato. *The Symposium and the Phaedrus: Plato's Erotic Dialogues.* Translated by William S. Cobb. Albany: State University of New York Press, 1993.

Rosenzweig, Franz. *The Star of Redemption.* Translated by William W. Hallo. London: Routledge & Kegan Paul, 1971.

————. *The New Thinking.* Edited and translated by Alan Udoff and Barbara E. Galli. Syracuse: Syracuse University Press, 1999.

Sartre, Jean-Paul. *Being and Nothingness.* Translated by Hazel E. Barnes. New York: Washington Square Press, 1956.

Secondary Works

Ainley, Alison, Peter Hughes, and Tamra Wright. "The Paradox of Morality: An Interview with Emmanuel Levinas." In Bernasconi and Wood, *The Provocation of Levinas: Rethinking the Other,* 168–80.

Albeck, Chanoch. *Midrash Genesis Rabbah.* In Julius Theodor, ed., *Minhat Yehuda.* Jerusalem: Shalem Books, 1996. In Hebrew.

Allen, Sarah. *The Philosophical Sense of Transcendence: Levinas and Plato on Loving beyond Being.* Pittsburgh: Duquesne University Press, 2010.

Beistegui, Miguel de. *Heidegger and the Political: Dystopias.* London: Routledge, 1998.

Bergo, Bettina. *Levinas between Ethics and Politics: For the Beauty that Adorns the Earth.* Pittsburgh: Duquesne University Press, 2003.

———. "Levinas's Weak Messianism in Time and Flesh, or the Insistence of Messiah Ben-David." *Journal for Cultural Research* 13, nos. 3–4 (2009): 225–48.

Bernasconi, Robert. "Different Styles of Eschatology: Derrida's Take on Levinas' Political Messianism." *Research in Phenomenology* 28 (1998): 3–19.

Bernasconi, Robert, and Simon Critchley, eds. *The Cambridge Companion to Levinas.* Cambridge: Cambridge University Press, 2002.

———. *Re-Reading Levinas.* Bloomington: Indiana University Press, 1991.

Bernasconi, Robert, and David Wood, eds. *The Provocation of Levinas: Rethinking the Other.* London: Routledge, 1988.

Bernet, Rudolf. "L'autre du temps." In Marion, *Positivite et transcendence,* 143–63.

Bernstein, Richard J. *The New Constellation.* Cambridge: Polity Press, 1991.

———. "Evil and the Temptation of Theodicy." In Bernasconi and Critchley, *The Cambridge Companion to Levinas,* 252–67.

Birmingham, Peg. "The Time of the Political." *Graduate Faculty Philosophy Journal* 14–15 (1991): 25–45.

Blattner, William D. *Heidegger's Temporal Idealism.* Cambridge: Cambridge University Press, 1999.

———. "Temporality." In Dreyfus and Wrathall, *A Companion to Heidegger,* 311–24.

Blidstein, Jerald J. *The Death of Moses: Readings in Midrash.* Alon Shvut: Tvunot, 2008. In Hebrew.

Blitz, Mark. *Heidegger's Being and Time and the Possibility of Political Philosophy.* Ithaca, NY: Cornell University Press, 1981.

Bovo, Elena. "Le temps, cette altérité intime: La critique de la temporalité husserlienne par Levinas." *Cahiers d'etudes Lévinassiennes* 1 (2002): 7–20.

Bruns, Gerald L. "The Concept of Art and Poetry in Emmanuel Levinas's Writings." In Bernasconi and Critchley, *The Cambridge Companion to Levinas*, 206–33.

Bury, R. G., ed. *The Symposium of Plato.* Cambridge: W. Heffer and Sons, 1973.

Caputo, John D. *Demythologizing Heidegger.* Bloomington: Indiana University Press, 1993.

Caygill, Howard. *Levinas and the Political.* London: Routledge, 2002.

Chalier, Catherine. "Levinas and the Talmud." In Bernasconi and Critchley, *The Cambridge Companion to Levinas,* 100–18.

Chanter, Tina, ed. *Feminist Interpretations of Emmanuel Levinas.* University Park, PA: The Pennsylvania State University Press, 2001.

———. *Time, Death and the Feminine: Levinas with Heidegger.* Stanford: Stanford University Press, 2001.

Ciaramelli. Fabio. "Le déformalisation du temps et la structure du désir." *Cahiers d'etudes Lévinassiennes* 1 (2002): 21–37.

———. "Un temps achevé? Question critiques à propos du messianique chez Lévinas. *Cahiers d'Etudes Lévinassiennes* 4 (2005): 11–19.

Cohen, Richard A., ed. *Face to Face with Levinas.* Albany: State University of New York Press, 1986.

Cohen, Richard A. *Elevations: The Height of the Good in Rosenzweig and Levinas.* Chicago: The University of Chicago Press, 1994.

———. *Ethics, Exegesis and Philosophy: Interpretation after Levinas.* Cambridge: Cambridge University Press, 2001.

———. *Levinasian Meditations: Ethics, Philosophy, Religion.* Pittsburgh: Duquesne University Press, 2010.

———. "Responsible Time." *Cahiers d'etudes Lévinassiennes* 1 (2003): 39–53.

Conesa, Dolores. "Urimpression husserliana y diacronía levinasiana: ¿continuidad o ruptura?" *Revue Philosophique.* 4 (2010): 435–54.

Critchley, Simon. *The Ethics of Deconstruction: Derrida and Levinas.* Cambridge, MA: Blackwell, 1992.

———. *Ethics-Politics-Subjectivity: Essays on Derrida, Levinas and Contemporary French Thought.* London: Verso, 1999.

———. "Five Problems in Levinas's View of Politics and the Sketch of a Solution to them." *Political Theory* 32, no. 2 (2004): 172–85.

———. *Very Little…Almost Nothing: Death, Philosophy, Literature.* London: Routledge, 1997.

Dallmayr, Fred. *The Other Heidegger.* Ithaca, NY: Cornell University Press, 1993.

Deleuze, Gilles. *Bergsonism.* Trans. Hugh Tomlinson and Barbara Habberjam. New York: Zone Books, 2002.

Delhom, Pascal. "Le temps de la patience." *Cahiers d'Etudes Lévinassiennes* 4 (2005): 21–48.

Dewitte, Jacques. "Un beau risque à courir." *Cahiers d'Etudes Lévinassiennes* 1 (2003): 55–76.

Dreyfus, Hubert L., and Mark A. Wrathall, eds. *A Companion to Heidegger.* Malden, MA: Blackwell, 2005.

Durie, Robin. "Wandering among Shadows: The Discordance of Time in Levinas and Bergson." *Southern Journal of Philosophy* 48, no. 4 (2010): 371–92.

Fried, Gregory. *Heidegger's Polemos: From Being to Politics.* New Haven: Yale University Press, 2000.

Fritsche, Johannes. *Historical Destiny and National Socialism in Heidegger's Thought.* Berkeley: University of California Press, 1999.

Fynsk, Christopher. *Heidegger: Thought and Historicity.* Ithaca, NY: Cornell University Press, 1986.

Gibbs, Robert. *Correlations in Rosenzweig and Levinas.* Princeton, NJ: Princeton University Press, 1992.

———. "Jewish Dimensions of Radical Ethics." In Peperzak, *Ethics as First Philosophy,* 13–24.

———. *Why Ethics?: Signs of Responsibilities.* Princeton, NJ: Princeton University Press, 2000.

Gordon, Peter Eli. *Rosenzweig and Heidegger: Between Judaism and German Philosophy.* Berkeley: University of California Press, 2005.

Guenther, Lisa. "'Like a Maternal Body': Emmanuel Levinas and the Motherhood of Moses." *Hypatia* 21, no. 1 (2006): 119–36.

Guignon, Charles. "History and Commitment in the Early Heidegger." In *Heidegger: A Critical Reader,* edited by Hubert L. Dreyfus and H. Hall, 130–42. Cambridge, MA: Blackwell, 1992.

————. "The History of Being." In Dreyfus and Wrathall, *A Companion to Heidegger*, 392–406.

Hamblet, Wendy C. *The Lesser Good: The Problem of Justice in Plato and Levinas.* Lanham, MD: Lexington Books, 2009.

Hand, Seán, ed. *Facing the Other: The Ethics of Emmanuel Levinas.* Richmond: Curzon Press, 1996.

Hartman, David. *A Living Covenant.* London: Collier Macmillan, 1985.

————. *Love and Terror in the God Encounter.* Vermont: Jewish Lights Publishing, 2001.

Heschel, Abraham Joshua. "On Prayer." In Petuchowski, *Understanding Jewish Prayer*, 69–83.

Irigaray, Luce. "Questions to Emmanuel Levinas: On the Divinity of Love." Translated by Margaret Whitford. In Bernasconi and Critchley, *Re-Reading Levinas*, 109–18.

Jardine, Alice. "Introduction to Julia Kristeva's 'Women's Time.'" *Signs* 7, no. 1 (1981): 5–12.

Jovanovic, Spoma, and Roy V. Wood. "Speaking from the Bedrock of Ethics." *Philosophy and Rhetoric* 37, no. 4 (2004): 317–34.

Jung, Lee H. "Neither Totality nor Infinity: Suffering the Other." *Journal of Religion* 79, no. 2 (1999): 250–79.

Kalibansky, Raymond, Erwin Panofsky and Fritz Saxl. *Saturn and Melancholy: Studies in History of Natural Philosophy, Religion, and Art.* New York: Basic Books, 1964.

Kantor, Alon. "Time of Ethics: Levinas and the Électement of Time." *Philosophy and Social Criticism* 22, no. 6 (1996): 19–53.

Katz, Claire Elise. "For Love Is as Strong as Death: Taking Another Look at Levinas on Love." *Philosophy Today* 45, no. 5 (2001): 124–32.

————. *Levinas, Judaism, and the Feminine: The Silent Footsteps of Rebecca.* Bloomington: Indiana University Press, 2003.

Kelly, Michael R., ed. *Bergson and Phenomenology.* Basingstoke: Palgrave-Macmillan, 2010.

Kettering, Emil, and Gunther Neske, eds. *Martin Heidegger and National Socialism.* New York: Paragon House, 1990.

Kockelmans, Joseph J. *Heidegger's Being and Time: The Analytic of Dasein as Fundamental Ontology.* Lanham, MD: University Press of America, 1990.

Kook, Rav Abraham Issac. *Olat Raiyah: Commentary on the Siddur.* Vol. 1. Jerusalem: Mossad Harav Kook, 1962. In Hebrew.

Korab-Karpowicz, W. J. "Heidegger's Hidden Path: From Philosophy to Politics." *Review of Metaphysics* 61, no. 2 (2007): 295–315.

Kristeva, Julia. "Women's Time." In *The Kristeva Reader,* edited by Toril Moi, 187–213. New York: Columbia University Press, 1986.

Lacey. A. R. *Bergson.* London: Routledge, 1993.

Lawlor, Leonard. *The Challenge of Bergsonism.* London: Continuum, 2003.

Legros, Robert. "L'expérience originaire du temps: Lévinas et Husserl." *Cahiers d'Etudes Lévinassiennes* 1 (2003): 77–97.

Leibowitz, Yeshayahu. "Al Ha-Tfila." In *Judaism, Jewish People, and State of Israel,* 385–90. Tel-Aviv: Schocken, 1975. In Hebrew.

Levi, Ze'ev. *Otherness and Responsibility: A Study of Emmanuel Levinas' Philosophy.* Jerusalem: The Hebrew University Magnes Press, 2005. In Hebrew.

Lingis, Alphonso. "The Self in Itself." *Journal of American Academy of Religion* 54, no. 3 (1986): 529–34.

Llewelyn, John. "Levinas and Language." In Bernasconi and Critchley, *The Cambridge Companion to Levinas,* 119–38.

Lyotard, Jean-François. *Heidegger and "the Jews."* Translated by Andreas Michel and Mark Roberts. Minneapolis: University of Minnesota Press, 1990.

Manning, Robert John Sheffler. *Interpreting Otherwise than Heidegger: Emmanuel Levinas's Ethics as First Philosophy.* Pittsburgh: Duquesne University Press, 1993.

Marion, Jean-Luc, ed. *Positivite et transcendence: Suivi de Levinas et la phenomenologie.* Paris: Presses Universitaires de France, 2000.

Matthews, Eric. "Bergson's Concept of a Person." In Mullarkey, *The New Bergson,* 118–34.

McNeill, William. *The Time of Life: Heidegger and Ethos.* Albany: State University of New York Press, 2006.

Meir, Efraim. "How to Think Death from Time and Not Time from Death." In Emmanuel Levinas, *Death and Time,* translated by Eli-George Shitrit, 7–13. Tel Aviv: Resling, 2007. In Hebrew.

Midrash Rabbah. Translated by Harry Freedman and Maurice Simon. Vol. 1. London: The Soncino Press, 1977.

Miller, Hugh. "Phenomenology, Dialectic, and Time in Levinas's *Time and the Other*." *Philosophy Today* 40, no. 2 (1996): 219–34.

Morgan, Michael L. *Discovering Levinas*. Cambridge: Cambridge University Press, 2007.

Mullarkey, John, ed. *The New Bergson*. Manchester: Manchester University Press, 1999.

Nancy, Jean-Luc. "The Being-with of Being-there." *Continental Philosophy Review* 41, no. 1 (2008): 1–15.

Olivier, Paul. "L'être et le temps chez Emmanuel Lévinas." *Recherches de Science Religieuse* 71, no. 3 (1983): 337–80.

Pawliszyn, Aleksandra. "A Temporality of Dasein (Heidegger) and a Time of the Other (Levinas)." In *Analecta Husserliana: The Yearbook of Phenomenological Research*. Vol. 77, edited by Anna-Teresa Tymieniecka, 193–204. Dordrecht: Kluwer, 2002.

Peperzak, Adriaan Theodor, ed. *Ethics as First Philosophy: The Significance of Emmanuel Levinas for Philosophy, Literature and Religion*. London: Routledge, 1995.

———. "The One for the Other: The Philosophy of Emmanuel Levinas." *Man and World* 24, no. 4 (1991): 427–59.

———. *To the Other*. West Lafayette, IN: Purdue University Press, 1993.

Perpich, Diane. "Figurative Language and the 'Face' in Levinas's Thought." *Philosophy and Rhetoric* 38, no. 2 (2005): 103–21.

Petuchowski, J. Jakob, ed. *Understanding Jewish Prayer*. New York: Ktav, 1972.

Price, A. W. *Love and Friendship in Plato and Aristotle*. Oxford: Clarendon Press, 1989.

Putnam, Hilary. "Levinas and Judaism." In Bernasconi and Critchley, *The Cambridge Companion to Levinas*, 33–62.

Ricoeur, Paul. "Otherwise: A Reading of Emmanuel Levinas's *Otherwise than Being or Beyond Essence*." *Yale French Studies* 104 (2004): 82–99.

Robbins, Jill. *Altered Reading: Levinas and Literature*. Chicago: The University of Chicago Press, 1999.

———. "Who Prays?: Levinas on Remissible Responsibility." In *The Phenomenology of Prayer*, edited by Bruce Ellis Benson and Norman Wirzba. New York: Fordham University Press, 2005.

Rockmore, Tom. *On Heidegger's Nazism and Philosophy.* Berkeley: University of California Press, 1992.

Rosenthal, Sandra B. "A Time for Being Ethical." *Journal of Speculative Philosophy* 17, no. 3 (2003): 192–203.

Ross, W. D. *Aristotle's Physics.* New York: Oxford University Press, 1998.

Salem-Weisman, Jonathan. "Heidegger's Dasein and the Liberal Conception of the Self." *Political Theory* 31, no. 4 (2003): 533–57.

Sandford, Stella. "Masculine Mothers?: Maternity in Levinas and Plato." In Chanter, *Feminist Interpretations of Emmanuel Levinas,* 191–202.

Schatzki, "Early Heidegger on Sociality." In Dreyfus and Wrathall, *A Companion to Heidegger,* 233–47.

Schonfeld, Eli. "Philosophical Present and Responsible Present: Comments on Emmanuel Levinas's Philosophy of Time." *Naharaim* 2, no. 2 (2008): 188–209.

Schroeder, Brian, and Bettina Bergo, eds. *Levinas and the Ancients.* Bloomington: Indiana University Press, 2008.

Scott, David. "The 'Concept of Time' and the 'Being of the Clock': Bergson, Einstein, Heidegger, and the Interrogation of the Temporality of Modernism." *Continental Philosophy Review* 39 (2006): 183–213.

Simon, Ernst. "On the Meaning of Prayer." In Petuchowski, *Understanding Jewish Prayer,* 100–11.

Sluga, Hans. *Heidegger's Crisis: Philosophy and Politics in Nazi Germany.* Cambridge, MA: Harvard University Press, 1995.

Sperber, Daniel. *Midrash Yerushalem: A Metaphysical History of Jerusalem.* Jerusalem: World Zionist Organization, 1982.

Stähler, Tanja. *Plato and Levinas: The Ambiguous Out-Side of Ethics.* London: Taylor & Francis, 2010.

Sugarman, Richard I. "Emmanuel Levinas and the Deformalization of Time." In *Analecta Husserliana: The Yearbook of Phenomenological Research: Logos of Phenomenology and Phenomenology of the Logos, Book 3, Volume XC,* edited by Anna-Teresa Tymieniecka, 253–69. Dordrecht: Springer 2006.

Tauber, Alfred. "Outside the Subject: Levinas's Jewish Perspective on Time." *Graduate Faculty Philosophy Journal* 20–21 (1998): 439–59.

Taylor, C. Mark, ed. *Deconstruction in Context: Literature and Philosophy.* Chicago: The University of Chicago Press, 1986.

Thomson, Iain D. *Heidegger on Ontotheology: Technology and the Politics of Education*. New York: Cambridge University Press, 2005.

Vassilicos, Basil. "The Time of Images and the Images of Time: Levinas and Sartre." *Journal of British Society for Phenomenology* 34, no. 2 (2003): 168–83.

Vieillard-Baron, Jean-Louis, "Levinas et Bergson." *Revue Philosophique* 4 (2010) 455–78.

Villa, Dana R. *Arendt and Heidegger: The Fate of the Political*. Princeton, NJ: Princeton University Press, 1996.

Vogel, Lawrence. *The Fragile "We": Ethical Implications of Heidegger's Being and Time*. Evanston, IL: Northwestern University Press, 1994.

Ward, Graham. "On Time and Salvation: The Eschatology of Emmanuel Levinas." In Hand, *Facing the Other*, 153–71.

Ward, James F. *Heidegger's Political Thinking*. Amherst: University of Massachusetts Press, 1995.

Warren, Nicolas de. "Miracles of Creation: Bergson and Levinas." In Kelly, *Bergson and Phenomenology*, 174–200.

Wingenbach, Ed. "Liberating Responsibility: The Levinasian Ethic of Being and Time." *International Philosophical Quarterly* 36, no. 1 (1996): 29–45.

Wolin, Richard. *Heidegger's Children: Hanna Arendt, Karl Lowith, Hans Jonas, and Herbert Marcuse*. Princeton, NJ: Princeton University Press, 2001.

———. *The Politics of Being: The Political Thought of Martin Heidegger*. New York: Columbia University Press, 1990.

Wygoda, Shmuel. "Time in the Philosophy of Levinas." In *Analecta Husserliana: The Yearbook of Phenomenological Research, Volume XC: Logos of Phenomenology and Phenomenology of the Logos*, edited by Anna-Teresa Tymieniecka, 283–301. Dordrecht: Springer, 2006.

Wyschogrod, Edith. *Emmanuel Levinas: The Problem of Ethical Metaphysics*. The Hague: Martinus Nijhoff, 1974.

Zahavi, Dan. "Life, Thinking and Phenomenology in the Early Bergson." In Kelly, *Bergson and Phenomenology*, 118–33.

INDEX

Abraham, 10, 14, 16, 164–66, 168, 172, 179, 181, 183n14; and "Here I am," 8–9, 11–13. *See also Akedah,* the; Bible; father-son relation; Isaac

Akedah, the, 8, 11–13, 164. *See also* Abraham; Isaac

alterity, 2–5, 86, 171, 178, 180; absolute, 69–70, 82, 190n28; and constitution of time, 61–72, 111, 121, 169; demand of, 134, 136, 149–50; and diachrony, 114–15, 124–25, 130, 182n3; and individual, 16, 139, 149–50; insufficient, 56, 64; lacking in Bergson, 25; lacking in Heidegger, 49, 52, 60; and other, 92, 96, 103–04, 187n22; and prayer, 141, 153–55; reduction of, 138, 149, 151, 161; and subject, 78, 82; unreachable, 134

American Civil War, the, 29–30

Aristotle, 73, 96, 112, 125, 160; and the now, 18, 59, 187n11, 188n33, 190n32; *On Generation and Corruption,* 190n35; *Physics,* 62–63, 72, 98; and traditional interpretation of time, 33, 34, 36, 41, 101

asymmetry, 134, 139, 171, 177

asymmetrical relation, 89, 92–93, 112–13, 151, 154

authenticity, 40, 41, 44–47, 77

Autrui, 71, 74. *See also* Other, the

becoming, 23, 57, 89, 100, 101, 119

being, 33, 38, 48, 50–52, 58, 61, 66, 69, 70, 94. *See also* being-toward-death; Dasein; Heidegger, Martin

being-toward-death, 37, 40, 51, 52, 68, 98

Beistegui, Miguel de, 41, 48

Bergo, Bettina, 139, 175

Bergson, Henri, 61, 68–70, 101, 120, 125, 173, 184n7; *Creative Evolution,* 24, 25, 31; duration *(durée),* 18–20, 65, 96–97; and ethics, 20–25; and future and past, 75–76; and Levinas, 3, 15–16, 54–58, 110–11; "Hommage à Bergson" (Levinas), 159–60; and society, 25–32; and temporality, 80, 160; and time, 63–64, 72, 73, 117; *Time and Free Will,* 17, 20, 24, 26, 27; *Two Sources of Morality and Religion,* 23, 25, 30, 31

Bernet, Rudolf, 96

Bernstein, Richard, 106

Bible: Genesis, 58; Cain and Abel, 164; Caleb, 169–70; Ishmael, 12; Jacob and Esau, 164; Joshua, 169–70; Saul and Jonathan, 164. *See also* Abraham; Isaac; Moses

biological relations, 88, 87, 94, 100, 101

Blanchot, Maurice, 90–93, 97, 99, 100, 125, 126, 129. *See also* substitution

Blattner, William D., 33, 38

Blidstein, Jerald, 169, 170

Blitz, Mark, 44

Bovo, Elena, 64

Buber, Martin, 92, 144

207